BOOM BUST OLOGY

BOOM
SPOTTING FINANCIAL BUBBLES
BUST
BEFORE THEY BURST
OLOGY

Vikram Mansharamani, PhD

WILEY

John Wiley & Sons, Inc.

Published by John Wiley & Sons, Inc., Hoboken, New Jersey.
Published simultaneously in Canada.

For general information on our other products and services or for technical support, please contact our Customer Care Department within the United States at (800) 762-2974, outside the United States at (317) 572-3993 or fax (317) 572-4002.

Wiley also publishes its books in a variety of electronic formats. Some content that appears in print may not be available in electronic books. For more information about Wiley products, visit our web site at www.wiley.com.

Library of Congress Cataloging-in-Publication Data:
Mansharamani, Vikram, author.
    Boombustology : Spotting Financial Bubbles Before They Burst /
Vikram Mansharamani.
      p. cm
     Includes index.
     ISBN 978-0-470-87946-7 (hardback); ISBN 978-1-118-02857-5 (ebk);
  ISBN 978-1-118-02855-1 (ebk); ISBN 978-1-118-02856-8 (ebk)
      1. Business cycles.   2. Financial crises.   3. Business forecasting.   I. Title.
HB3711.M354   2011
338.5′42–dc22

                          2010045668

Printed in the United States of America

10 9 8 7 6 5 4 3 2 1

To my family, for their love and support

Contents

Foreword

Vikram Mansharamani's *Boombustology* serves an important purpose in reminding us that narrow, model-driven approaches to understanding financial markets frequently fail. His subject, financial crises, bedevils market modelers, because crises reside in the notoriously difficult-to-assess fat tails of distributions of security returns. Not only are the fat tails hard to parse, but their impact is disproportionate to their size. Extreme events, good and bad, do more to determine longrun results for investors than do the run-of-the-mill events that fall in the center of distributions. Sensible investors pay close attention to low probability extreme negative events, like financial crises, that have the potential to wreak havoc with their portfolios.

Successful approaches to making investment decisions require more than applying state-of-the-art finance theory. In the 25 years that I have had responsibility for managing Yale University's endowment fund, I have hired a large number of young professionals, most of them immediately after graduation from college. Many of my new hires have formal training in economics and finance, with an emphasis on model-based approaches to understanding markets. The financial world presented in the classroom is populated by rational transactors armed with perfect information. Perhaps the most fundamental difference between the academic world where students learn about markets and the real world where analysts operate in markets is the real world's population of flesh-and-blood economic actors.

After a prospective employee signs up for a stint with the Investments Office, I supply him or her with a number of books that illustrate a common theme—the importance of actions of individuals in the functioning of our financial markets. The reading list includes *Den of Thieves*, James Stewart's story of the junk bond scandals of the 1980s; *When Genius Failed*, Roger Lowenstein's depiction of the collapse of Long-Term Capital Management; *Conspiracy of Fools*, Kurt Eichenwald's tale of the Enron fraud; and *The Big Short*, Michael Lewis's account of the subprime mortgage crisis. These books describe, in a thoroughly engaging manner, individual behavior that fails to correspond to the rational actions presupposed by academic modelers. Moreover, in each instance, the actions of all-too-human individuals profoundly influence the world's financial markets.

Armed with the knowledge that making high-quality investment decisions requires a combination of rigorous financial modeling and informed market judgment, my colleagues in the Investments Office stand well prepared to operate in markets. By employing the best that finance theory offers, investors bring an analytical perspective to the table. By including an appreciation of the human elements of market behavior, investors exhibit a healthy skepticism of neatly packaged model results. The combination of analytical rigor and reasoned judgment informs not only the evaluation of bottom-up security selection decisions, but also the analysis of top-down asset allocation studies.

In *Boombustology*, Vikram Mansharamani advocates a similarly broad-based approach to understanding financial booms and busts, describing the financial world as seen through the five lenses of microeconomics, macroeconomics, psychology, politics, and biology. By employing an unusually diverse set of perspectives to increase understanding of the character of financial crises, Mansharamani gives his readers a valuable set of guideposts to help them find a safe path through future market disruptions.

A financial crisis challenges even the most thoughtful decision-making process. During my career at Yale, the endowment faced a number of major market dislocations—the market crash in October 1987, the near collapse of the financial system in 1998, the bursting of the Internet bubble in 2000, and the financial debacle of 2008. In each instance, the extreme market moves produced pitfalls and opportunities.

The crash in October 1987 highlighted the importance of a disciplined approach to maintaining asset allocation targets. On October 19, 1987, as many recall, stock markets around the world declined more than 20 percent. Less well remembered was the strong flight-to-quality rally in U.S. Treasury securities. The decline in stock prices and increase in Treasury prices presented investors with an opportunity to buy stocks low and sell Treasuries high. In fact, as I describe in my book, *Pioneering Portfolio Management,* fearful investors did the opposite, selling (now cheaper) stocks and buying (now more expensive) bonds. Did investors forget that buying high and selling low damages portfolio returns? In contrast, a disciplined rebalancing approach called for purchases of stocks and sales of bonds, positioning the portfolio for future success.

The September 1998 collapse of Long-Term Capital Management (LTCM) showed investors the importance of insulating portfolios, to greatest extent possible, from the actions of others. Nearly all of the positions held by LTCM made fundamental economic sense. What made no sense whatsoever was the staggering level of leverage in the LTCM portfolio, which ran as high as 250 to 1. Because of the underlying sensibility of LTCM's positions, many other investors (including large numbers of hedge funds and the trading desks of Wall Street banks) put on similar trades. When LTCM experienced an unexpected loss, lenders began forcing sales of positions. As LTCM liquidated its massive portfolio, spreads on their otherwise sensible trades widened; that is, cheap assets became cheaper and expensive assets became more expensive. A substantial number of hedge funds suffered, as frightened investors rushed for the exits. In fact, the impact on portfolios exceeded the actual demand for liquidity, since hedge funds raised massive amounts of cash in anticipation of redemption demands. Funds that promised levels of liquidity to investors that were inconsistent with the investment horizon of underlying security positions found themselves forced to raise high levels of cash at the point of maximum opportunity. Investors in funds with sensible lockups and investors with separate accounts faced no such pressure to raise cash and positioned themselves to produce superior results. While no investor can avoid the short-term impact of adverse price moves, steadfast investors can maintain positions and benefit from the ultimate return to fair value of both cheap and expensive securities.

The March 2000 bursting of the Internet bubble showed investors the rewards of persistence in the face of market headwinds. For a number of years prior to the collapse in prices, the market for Internet stocks exhibited unmistakable signs of speculative excess. The irrational increase in prices caused pain for investors who failed to participate in the mania and even greater pain for investors who bet on a return to rationality by taking short positions in Internet

stocks. Yet, those investors who persevered with bets against speculative excess not only benefited from dramatic declines in Internet
stocks, but also benefited from superior performance of value-
oriented securities held in the place of their speculative cousins.

The financial crisis of 2008 forced investors to confront the
importance of liquidity. As markets seized up and ready access to
funds disappeared, investors found that many formerly liquid assets
(e.g., money market funds) became less liquid. Confronted with
demands for liquidity to fund operations and to support portfolio management activities, investors generated funds from sources
not disruptive to the portfolio (e.g., external borrowing) and from
sources disruptive to the portfolio (e.g., sales of illiquid partnership
interests). The quest for liquidity, particularly from sources that
did not disturb portfolio allocations, preoccupied many investors,
especially those whose portfolios emphasized allocations to private
equity and real assets. Better prepared investors, who had in-place
liquidity and borrowing facilities, fared much better than those who
scrambled to raise funds in the chill of the crisis.

The admittedly brief descriptions of lessons learned from past
crises illustrate not only the difference in character of each of the
crises, but also the importance of following sensible portfolio management principles throughout a period of market disruption, a
time when many investors lose their bearings. In *Boombustology*,
Vikram Mansharamani assists investors by rolling up his sleeves and
applying his perspective to analyses of five past crises, ranging from
Tulipmania in seventeenth-century Holland to the subprime mortgage catastrophe in twenty-first-century America. He may be correct
that the crises share "many similar characteristics" (although I am
often struck by their differences), but he is certainly correct that
the study of crises is most useful "if it helps one to make money,
avoid losses, or, ideally, both." Where Mansharamani falls short in
his quest to help his readers make money is in addressing the critical element of timing.

The investment world fails to distinguish between early and
wrong. Managers who underweighted Japan in the face of absurd
valuations in the late 1980s suffered as Nikkei marched to ever
higher levels, ultimately peaking at nearly 39,000 in December
1989. Investors who recognized the bubble early incurred opportunity costs (by underweighting Japan) or direct costs (by short-
ing Japan). In all too many instances, investors locked in losses by

abandoning correct, but out-of-favor, positions when the pain of losses became intolerable. In other instances, investors profited from their anti-bubble bet, but reduced the profitability of their position by starting too soon. Precisely the same problem confronted investors during the Internet bubble in the late 1990s. Early looks a lot like wrong.

In the introduction to his book, Vikram Mansharamani makes an interesting distinction between puzzles (for which a solution exists) and mysteries (for which a solution does not yet exist). Even though his work will not assist investors in dramatic fashion unless he addresses the core (perhaps, unsolvable) mystery of the timing of market crises, Mansharamani's broad-based approach to examining financial crises helps investors by making these extraordinarily important market events less mysterious and more puzzle-like.

David F. Swensen
Chief Investment Officer
Yale University
New Haven, Connecticut
January 4, 2011

Is There a Bubble in Boom–Bust Books?

W hile I sincerely hope that *Boombustology* becomes a timeless classic for students, academics, policymakers, and investors alike, my current goal is considerably more modest. I have written this book because I believe it timely. The world is in the midst of an accelerating sequence of boom and bust cycles, and despite these developments, no organized, multidisciplinary framework exists for thinking about them. This book hopes to provide that framework. Lacking such a framework, we are destined to a world of massive unintended consequences and the continual escalation of extremes—the ultimate outcome of which may be quite destructive to society and the socioeconomic–political world as we know it.

Might it be possible that our attempts to deal with apparent Japanese economic dominance resulted in the Japanese bust, which drove the Asian financial crisis, which drove the dot-com bubble, which resulted in the U.S. housing boom and bust, which is currently creating unsustainable debt loads at the government level around the world? Might it have been possible to identify these booms before they busted so as to prevent the numerous unintended consequences that follow in the wake of our attempts to address each bust? This book will address these topics.

The market for books about financial booms and busts has itself boomed over the past several years, accelerated in no small part by the recent financial crisis. Why then does it make sense to add to the noise with another treatise on financial bubbles and crashes? Surely all previously written work has addressed any pertinent issues. What can a practicing money manager and part-time college lecturer possibly add to the overflowing bookstore business section?

The mere fact that this book exists and that you stand here reading it answers these somewhat rhetorical questions. This book, which is a written version of a course that I have taught at Yale, provides a new perspective on financial booms and busts. The fact that I chose to design a course to teach at an undergraduate liberal arts college (rather than an undergraduate or graduate business school) is a telling statement about my perspective. Social occurrences are difficult to categorize as solely economic, psychological, political, or biological—they are, in fact, a complex concoction of all such phenomena. Why, then, should one limit oneself to a simple unidisciplinary lens when studying financial markets, perhaps the most complicated of social phenomena?

Financial markets are extremely complex phenomena; competing within them with the handicap of a single lens seems in many ways illogical. Unfortunately, our entire society and educational infrastructure is designed toward specialization and single-discipline analysis. Even among the leading liberal arts schools, virtually all college students are eventually channeled toward a disciplinary major such as economics, political science, psychology, history, literature, biology, or chemistry. While there are meaningful benefits in developing expertise, few multidisciplinary options are offered, let alone pursued. This is exacerbated in graduate and professional schools, and although such specialization is necessary and beneficial in most scientific pursuits, it has the potential to be counterproductive in social pursuits.

Since I entered Yale University as a college freshman, I have resisted the tendency of the establishment to channel me into a particular discipline or "box." Rather than merely study economics or political science, I majored in Ethics, Politics and Economics—a multidisciplinary major offered at Yale and modeled after the program in Philosophy, Politics, and Economics at the University of Oxford. Incidentally, I double-majored with East Asian Studies, another multidisciplinary major.

Resisting the channel toward a specialization was tougher while pursuing a doctorate, but even here I think I managed to evade the "you must be a single-discipline expert" police that have permeated almost every corner of academia. I sought out PhD programs in the study of innovation and entrepreneurship, inherently multi-/interdisciplinary topics, and was accepted into one such program at the Massachusetts Institute of Technology. The degree I pursued was housed at the Sloan School of Management and was offered by a program called the Management of Technological Innovation and Entrepreneurship. My coursework included economics, psychology, political science, sociology, history, and law.

Even after completing my education and seeking positions in the money management business, the tendency for immediate specialization was ubiquitous. Virtually every firm with which I interviewed wanted me to become an industry analyst focused on one or two industries. Several firms suggested that it would be best to also focus on a singular geography as well. I soon determined that the established system was based on a strong and widely held view that specialization in the financial markets was a source of advantage. In effect, the industry had created a strong and pervasive culture of "siloed" thinking in which specialists were focusing on geographies and industries. It was, in the language of Isaiah Berlin, an industry of hedgehogs—people who knew "one big thing." I instead became a fox.

In the course of forming my own investment philosophy and approach to thinking about the financial world, I developed a strong belief that a generalist approach (i.e., being a fox) was superior and that competitive insights were found not by competing against other experts but rather by looking between and across the silos. The saying "To a man with a hammer, many things look like nails" is particularly pertinent to the money-management industry, as many industry analysts are organized in silos. There are times when the worst energy idea may be better than the best consumer idea, yet such insights get lost with expert-oriented approaches. Seeking to continue my multidisciplinary life into the money-management industry, I operate as a global generalist.

■ ■ ■

Before describing what the book is, let me begin by describing what it is not. It is not a book about making day-to-day investment decisions or about the proper investment approach for a particular market. It is not about market timing. Nor is it a book that presents a unique investment philosophy. Many fine books have been written about these topics. Rather, this book is about the context in which these decisions and philosophies are implemented. It is about deciphering the needle-moving extremes that have the potential to render many traditional investment approaches useless. Rather than providing you with a map of how markets may move, *Boombustology* hopes to provide you a seismograph that can help identify forthcoming quakes.

Given my firm belief that insight is found by looking across and through multiple disciplines, it should come as no surprise that this book provides a multidisciplinary framework for evaluating the extremely complex social phenomenon of financial market booms and busts. This book differs from other treatments of financial extremes in three primary ways: (1) it develops and utilizes a multidisciplinary perspective, based on the findings of economics, psychology, and other disciplines; (2) it utilizes historical case studies to illustrate the power of multiple lenses; and (3) it summarizes these findings into a forward-looking framework useful in understanding and identifying future financial extremes. Upon conclusion of this book, the reader will be left with a robust understanding of the dynamics that precede, fuel, and ultimately reverse financial market extremes. It is also hoped that the reader will be well versed in the numerous indicators that telegraph the existence of a bubble.

This book is based on a course I teach at Yale that emphasizes a liberal arts approach to thinking about booms and busts. The focus is upon asset class bubbles. The book mimics the course in that it is divided into three parts. The first focuses on the five lenses that I consider to be most useful in the study of booms and busts: microeconomics, macroeconomics, psychology, politics, and biology. Why did I choose these lenses? Both micro- and macroeconomic lenses are too obvious to exclude and the recent emphasis on behavioral approaches necessitates its inclusion. Given the role of politics in developing the very foundation on which booms and busts develop, I included it as well. Space constraints limited me to five lenses, and I chose biology as the fifth to illustrate the power of a perspective external to the social sciences. I chose biology over physics as the economic emphasis on equilibrium is itself derived from physics.

Booms and busts that affect entire asset classes (versus those that might affect a particular industry or sector) are actually quite rare. As such, the second part of the book applies the five lenses to five case studies to generate a "bubble-spotting" theory. The cases chosen (Tulipmania, the Great Depression, the Japanese bubble, the Asian financial crisis, and the U.S. housing boom) were selected to represent variation in geography and time.

The third and final part of the book takes the lessons learned from Parts One and Two and develops a framework for proactively thinking about and identifying financial bubbles before they burst. The theory generated in the book is summarized in a framework presented in Part Three; I encourage researchers to test the importance of each indicator.

Topics included in the course but not in the book are the benefits of booms and busts and the coincidence of frauds and swindles with busts. Both are excluded here because they are not explicitly about the topic of identifying bubbles. Frauds, swindles, and scams are not-infrequent occurrences in boom times, but because they are unfortunately not revealed until after a bust is well developed, they are a lagging (and therefore less useful) indicator.

■ ■ ■

Chapter 1 focuses on the microeconomics of booms and busts, paying special attention to the tendency of prices under various circumstances. Given the dominant microeconomic ideas of market efficiency and supply and demand–driven equilibrium, the chapter describes them and various alternatives. The theory of reflexivity, developed by George Soros, is presented as a viable alternative to the equilibrium-seeking world of traditional microeconomics. The chapter concludes with a reconciliation of the disequilibrium suggested by reflexivity and the equilibrium assumed by microeconomics.

Chapter 2 focuses on credit cycles and financial instability. Three primary theories serve as the focus of the chapter: Irving Fisher's debt-deflation theory of depressions, Hyman Minsky's financial instability hypothesis, and the Austrian business cycle theory. The chapter concludes with a framework for thinking about credit cycles and their impact on asset prices.

Chapter 3 is about the cognitive biases found in most human decision making. The behavioral lens presented in this chapter focuses on the representativeness and availability heuristics that have historically guided human decision making toward appropriate answers, but that, in today's increasingly complex, uncertain, and interconnected world, have great potential to lead us astray. Other findings from the research on decision making are considered and presented, including biases caused by anchoring and insufficient adjustment, mental accounting, fairness, and existing endowments.

Chapter 4 focuses on the politics of property rights and the means through which a society determines the relative value of its goods (i.e., prices). The logic and ramifications of politically motivated price floors and price ceilings are considered, and the chapter concludes with a short discussion of tax policies and how they have the ability to impact asset prices by motivating (or disincentivizing) particular investment decisions by investors.

Chapter 5 attempts to take an emergent perspective from the study of biology and apply it to financial markets. Epidemics, herd behavior, and swarm logic/intelligence are the focus. The chapter focuses on two key lessons: how the study of epidemics and the diffusion of diseases can inform our study of booms and busts—with specific value in helping one understand the relative maturity of a bubble—and how group behavior can have a profoundly conforming impact on its seemingly individualistic members.

Part Two of the book presents five historical cases and utilizes the five lenses from Part One to evaluate them. Specifically, Chapter 6 evaluates the Tulipmania of the 1630s, Chapter 7 applies the lenses to the Florida land boom of the mid-1920s and the Great Depression, Chapter 8 is about the Japanese boom and bust, Chapter 9 presents the Asian financial crisis, with special attention paid to Thailand as the epicenter of the events that unfolded, and Chapter 10 evaluates the U.S. housing boom and bust of the 2000s.

Chapter 11 summarizes the five lenses and the five cases in a matrix-style analysis that attempts to generate a generalized framework for identifying bubbles before they burst. Key indicators or signposts of a financial bubble are formulated, and a checklist-style evaluation emerges as a means to gauge the likelihood of an unsustainable boom.

Chapter 12 applies the framework of Chapter 11 to one of the most controversial investment considerations in the world today: China. While China has emerged to be one of the best economic growth stories of the past 30 years, there are reasons to pause and think this may not continue. At the risk of giving away the punch line, Chapter 12 concludes that many indicators are highlighting an elevated probability that China is in the midst of a bubble that may burst. The *Boombustology* seismograph is picking up increased prequake rumbles.

The framework developed over the following pages has helped me navigate through recent financial booms and busts. I hope it will help you do the same, for in the wise words of Mark Twain, "Although history rarely repeats itself, it often does rhyme."

Vikram Mansharamani
Brookline, MA
December 2010

Acknowledgments

The ultimate origin of this book lies on a squash court in New Haven. After an exhausting and grueling squash match against a formidable competitor (I won), I sought his advice. "I'd like to put my PhD to work and perhaps teach a course here at Yale. What do you think?" His response set the wheels in motion: "I think it's a great idea! See if you can teach it as a college seminar." So it is that I must begin by thanking David Swensen for his encouragement and support in teaching a class at Yale. David is a fierce competitor, a loyal Yalie, a caring mentor, and overall class act. I feel extraordinarily lucky to have him as a friend. A course does not, however, a book make. Charley Ellis encouraged me to convert the course into a book and provided numerous introductions to facilitate its publication. Without his guidance and help, this book would not have been written.

I thank the many students I have had the pleasure of teaching. Over the course of my graduate education and subsequent years of teaching, I have met no group of students more motivated, insightful, intelligent, and analytical than the undergraduates at Yale University. They are, simply put, an absolute pleasure to teach because they exhibit natural curiosity, analytical rigor, and intellectual honesty. They have challenged me to think about this material more deeply and have helped refine my thinking.

My graduate education at MIT was an amazing experience that opened my eyes to a new way of thinking. I am particularly thankful to Michael Cusumano, my dissertation committee chair, for his patience as I wandered between academic and nonacademic pursuits. Professor Harvey Sapolsky of the Security Studies Program was a constant friend and mentor.

From a professional perspective, I have had the pleasure of working with many fine individuals over the past 20 years. Several have left major imprints on my way of thinking and have indirectly influenced the work presented here. While there are too many to mention, four of them selflessly took time to provide me with feedback, guidance, and encouragement as I wrote this book: Christopher Bodnar, Douglas Suliman, William Vens, and Matthew Vettel. I also particularly thank Dee Keesler for encouraging my teaching efforts at Yale and providing a professional environment supportive of "fox" thinking. Additional gratitude is owed to Hank Blaustein for rapidly and creatively capturing the spirit of Chapter 12.

My parents, Shobha and Vishnu Mansharamani, deserve special thanks. Without their sacrifices (financial and otherwise), I likely would not have had the opportunities in life that I have had.

Any working professional with a young family knows that time is scarce. It should therefore come as no surprise that my greatest debt of gratitude is to my family for their support in providing the time to write this book. Special acknowledgment is owed to my wife, Kristen Hanisch Mansharamani, who has tirelessly read every word. Her editorial capabilities have been tested repeatedly, initially through the writing of three graduate theses, and now through a book. Her dedication and commitment were steadfast. All errors remain hers. Actually, I think it is customary for me to take credit for the errors, but, as any spouse understands, blame is a matter of perspective!

Finally, I want to thank the editorial staff at John Wiley & Sons (especially Meg Freeborn, Claire Wesley, and Bill Falloon) for their persevering attention to detail and their unwavering commitment to my efforts, inconsistent as they may have been.

BOOM
BUST
OLOGY

The Study of Financial Extremes

ONE-ARMED ANALYSTS, SECRETS, MYSTERIES

Among the many noteworthy comments made by U.S. presidents over the years, perhaps one of the most pertinent with respect to the study of financial booms and busts was made by President Harry Truman: "Someone give me a one-armed economist!" The statement, made in response to the constant "on the one hand . . . on the other hand" presentation of analysis to him by his advisors, captured the discomfort most decision makers have with ambiguity and uncertainty. For better or worse, the world in which we now find ourselves is plagued with ambiguity and uncertainty. Globalization, economic interconnectedness, global warming, and international financial linkages are the reality of our sociopolitical-economic existence.

Boombustology takes President Truman's memorable phrase and flips it on its head. "Someone give me a five-armed analyst!" is my mantra. It is no longer enough for us to evaluate the bipolar possibilities suggested by a two-armed individual. The world is more complex, more uncertain, more dynamic, and more volatile than ever before. It is no longer enough to evaluate developments via a single perspective. Ambiguities rule the day, and as reflected by the title of Robert Rubin's insightful coauthored book, we live "in an uncertain world."

The fall of the Soviet Union was a defining moment of late twentieth-century world history, but it drove an existential reevaluation for government organizations like the U.S. Central Intelligence Agency. The Agency literally had its entire existence questioned, with many calling for its immediate abolishment.[1]

1

Rather than succumb to such pressure, the intelligence community instead rigorously reevaluated its purpose in a new world facing new threats and plagued with innumerable uncertainties. Although much of this thinking has broad applicability to the world in which we live today, very little has surfaced in a manner applicable to the dynamic financial and economic uncertainties that have recently dominated popular attention.

Secrets versus Mysteries

One of the primary insights from this intelligence community introspective analysis is that an inherent and profound difference exists between problems for which an answer exists and must be found versus problems for which no answer (yet) exists. The former case has been labeled a "puzzle" or "secret" while the latter case is considered a "mystery." Two leading scholars on these distinctions in the U.S. intelligence community are Gregory Treverton and Joseph Nye. Both have highlighted the significant ramifications of this seemingly simple distinction on the approach to generating intelligence.

Treverton eloquently explains the difference between secrets and mysteries in a *Smithsonian Magazine* article titled "Risks and Riddles." In it, he says:

> There's a reason millions of people try to solve crossword puzzles each day. Amid the well-ordered combat between a puzzler's mind and the blank boxes waiting to be filled, there is satisfaction along with frustration. Even when you can't find the right answer, you know it exists. Puzzles can be solved; they have answers.
>
> But a mystery offers no such comfort. It poses a question that has no definitive answer because the answer is contingent; it depends on a future interaction of many factors, known and unknown. A mystery cannot be answered; it can only be framed, by identifying the critical factors and applying some sense of how they have interacted in the past and might interact in the future. A mystery is an attempt to define ambiguities.[2]

Nye goes on to clarify the distinction in more explicit intelligence community terminology:

A secret is something concrete that can be stolen by a spy or discerned by a technical sensor, such as the number of SS-18 missiles in the Soviet Union or the size of their warheads. A mystery is an abstract puzzle to which no one can be sure of the answer. For example, will Boris Yeltsin be able to control inflation in Russia a year from now? No one can steal that secret from Yeltsin. He does not know the answer. He may not even be in office a year from now.[3]

The distinction these intelligence community scholars make between puzzles and mysteries has broad pertinence to financial markets. Consider the early 2007 *New Yorker* article "Open Secrets" written by Malcolm Gladwell. In it, Gladwell highlights the "perils of too much information" and how understanding the difference between puzzles and mysteries leads to a radical reinterpretation of the Enron scandal. Gladwell notes that the truth about Enron's transactions was openly revealed in public filings and all it took was a diligent *Wall Street Journal* reporter to unveil the issues at hand. The needed capability was not the ability to find particular information, but rather the skill to assemble disparate data points into a clear image of the whole. The problem is not one of inadequate information, but instead one of too much information overwhelming the processing capabilities of "one-armed" analysts.

Different Problems Necessitate Different Approaches

Given that puzzles (i.e., problems for which there are indeed knowable answers) and mysteries (i.e., problems for which there are not knowable answers) are fundamentally different, it should come as no surprise that they necessitate radically different approaches. Consider the relative importance of information and data gathering in each problem.

In the case of a puzzle, the problem is simple: a lack of specific information (i.e., the answer) drives the need for more and more data. More information may contain the answer, so the best approach to addressing a puzzle is to get more information. As mentioned by Treverton above, the Soviet Union was a puzzle. The American intelligence community simply needed to gather more data (via satellites, aerial photography, and human intelligence, for starters) to seek the answer.

Mysteries, on the other hand, are less clear. Information is plentiful, and additional data is unlikely to enhance understanding. In addressing mysteries, more information is likely to make the problem more difficult to understand. There is no answer per se in the form of specific data. Rather, insight exists in how the data comes together. In describing the role of the intelligence analysts in the post-Soviet era, Nye noted that they are "people assembling a jigsaw puzzle who have some nifty nuggets inside a box but need to see the picture on the cover to see how they fit."[4] Finding the pieces is "puzzle work." Forming the cover image is "mystery work."

To understand mysteries, we need sophisticated analysis that looks across differing sources of data and evaluates existing information through multiple lenses to uncover a probabilistic answer of how best to understand the mystery. It is only through the use of multiple lenses that we might be able to get a sense of the picture on the jigsaw puzzle box. One lens might only consider color, another might consider the shapes of the pieces, noting the existence of straight edges, a third might focus on anticipated images that are being formed from the other lenses, and so forth.

Nye notes the problem of what I call single-lens analysis in highlighting how the perspectives of the State Department might materially differ from those of the Department of Defense:

> In policy circles, the old adage is that where you stand depends on where you sit. In intelligence, what you foresee is often affected by where you work. The primary duty of departmental analysts is to respond to the needs of their organizations. Diplomats are supposed to negotiate solutions. Even in apparently hopeless situations, they tend to press departmental analysts for the one chance in a hundred that might permit success. Generals are supposed to win battles. Even in hopeful situations, they tend to press their intelligence analysts for estimates of what they will have to face if worst comes to worst . . . The best solution to such human and bureaucratic problems is multiple points of view that are brought together in one place . . .[5]

Given insights that help elucidate mysteries exist within the mountains of already-available information and data, the key to understanding mysteries lies in filtering and data analysis. Further, as described by Nye, any one filter is necessarily going to be biased—a reality that necessitates the need for multiple lenses. More information (i.e., solving puzzles) will only exacerbate these biases, whereas multiple perspectives will help filter and extract insight from information (i.e., understanding mysteries).

Balancing the general's desire for a worst-case scenario with the diplomat's desire for a best-case scenario will lead to a more calibrated, reasoned, and balanced perspective on the reality of a situation. Likewise, as shall be argued below, financial booms and busts can be best understood when one balances an economist's focus on efficiency with a psychologist's focus on cognitive biases with the insights gained via the use of other lenses.

Financial Booms and Busts as Mysteries

Financial booms and busts are mysteries; they are, particularly from an a priori perspective, probabilistic events for which multidisciplinary analysis is essential. Addressing financial booms and busts as a puzzle may not only prove to be without value, it may in fact have negative impacts and lead to gross misunderstandings.

Thinking of booms and busts as puzzles will lead to a greater emphasis on singular perspectives. It leads to an emphasis on depth of data versus breadth of information. It leads to deeper and more thorough understanding of particular information, but it misses the point that information is not the essential element. There are plenty of "dots" but connections between them are lacking. We need a framework for connecting the dots in a manner that helps extract insight from the tremendous amounts of information and data that are already available.

As noted by Gladwell, "A puzzle grows simpler with the addition of each new piece of information" while "mysteries require judgment and the assessment of uncertainty."[6] Conceiving of financial booms and busts as a mystery necessitates the application of different lenses to develop a probabilistic interpretation of the facts to better understand the situation.

This book provides a framework through which the application of five key disciplines results in a more robust understanding of boom and bust mysteries. The five lenses are microeconomics, macroeconomics, psychology, politics, and biology. Almost by definition, each lens is based on the underlying worldview and beliefs that each discipline is based on. By melding insights from and across these fields, *Boombustology* will help you become a five-armed analyst. While the one-armed analyst sought by Truman might make for *easier* decisions, the five-armed analyst is likely to guide leaders toward *better* decisions.

PART

I

Five Lenses

Part One surveys five disciplines: microeconomics, macroeconomics, psychology, politics, and biology. Each discipline, or lens, is presented as a useful tool in deciphering the mysteries of bubbles before they burst. Specific topics emerging from these five lenses include equilibrium tendencies, reflexivity, credit dynamics, overconfidence, anchoring and adjustment, price mechanisms, property rights, epidemics, and emergence.

CHAPTER 1

Microeconomic Perspectives
TO EQUILIBRIUM OR NOT?

The most interesting, and profitable, times to be involved in investment management are when Mr. Smith's invisible hand is visibly broken.

—Paul A. McCulley

I n this opening chapter, we begin our discussion of the various lenses that prove useful in the study of booms and busts by focusing upon a critically important and far-reaching element of traditional microeconomic theory: supply and demand–driven financial equilibrium. Two competing and seemingly contradictory theories are presented and discussed—the efficient market hypothesis and the theory of reflexivity.

There are many ways in which to illustrate the concept of equilibrium, but it is perhaps best analogized with a ball on a curved shape (see Figure 1.1). A situation in which equilibrium is possible is one in which over time, if left to its own devices, the ball will find one unique location. Overshooting and undershooting this unique location is self-correcting. A situation of disequilibrium, however, is one in which the ball is unable to find a unique location. A ball in such a state does not generate self-correcting moves that dampen its moves toward a theoretical "equilibrium" or resting spot; rather,

9

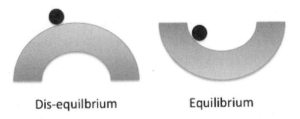

Dis-equilbrium   Equilibrium

Figure 1.1   Equilibrium in Pictures

disequilibrium generates motion that is self-reinforcing and accelerates the ball's move away from any stable state.

The application of these concepts to the financial arena is very straightforward. The concept of a stable point is best analogized with a price or valuation level in the financial arena. The general idea behind price equilibrium stems from the powerful forces of supply and demand. Inherent in most equilibrium-oriented approaches is a belief that higher prices generate new supply that tends to push prices down. Likewise, it is believed that lower prices generate new demand that tends to push prices up. In this way, deviations from an appropriate price level are self-correcting.

We begin with the traditional economic lens that adopts an equilibrium-oriented view of the financial world. In addition to being based on intuitive supply (the higher the price, the more will be produced) and demand (the higher the price, the lower the demand) logic, the argument in favor of equilibrium is seductively simple. Following a discussion of the efficient market hypothesis and its implications for financial equilibrium, the chapter then turns to the theory of reflexivity. Developed by billionaire George Soros, the theory states that misperceptions about reality may become self-fulfilling, driving prices to ever-greater distances from any supposed stability point.

The careful reader will complete this chapter with the tools to consider financial developments as being equilibrium-oriented or not—which in and of itself should prove valuable in the study of and participation in financial markets. The chapter concludes with a plausible framework for combining the usefulness of both equilibrium and reflexivity lenses.

"Random Walks" and Accurate Prices: The Efficient Market Hypothesis

Adam Smith observed in 1776 that individual, selfish pursuits are able to achieve optimal group outcomes better than if individuals selflessly pursued what they each deemed best for the group. It was as if the self-interested individual is "led by an invisible hand to promote an end which was no part of his intention . . . [B]y pursuing his own interest, he frequently promotes that of society more effectually than when he really intends to promote it."[1]

Economic thinking has been profoundly influenced by this early idea that selfish pursuits allocate scarce resources more efficiently than any individual might, despite the noblest of intentions. The laws of supply and demand drive the most efficient allocation of resources, and prices provide accurate signals for the increasing (or decreasing) of supply, with demand rising as prices fall or falling as prices rise.[2] An analogous construct in finance is the efficient market hypothesis, a theory that posits prices of financial securities embody all known information and therefore only move randomly.

The early origins of the efficient market hypothesis can be traced back to George Rutledge Gibson, who in 1889 asserted that the prices of shares that were well known in an open market embodied "the judgment of the best intelligence concerning them."[3] The statement captures one of the two key building blocks upon which the efficient market hypothesis was built, namely that prices "contain" or "embody" all available public information. This assertion, which was later developed with greater rigor and precision in the twentieth century, was combined with early econometric work asserting that security prices move in a random manner. This latter claim, developed primarily by MIT economist Paul Samuelson and University of Chicago economist Eugene Fama, essentially stated that stock prices were not predictable based on their prior movements.

Fama and Samuelson, who were both building upon an unpublished dissertation by Louis Bachelier written in 1900 titled "The Theory of Speculation," provided a compelling framework for understanding the behavior of stock prices through further conceptual development of the efficient market hypothesis.[4] In particular, Fama extended, refined, and further developed the theory by articulating three forms of efficiency that exist in the financial markets: weak, semi-strong, and strong.

Before describing each of these three forms of efficiency in greater detail, it is useful to consider the market conditions (i.e. assumptions) on which the theories of efficiency are based. In particular, the efficient market hypothesis requires that participants (in the aggregate) are on average correct and that information is immediately and without friction incorporated by these participants. There is no explicit requirement that individuals be rational or even correct. The only requirement is that individual participants not systematically be irrational in the same manner. This means that any irrationality exhibited at the individual level must be offset by contrary irrationality among other individuals such that the "average" individual is not irrational.

As will be questioned below and again in Chapter 3, one of the root underlying assumptions or beliefs in efficient pricing is that all information is interpreted by all participants in exactly the same way. In reality, however, each individual participant may interpret data differently or come to unique conclusions about its importance. To say that all individuals have the same information does not necessarily imply that all individuals come to the same conclusion. In fact, as described below, misinterpretations can compound upon themselves as differing conclusions from common data might reinforce themselves.

Now, let us turn to the three forms of efficiency. The weak form of market efficiency describes a situation in which prior security prices provide no predictive value with respect to future security prices. According to weak form efficiency, evaluating historical stock price movements proves futile in the search for outperformance in the long run. In the language of today's financial analysts, weak form efficiency is a theory that technical analysis—the study of prior price movements as the basis to predict future price movements, independent of any fundamental developments—does not work. Weak form efficiency does not imply that fundamental analysis is not fruitful, just that price movements exhibit no predictable pattern. Stock prices stumble through time in what Fama describes as a "random walk."[5]

The semi-strong form of market efficiency describes a scenario in which publicly available information fails to provide any predictive value with respect to future security prices. Thus, semi-strong efficiency is really a statement about the rapidity of information incorporation. It implies that share prices instantaneously adjust to new information such that consistently profitable trading on the revelation of such information is not possible. Semi-strong efficiency builds on the weak form's belief that technical analysis is useless and implies that fundamental analysis is also useless.[6]

Finally, the strong form of the efficient market hypothesis suggests that all information (private, public, and otherwise) is fully reflected within the prices of securities, and as such, prices are always correct in that there is no information that provides predictive value with respect to future security prices.[7] Table 1.1 summarizes these three forms of efficiency.

Although the theory of market efficiency was clearly intended to be a simplifying construct and a model useful in helping to explain reality, it was extremely well received by those seeking to understand the volatile (and range-bound) equity markets of the 1960s and 1970s. Specifically, corporate America, Wall Street, and regulators greeted the efficient market hypothesis with a warm reception—resulting in its deep burrowing into the fabric of finance.

Implications of Financial Efficiency

The rapid acceptance of the efficient market hypothesis in financial and regulatory communities was a result of its elegance. The seemingly simple idea that security prices fully reflect all available information meant that markets were "right," and that price moves were accurate reflections of changing fundamentals. Although this logic imbued many facets of the financial industry, the most important manifestations of it are found in the realm of regulatory philosophy and money-management practices.

Table 1.1   The Three Forms of Market Efficiency

	Weak	Semi-strong	Strong
Price Information	Prices move in random ways	Prices incorporate all publicly available information	Prices fully reflect all public, private, and other information
Role of Technical Analysis	Not useful	Not useful	Not useful
Role of Fundamental Analysis	Useful	Not useful	Not useful
Role of "Inside"/ Non-Public Information	Useful	Useful	Not useful
Method for generating outperformance	Traditional fundamental research	Seeking a nonpublic "edge"	None

Time columnist Justin Fox, in *The Myth of the Rational Market*, succinctly summarizes the impact of this warm reception:

> It was a powerful idea, helping to inspire the first index funds, the investment approach called modern portfolio theory, the risk-adjusted performance measures that shape the money management business, the corporate creed of shareholder value, the rise of derivatives, and the hands-off approach to financial regulation that prevailed in the United States from the 1970s on.[8]

If one believes that security prices are right and completely reflect all available information and expectations, then there is absolutely no room for the consideration that prices are excessively depressed or overly ebullient. Bubbles do not exist in this world, and as such, asset prices are not and should not be a consideration for policymakers. Further, securities regulations need only focus on the creation of a level playing field vis-à-vis insider information, the protection of the public from untrue and unscrupulous marketing, and the prevention of illegal manipulation. Matters such as margin rates, counterparty risk, disclosure requirements, and other mechanical considerations become secondary. This overarching philosophy that "markets know best" has been the guiding light behind much of western-style democratic capitalism since the 1970s, due largely to the broad intellectual appeal and elegant simplicity of the efficient market hypothesis.

Another dramatic implication was that efficiency obviates the need for active portfolio management, whereby investors attempt to outperform the market. After all, if security prices already reflect all available information and there is no predictive value in any information, what value is there in conducting analysis using available information? Better instead to simply "buy the whole market" in a passive manner and not pay the fees associated with active management. The growth of passive money management (primarily manifested in the rapid rise of index funds) has been enormous since the 1970s and at least partially reflects the mass appeal of this efficiency argument.

The Boom and Bust of Efficiency

The common sense critique of the efficient market hypothesis is best captured by the often-quoted joke about the economist and a friend walking down the street. After stumbling upon a $100 bill lying on the ground, the economist's friend reaches down to pick it up, marveling at her good fortune. Before she actually picks it up, however, the economist says, "Don't waste your efforts. If it were a genuine $100 bill, it would already have been picked up by someone else."

The absolute domination of the efficient market hypothesis over economic affairs around the world cannot be overstated. In fact, the 1997 Nobel Prize in Economic Sciences was awarded to Robert C. Merton and Myron Scholes for "a new method to determine the value of derivatives."[9] At the very root of their contribution was a belief that rational, efficient pricing of assets was inevitable and prices would tend toward identifiable equilibria. These two academics were also moonlighting as financiers helping to manage what at the time appeared to be one of the most successful hedge funds of all time, Long-Term Capital Management (LTCM).

LTCM employed a strategy of identifying small inefficiencies in which prices had deviated from their model-derived equilibrium price. The fund then used massive amounts of borrowed money to magnify their bets. In some instances, their bets were magnified through the use of more than $100 of borrowed money for each $1 of invested capital.[10] Although complicated, Nobel-prize winning, mathematically advanced formulas were behind the fund's strategies, one basic underlying premise served as the foundation of their worldview on which the whole firm's approach was based: Prices tended toward identifiable equilibria. The firm had billions and billions of dollars (some argue almost a trillion dollars) at risk behind a belief that prices operated according to the right-hand picture in Figure 1.1.

Despite the enormous leverage involved, LTCM had never had a monthly loss of greater than 3 percent prior to 1998.[11] Global economic uncertainty driven by the Asian financial crisis and the Russian debt default, however, were enough to cause not one, but two days (August 21, 1998 and September 21, 1998) of more than $500,000,000 in losses.[12] According to the LTCM equilibrium-oriented financial models, the likelihood of having one such day was 1 in 50 million. The likelihood of two such days was incalculably small. Needless to say, the revelation of the flawed framework, as well as the huge monetary losses, were shocking to the LTCM financial wizards in Greenwich. Not surprisingly, author Michael Lewis described August 21, 1998 as "the worst day in the young history of scientific finance."[13]

The most ironic element of the story, of course, is that a team of efficiency-committed, Nobel prize–winning "equilibriumists" effectively undermined their intellectual position by first demonstrating it was possible to generate excess returns (i.e., that markets were not in fact efficient) and then by blowing up due to massive market inefficiency.

More recently, Alan Greenspan, "a card-carrying member of the free market brigade"[14] and Ayn Rand devotee, testified to the U.S. Congress that "I do have an ideology. . .that free, competitive markets are by far the unrivaled way to organize economies."[15] In response to later questioning about how his philosophy might reconcile with regulation, his response was straightforward: "We've tried regulations. None meaningfully worked."[16] As a result of this philosophy, the Chairman of the Federal Reserve took an extraordinarily (but not entirely) hands-off approach to the financial markets. I say "not entirely" because the very existence of a central bank is in fact contradictory to a free market perspective. By basically setting the short-term interest rate in America, the Federal Reserve is effectively a central planner that dismisses supply and demand fundamentals in the money market and chooses a price for money that it deems appropriate. As we will see in Chapter 2, a small group of economists (collectively known as the Austrian school of economics) have argued that such meddling in the money markets is perhaps *the* root cause of booms and busts.

Nevertheless, by the fall of 2008, amid one of the most severe economic downturns since the Great Depression, Greenspan indicated to Congress that he had found a flaw in his model of how the financial world works. In fact, he went on to describe the greater impact of the credit crunch on the philosophy of market efficiency, saying, "The whole intellectual edifice collapsed in the summer of last year."[17] For this devout free-marketeer and devotee of market efficiency, such a statement was equivalent to serving pork for lunch during Ramadan in the holy mosques of both Medina and Mecca.

Constant Instability and Inefficiency: The Theory of Reflexivity

George Soros, the hedge fund manager famous for speculating on the dynamics of financial markets, is more known for his financial wizardry than his philosophical musings. Nevertheless, his theory of reflexivity provides a tremendously powerful lens through which to (re)consider market efficiency. Using a "reflexive" lens to view booms and busts proves quite useful, and this section will explain the theory of reflexivity and its primary implications for financial markets.

At its roots, Soros' theory of reflexivity is a theory on the limits of human knowledge. If this is not a grandiose enough topic, the underlying focus of the theory is on the determination of reality and truth in complex social phenomena (like financial markets). The theory is a product of his intellectual devotion to Karl Popper, the early twentieth-century Austrian philosopher and author of *Open Society and Its Enemies.*

Popper's primary philosophical contributions relate to the asymmetry in the development and falsification of theory. The fundamental problem of science, claimed Popper, is that it cannot prove anything. Rather, virtually all efforts to produce knowledge are based on induction and induction is inherently problematic. The "problem of induction," relates to the fact that while all confirmatory evidence cannot prove a fact, one contrary piece of evidence can indeed falsify a supposed fact. Thus, although the sun has risen and set every day (thereby leading to a theory that the sun is on a cycle of rising and falling every 24 hours), the mere fact that it has occurred does not mean that it will continue to occur. However, if the sun were to ever not rise and set in a 24-hour period, the theory would be proven false.[18]

Soros goes on to identify two primary "functions" in the social arena. The first, called the cognitive function is the act through which a participant observes the social situation in which he finds himself. The second, the participating function, is the act by which participants participate in (and therefore affect) the social situation. The operation by which these two functions interact is reflexivity. He summarizes: "Reflexivity is, in effect, a two-way feedback mechanism in which reality helps shape the participants' thinking and the participants' thinking helps shape reality in an unending process in which thinking and reality may come to approach each other but can never become identical."[19] This delta between reality and thinking is known as the participants' bias.

A key implication of this two-way feedback mechanism is that social phenomena have an indeterminacy not present in the natural sciences. There is, according to Soros, no objective truth, and perceptions affect reality as much as reality affects perceptions.

While many have suggested that observers might affect the reality they seek to observe, Soros is unique in suggesting that observers actually change the reality that they are diligently trying to observe, and that this changed reality in turn affects their perception, creating a self-reinforcing cycle that compounds misperceptions.

Rather than suggesting an additional or alternative lens through which to view reality, Soros actually goes further to suggest that the scientific method and the basis on which supposed knowledge has been generated is not applicable to the social sciences. Given that economics is the social science that most emulates the natural sciences (thought by many to be the result of "physics envy"), Soros is effectively attacking the supposed rigor of the economic approach. The theory of reflexivity suggests that when it comes to events that have thinking participants, there is no such thing as objective knowledge. Participants act based on their beliefs, which are derived from observing the actions of participants, which are based on their own beliefs, and so on.

Soros bluntly stated his conclusion in a 1994 speech to the MIT Department of Economics: "Thinking participants cannot act on the basis of knowledge. Knowledge presupposes facts which occur independently of the statements which refer to them, but being a participant implies that one's decisions influence the outcome."[20] Soros fully admits that reflexivity does not occur in every case, but that when it does occur, the dynamics of the situation make traditional scientific approaches (meaning those based on observation) less useful. Figure 1.2 demonstrates how reflexivity is not merely a different way of observing, but rather a radically different process through which reality unfolds.

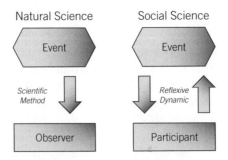

Figure 1.2   Natural vs. Social Science: Key Observational Distinctions

The key point, then, is that reflexivity is significant because it describes a situation in which misperceptions can be self-reinforced into reality. For this to occur, a strong interaction between the participant and the event must exist to transform the misperception into reality: "What renders reflexivity significant is that it occurs only intermittently. If it were present in all situations all the time, it would merely constitute a different way of looking at events and not a different way for events to evolve."[21]

Implications of Reflexivity

For Soros, a Hungarian-born Jew whose family had avoided Nazi persecution through wily tactics such as name changing and secretive movements, it was virtually impossible to believe that truth was knowable or even useful as a concept. The implications of reflexivity on financial markets are quite profound, particularly with regard to the existence of an equilibrium price. Soros describes these implications in his own words quite succinctly:

> Instead of a tendency towards some kind of theoretical equilibrium, the participants' views and actual state of affairs enter into a process of dynamic disequilibrium, which may be self-reinforcing at first, moving both thinking and reality in a certain direction, but is bound to become unsustainable in the long run and engender a move in the opposite direction.[22]

In fact, his 1994 testimony to the House Banking Committee eloquently summarizes his theory of reflexivity and how it can occasionally rear its head in financial markets:

> I must state at the outset that I am in fundamental disagreement with the prevailing wisdom. The generally accepted theory is that markets tend towards equilibrium and on the whole discount the future correctly. I operate using a different theory, according to which financial markets cannot possibly discount the future correctly because they do not merely discount the future, they help to shape it. In certain circumstances, financial markets can affect the so-called fundamentals which they are supposed to reflect. When that happens, markets enter into a state of dynamic disequilibrium and behave

quite differently than what would be considered normal by the theory of efficient markets. Such boom/bust sequences do not arise very often, but when they do, they can be very disruptive, precisely because they affect the fundamentals of the economy.[23]

Soros goes on to claim that financial extremes are characterized by two primary components: a prevailing trend that exists in reality and a misconception relating to it. He often uses real estate as an example to illustrate this point. The prevailing trend in reality is that there is an increased willingness to lend and a corresponding rise in prices. The misconception relating to this trend is that the prices of real estate are independent of the willingness to lend.[24] Further, as more banks become willing to lend, and the number of buyers therefore rises, the prices of real estate rise—thereby making the banks feel more secure (given higher collateral values) and driving more lending.

The Reluctant Recognition of Reflexivity

George Soros has used his theory of reflexivity to make billions of dollars for his investors and himself. This does not imply, however, that he has been completely accurate in his predictions. Rather, Soros has been good at managing risk. At the very root of his philosophy is an understanding that he does not know (actually, that he cannot know) anything with 100 percent certainty.

Soros has been glaringly wrong (or perhaps just very early) in some of his predictions. In his 1998 book, *The Crisis of Global Capitalism,* Soros boldly predicted "the imminent disintegration of the global capitalist system."[25] In 2001, he later admitted during a seminar in New York that he "got carried away" and that he now has "egg on his face."[26] Despite the bold (and at the time wrong) prediction about the implosion of capitalism, recent events have turned in favor of his arguments. In fact, his 2008 testimony to Congress captures the essence of his current thinking:

> The salient feature of the current crisis is that it was not caused by some external shock like OPEC raising the price of oil or a particular country or financial institution defaulting. The crisis was generated by the financial system itself. This fact—that the

defect was inherent in the system—contradicts the prevailing theory, which holds that financial markets tend toward equilibrium and that deviations from the equilibrium either occur in a random manner or are caused by some sudden external event to which markets have difficulty adjusting. The severity and amplitude of the crisis provides convincing evidence that there is something fundamentally wrong with this prevailing theory . . . Usually markets correct their own mistakes, but occasionally there is a misconception or misperception that finds a way to reinforce a trend that is already present in reality and by doing so reinforces itself. Such self-reinforcing processes may carry markets into far-from-equilibrium territory. Unless something happens to abort the reflexive interaction sooner, it may persist until the misconception becomes so glaring that it has to be recognized as such . . .[27]

The fact that the theory of reflexivity has been so effective at explaining the most impactful events in financial markets (i.e., the extremes) has been the basis of its recent, albeit reluctant, recognition by practitioners and academics. While it has yet to be fully-accepted, the glaring failures of the efficiency arguments over the past 20 years have resulted in an increasing openness to alternatives. Simply put, the existing efficiency framework is not always accurate, and reflexivity helps fill in the holes when it fails. Stability is not ensured by simple supply and demand dynamics. Rather, there are times in asset markets when higher prices generate more demand (not more supply) and when lower prices generate more supply (not more demand). As noted by Soros above, these self-reinforcing processes can generate instability from within the system.[28]

Reconciling Efficiency and Reflexivity

By attempting to reconcile the seemingly incompatible approaches of the efficiency and reflexivity lenses, this chapter concludes by suggesting a contingent approach to using the lenses. Even though Soros adamantly opposes the logic of efficiency, he does concede that markets usually correct themselves. Thus, the efficiency argument for a stable equilibrium that results in events tending toward it seems viable—most of the time. However, it also seems likely that

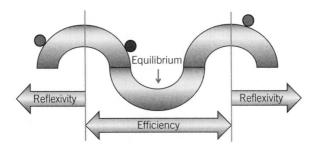

Figure 1.3   Reconciling Efficiency and Reflexivity

events that occur far from equilibrium or are reinforced beyond a certain distance from that equilibrium are unlikely to return to it.

Figure 1.3 attempts to capture these two distinct phases using the balls and hills logic utilized earlier in the chapter. In the figure, one can notice that events transpiring in the efficiency band will tend toward an equilibrium point. The same is not true, however, for the balls that have entered the realm of far-from-equilibrium reflexive developments. These balls are unlikely to stabilize in any specific condition unless assisted by an external force.

Most of the time, efficiency logic works and deviations from equilibria tend to self-correct. However, there are instances in which reflexive dynamics are able to overcome the self-correcting force and create self-fulfilling extremes. The investment implications of this efficiency/reflexivity duality are that Adam Smith's invisible hand, which normally drives an appropriate price discovery process, occasionally breaks down. It is precisely when such dynamics take over that extremes become increasingly likely.

2

Macroeconomic Perspectives

THE IMPACT OF DEBT AND DEFLATION
ON ASSET MARKETS AND PRICES

It may sometimes be expedient for a man to heat the stove with his furniture. But he should not delude himself by believing that he has discovered a wonderful new method of heating his premises.
                                                    —Ludwig von Mises

The chapter makes a leap to macro thinking from the micro considerations of the last chapter. Though not shocking, it seems that what makes sense for the individual may not always make sense for the group. Highlighting how this paradox of aggregation operates, Paul McCulley notes:

> Anybody who's ever been a spectator at a crowded ball game has witnessed the difference between microeconomics and macroeconomics: from a micro perspective, it is rational for each individual to stand up to get a better view; but from a macro perspective, each individual acting rationally will produce the irrational outcome of everybody standing, but nobody having a better view.[1]

In economic spheres, this fallacy of composition can be more extreme and have more dramatic impacts on society. Specifically, analysis conducted at an individual unit of analysis may not apply to groups.[2] Consider home finance. Though it may be reasonable for an individual bank to believe that it can foreclose and sell the house for a value in excess of the mortgage amount, this conclusion is very suspect when considering millions of homes simultaneously being sold. This latter case will crash the market for homes and result in significantly lower prices.

The underlying premise evaluated in this chapter is that debt and the amplification of debt by deflation can have deleterious impacts on individuals, companies, and in aggregate, markets. Before diving into the conditions under which these effects can snowball in dramatic fashion, we first review the mechanics of debt. More specifically, understanding leverage and how it impacts equity values is essential to grasping how debt exacerbates ups and downs into booms and busts. After describing the mechanisms through which debt amplifies returns, the chapter turns to a somewhat less traditional perspective on the role of money and credit in the creation of booms and busts—Hyman Minsky's Financial Instability Hypothesis. We then explore Irving Fisher's debt-deflation theory, as well as the Austrian Business Cycle Theory and conclude the chapter by integrating these perspectives into a single macroeconomic framework.

The Magnifying Power of Leverage

Suppose you purchased a house for $100 (a real steal!). Because you didn't have all the money needed to buy the house, you decide to take out a loan for a portion of the purchase price. The amount you put down will be your equity in the home, and mortgage value will be your debt. Now let us consider two separate scenarios. The first, called "Happy Times," is one in which the value of your newly purchased home rises by 10 percent. The second, "Sad Times," is a situation in which the price of your newly purchased home falls by 10 percent.

What happens to your investment in each of these scenarios? Table 2.1 summarizes the impact on your investment for a range of down payments under each case. Four rows are highlighted to demonstrate the impact of debt: 10 percent down, 20 percent down, 50 percent down, and 100 percent payment in full.

Table 2.1   Debt's Amplification Power

Initial Value	Initial		Happy Times				Sad Times			
	% down	Equity	Value	Debt	Equity	Return	Value	Debt	Equity	Return
$100	0%	$0	$110	$100	$10	Infinite	$90	$100	($10)	Infinite
$100	10%	$10	$110	$90	$20	100%	$90	$90	0	(100%)
$100	20%	$20	$110	$80	$30	50%	$90	$80	$10	(50%)
$100	30%	$30	$110	$70	$40	33%	$90	$70	$20	(33%)
$100	40%	$40	$110	$60	$50	25%	$90	$60	$30	(25%)
$100	50%	$50	$110	$50	$60	20%	$90	$50	$40	(20%)
$100	60%	$60	$110	$40	$70	17%	$90	$40	$50	(17%)
$100	70%	$70	$110	$30	$80	14%	$90	$30	$60	(14%)
$100	80%	$80	$110	$20	$90	13%	$90	$20	$70	(13%)
$100	90%	$90	$110	$10	$100	11%	$90	$10	$80	(11%)
$100	100%	$100	$110	$0	$110	10%	$90	$0	$90	(10%)

In the scenario in which you do not borrow any money and pay for your house with $100 (i.e., 100 percent down), your investment return in each case is equal to the change in the asset value (i.e., +10 percent in home value = +10 percent in equity value). As the amount of debt utilized increases, however, the return on your invested capital is a multiple of the return. For instance, if you purchased your home with $50 down and a $50 mortgage, then a 10 percent move in the house price equated to a 20 percent move in your equity value. Likewise, with 20 percent down, a 10 percent move in the house price equates to a 50 percent move in your equity value. In each of these cases, the return on your equity is equal to a multiple of the return on the house. More precisely, the equity return is equal to

$$\text{Return of asset} \times (1 \; / \; \% \; \text{Down})$$

In sum, debt amplifies your returns—you make more money when asset values rise, and you lose more money when asset values fall. Given the powerful amplification feature of debt, it should come as no surprise that some of the most persuasive arguments explaining boom and bust cycles are based on debt and debt cycles.

Collateral Rates and Debt Dynamics

To understand debt dynamics in a more granular way, let us look at three different families: the Safe Smiths, the Optimistic Osbornes, and the Carefree Carrolls.[3] As you meet each of these families, pay attention to their risk profiles and how each fares under Happy Times and Sad Times. Here are some facts that apply to all three families:

- All houses cost $100
- Each family earns $25 per year before taxes ($15 after taxes)
- Each family has nonmortgage expenses of $10 per year
- Money available for mortgage payments each year is therefore $5
- All mortgages are obtained from Local Bank ABC, must be refinanced or paid off at the end of five years, and are available with the terms shown in Table 2.2 thanks to a government program guaranteeing access to home purchase finance

The Safe Smiths are a conservative bunch. Mr. and Mrs. Smith both work and the family lives within its means. Like all other families in the neighborhood, the Safe Smiths purchased a home this year for $100. Although they have savings in excess of $100, they decided to purchase the home with $40 down and a $60 mortgage. Because they put 40 percent down and their mortgage amount is less than $100, the rate that they obtained for their mortgage was 4 percent. Their yearly interest payments to the bank are therefore $2.40, and if they are interested in paying off their mortgage in 30 years, their

Table 2.2   Local Bank ABC Loan Rates

	Loan Amount	
Down Payment	<$100	$100 +
0%	7.00%	7.50%
10%	6.25%	6.75%
20%	5.50%	6.00%
30%	4.75%	5.25%
40%	4.00%	4.50%
50%	3.25%	3.75%

annual payment (i.e., principal and interest) is equal to $3.44. Given they have $5 available for mortgage payments, the Safe Smiths sleep well at night and are not worried about their budget.

The Optimistic Osbornes are a bit more aggressive. They believe the future is bright, and are willing to plan on a better tomorrow. They haven't saved as much as the Safe Smiths, but have enough capital for a 20 percent down payment. Thus, they take out an $80 mortgage and the bank gives them a mortgage rate of 5.5 percent. Their yearly interest payments to the bank are $4.40, and if they are interested in paying off their mortgage in 30 years, their monthly payment is equal to $5.45. Like all other families in the neighborhood, the Optimistic Osbornes only have $5 available for mortgage payments, so they opt for an "interest only" mortgage and agree to pay the $4.40 per year. The family is optimistic that Mr. Osborne may get a promotion (with an accompanying increase in salary) or that the house will appreciate in the near future. Even if they cannot begin paying the full $5.45 per year, the Osborne family is confident that they can refinance the house once it has appreciated and get a lower interest rate on their mortgage.

Finally, the Carefree Carrolls are an optimistic lot who live solely in the present. They don't think about the future and believe tomorrow is always better than today, that house prices always go up, and that budgeting is a worthless task. The Carefree Carrolls love to consume and have not saved very much over the years. As a result, they have no money for a down payment and must seek $100 of financing. Thanks to government programs encouraging homeownership, they are able to get the mortgage at a rate of 7.5 percent, with a flexible payment schedule. For the first three years of ownership, they are allowed to pay what they are able and any unpaid interest will be added to the principal of the loan. Their yearly interest payments to the bank are $7.50, and if they are interested in paying off their mortgage in 30 years, their annual payment is equal to $8.39. Given they only have $5 available for mortgage payments, the bank has arranged to let the Carefree Carrolls pay $5 and let $2.50 be added to the balance of the mortgage at the end of the year. The family is ecstatic they're able to buy their new home and, given the stories they've heard of people making money in real estate, are looking forward to real estate riches.

Table 2.3 summarizes the financial obligation structures for these three families.

Table 2.3   Comparing the Safe Smiths, Optimistic Osbornes, and
Carefree Carrolls

	Safe Smiths	Optimistic Osbornes	Carefree Carrolls
Purchase Price	$100	$100	$100
Down Payment	$40	$20	$0
Mortgage	$60	$80	$100
Interest Rate	4.0%	5.5%	7.5%
Payments			
Interest	$2.40	$4.40	$7.50
Principal + Interest	$3.44	$5.45	$8.39

To see how each family does in Happy Times and Sad Times, look at their financial conditions at the end of year one. To simplify the analysis, let's assume that each family pays the entire $5 to the bank in year one, meaning that the Safe Smiths pay $2.40 in interest and the remaining $2.60 as principal repayment to the bank. Likewise, the Optimistic Osbornes pay $4.40 in interest and $0.60 as principal. The Carefree Carrolls will pay $5 towards interest, and borrow an additional $2.50 to pay interest. Table 2.4 summarizes each family's equity return after one year in both Happy Times and Sad Times.

Let us now consider two new scenarios, Very Happy Times and Very Sad Times, in which house prices rise and fall, respectively, by 25 percent over five years. How do each of the families fare? Again, for simplicity, let's assume that each family pays only interest for the five years and applies all saved money (i.e., annual savings = $5 minus the interest payment) to principal at the end of the five years. Table 2.5 summarizes the resulting outcomes for the families in both Very Happy Times and Very Sad Times.

Given that each party has a mortgage balance at the end of the five years and must refinance the loan, let's examine the how each family's down payment (i.e., the equity value) changed as a percentage of the home value, and the new resulting interest rate.

For the Safe Smiths, neither Very Happy Times nor Very Sad Times greatly affect their refinancing terms. In Very Happy Times, they can refinance at a rate of 3.25 percent because their down payment is now effectively >50 percent. In very sad times, they can refinance for 4.75 percent with their yearly interest payment due as $2.23, still comfortably below their $5 budget.

Table 2.4   Happy Times and Sad Times

	Safe Smiths	Optimistic Osbornes	Carefree Carrolls
Happy Times			
House Value	$110.00	$110.00	$110.00
Mortgage	$57.40	$79.60	$102.50
Equity Value	$52.60	$30.40	$7.50
Original Equity	$40	$20	$0
Return	31.5%	52.0%	*infinite*
Sad Times			
House Value	$90.00	$90.00	$90.00
Mortgage	$57.40	$79.60	$102.50
Equity Value	$32.60	$10.40	($12.50)
Original Equity	$40	$20	$0
Return	−18.5%	−48.0%	*infinite*

Table 2.5   Very Happy Times and Very Sad Times

	Safe Smiths	Optimistic Osbornes	Carefree Carrolls
Very Happy Times			
House Value	$125.00	$125.00	$125.00
Mortgage	$47.00	$77.00	$112.50
Equity Value	$78.00	$48.00	$12.50
Original Equity	$40	$20	$0
Return	95.0%	140.0%	*infinite*
Very Sad Times			
House Value	$75.00	$75.00	$75.00
Mortgage	$47.00	$77.00	$112.50
Equity Value	$28.00	($2.00)	($37.50)
Original Equity	$40	$20	$0
Return	−30.0%	−110.0%	*infinite*

The Optimistic Osbornes, however, are greatly affected by the difference between Very Happy Times and Very Sad Times. In Very Happy Times, they're able to refinance to 4.75 percent (because their down payment is effectively 38 percent), leaving them with an interest payment of $3.88 and interest + principal payment scheme

Interest Rates and Asset Prices: Affordability-Based Valuation

Though it may seem obvious that lower interest rates make assets such as homes more affordable, they also have the potential to inflate asset prices. Consider the following example, in which a house is originally purchased for $100, when the cost of money (i.e., the interest rate) was 5 percent. For ease of calculation, let's assume that the house was purchased with 100 percent financing and no money down.

In this case, the buyer's annual payments in interest would be equal to $100 × 5 percent or $5. Now let us suppose that interest rates fall by 1 percent. One impact may be that a buyer might again pay $100 and have an annual carrying cost of $4, but another very possible impact is that the buyer's budget of $5 is fixed, and he's willing to now pay up to $5/4% or $125 for the home. Similarly, if interest rates rise by 1 percent, the buyer might be willing to pay $100 and have a higher carrying cost of $6 per year—or perhaps the buyer retains the $5 budget and is willing to pay only $5/6% or $83.

Clearly, interest rates can meaningfully affect asset valuations, particularly when buyers may be budget constrained.

of $4.80 for a 30-year payoff (both of which are within their $5 budget). In Very Sad Times, however, they must refinance at a rate of 7 percent, leaving them with interest payments of $5.39—meaning they must borrow more each year simply to make the payments.

For the Carefree Carrolls, Very Happy Times allow them to continue their lives effectively "as is." They're able to refinance at a lower rate of 6.75 percent, but due to the extra money they've borrowed over the years, their yearly interest payment ($7.59) remains in excess of their $5 budget. Very Sad Times, however, are very sad indeed for the Carefree Carrolls. Because they have a loan amount that is far in excess of the house's value, the bank is not willing to refinance the property and instead forecloses.

As these examples have shown, the relationship between debt, collateral (i.e., down payment or equity amount), and asset prices has the potential to create a toxic cocktail that can greatly improve or deteriorate one's financial condition quite rapidly. The next section turns to a theory—the Financial Instability Hypothesis—that suggests these relationships result in a cyclical flow of credit that results in continuous financial instability.

Interest Rates and Corporate Investing

Corporations regularly make decisions regarding the projects in which to invest. As part of their decision-making processes, most businesses attempt to understand the financial returns likely to be generated by investing in the project. A key input in this analysis is the cost of funding, a variable directly influenced by interest rates. All else being equal, corporations will have many more profitable and financially worthwhile projects to take on when interest rates are lower than when they are higher.

Thus, interest rates affect the likelihood of investments taking place and lower interest rates make lower-return projects viable. The impact of rising rates, once projects are under way, however, can have disruptive impacts on many elements of a corporation, and in aggregate, on industries in which similar decision-making processes may exist.

Consider a steel mill that decides a $1 million investment in expansion makes sense because it generates a 10 percent return (based on current steel prices, etc.) while its cost of capital is 8 percent. However, if interest rates rise and the company's cost of capital is now 11 percent, the project is no longer profitable. In short, higher interest rates raise the hurdle for corporate investment decisions.

Hyman Minsky's Financial Instability Hypothesis

Hyman Minsky was an American economist and professor of economics at Washington University in St. Louis, Missouri. A graduate of the University of Chicago and Harvard University (where he studied under Joseph Schumpeter and Wassily Leontief), Minsky was a relatively unacknowledged economist until after his death in 1996. "With long, wild, white hair, Minsky was closer to counterculture than to mainstream economics."[4] Although his initial research was focused on poverty, he was taken by a seemingly simple question: Could the Great Depression happen again?[5] It was from this line of research that Minsky delved into the topic of financial crises and debt dynamics preceding, during, and subsequent to them. The outcome of this effort was the Financial Instability Hypothesis.

Recently, Minsky's theories have found a home among practicing financiers. In fact, UBS held a conference call in October 2009 titled "Minsky for Beginners" for their institutional clients.

During the call, George Magnus, former UBS chief economist, eloquently summarized the Financial Instability Hypothesis:

> Minsky's big contribution was the proposition that after long periods of economic stability, endogenous destabilizing forces in the economy begin to develop, forces that eventually lead to financial instability . . . [H]e argued that this happens through the progressively more interesting but then progressively more dangerous use of leverage.[6]

The roots of this internally produced instability, Minsky argues, are found in the three primary forms of debt structures that exist in a capitalist society, and their relative predominance in the system at various points in time. His three distinct income-debt relationships were labeled according to their respective ability (or inability) to pay interest and principal from normal cash flows as hedge, speculative, and Ponzi.[7]

Hedge financing takes place when one is able to pay back both the interest owed as well as the principal due via normal cash flows. This approach is not particularly risky and is not subject to changing market conditions. The Safe Smiths in our preceding examples can be classified as hedge financiers.

Speculative financing is a bit riskier because it is an approach in which interest expenses are paid, but the principal must be refinanced upon maturity. According to Minsky, "the speculation is that refinancing will be available when needed."[8] Greater risk is borne as the availability of debt for refinancing may be available at materially different prices than originally envisioned. The Optimistic Osbornes began as speculative financiers.

Finally, Ponzi financing takes place when one is dependent on the availability of additional debt in order to pay interest on existing debt. Given the inability to pay interest expense out of cash flows, the possibility of principal paydown is nonexistent in Ponzi financing structures. This structure is based on an operating assumption that values will continually rise, allowing for easier and more advantageous refinancing terms. The Carefree Carrolls are Ponzi financiers. Table 2.6 summarizes these three financing structures.

The Financial Instability Hypothesis that Minsky proposes is based on a shift in the mix of financing structures present in a society. In a working paper presented at Bard College, Minsky

Table 2.6   Minsky's Debt Descriptions

	Hedge	Speculative	Ponzi
Cash Flow Adequate to Pay Interest?	Yes	Yes	No, interest must be paid for with new debt
Cash Flow Adequate to Pay Principal?	Yes	No, principal must be refinanced with new debt	No, principal must be refinanced with new debt

eloquently summarized his theory, utilizing the language of equilibrium presented in the prior chapter:

> It can be shown that if hedge financing dominates, then the economy may well be an equilibrium-seeking and -containing system. In contrast, the greater the weight of Ponzi finance, the greater the likelihood that the economy is a deviation-amplifying system.[9]

Shifting economic conditions further complicate the distinctions of these financing structures, as hedge units could become speculative units or Ponzi units, and speculative units may well turn into Ponzi units in environments of degrading profitability.

Earlier, we observed a shift in the type of financing structure utilized by the Optimistic Osbornes depending on the state of asset prices. In Very Happy Times, the Optimistic Osbornes migrated from speculative financiers to hedge financiers. However, in Very Sad Times, they morphed from speculative to Ponzi financiers.

Minsky's argument about constant instability is straightforward: "Over a protracted period of good times, capitalist economies tend to move from a financial structure dominated by hedge finance units to a structure in which there is a large weight of units engaged in speculative and Ponzi finance."[10] Thus, in a self-fulfilling, reflexive manner, financing units get more and more aggressive as the lack of failure justifies this tendency. Eventually, however, the weight becomes unbearable and the structure implodes. This procyclical tendency of credit to grow in riskiness during good times is very destabilizing, and something I call the Minsky Migration.

McCulley eloquently summarizes Minsky's underlying point: "Put differently, stability can never be a destination, only a journey to instability."[11] McCulley coined the term the "Minsky Moment," representing that moment in time when the credit structure switches from getting more aggressive to less aggressive. After the Minsky Migration crosses the Minsky Moment, bad things happen. Speculative and Ponzi units begin to implode, and hedge units become vulnerable as the entire economy wobbles. Asset prices plunge as those units unable to obtain refinancing are forced to sell assets. This dynamic, which causes broad and great pain in an economy, is known as debt deflation.

Debt Deflation and Asset Prices

Irving Fisher[12] is most known for his unfortunately timed statement in 1929, days before the stock market crash, that "stock prices have reached what looks like a permanently high plateau." His insistence immediately after the crash and up until the economic contraction had acquired significant momentum that stock prices were destined to go higher, combined with the failure of a firm he started, led most people to dismiss him and his ideas entirely. His debt-deflation theory, in which he argued that deflation increased the real value of debts, did not receive serious attention until well after his death.

Although Fisher was a devout believer in general equilibrium theory prior to the Great Depression, he quickly rejected the idea of a stable equilibrium by 1933, noting that "there may be an equilibrium which, though stable, is so delicately poised that, after departure from it beyond certain limits, instability ensues, just as, at first, a stick may bend under strain, ready all the time to bend back, until a certain point is reached, when it breaks."[13] In fact, Fisher stated that he believed the concept of equilibrium to be "absurd" and that "at most times there must be over- or under-production, over- or under-consumption, over- or under-spending, over- or under-saving, over- or under-investment, and over- or under- everything else."[14]

Once the Great Depression was in full force, Fisher developed a cycle theory of booms and busts: the debt-deflation theory of great depressions. Embodied in his book *Booms and Depressions* and succinctly summarized in a 1933 *Econometrica* journal article, the theory is based on the premise that overindebtedness and deflation are a toxic combination, regardless of other factors that may be present. Fisher admitted that overinvestment, overconfidence, and overspeculation were important considerations, but further noted that "they would have far less serious results were they not conducted with borrowed money."[15]

At the root of the debt-deflation theory is an understanding that falling prices effectively increase the real value of debts, further burdening already stressed borrowers like the Osbornes and the Carrolls. This process usually results in forced and uneconomic selling of assets by overindebted companies and individuals, which results in further falling prices that results in an effective increase in real debt. Fisher summarizes the results of this process: "when overindebtedness is so great as to depress prices faster than liquidation, the mass effort to get out of debt sinks us more deeply into debt."[16]

Many scholars today argue that the twentieth century had experienced two serious bouts of debt deflation: the Great Depression and Japan's Lost Decade(s). Because data is significantly more available for the Japan case, recent (and ongoing) research on the Japan case has proven additive. In particular, Richard Koo's formulation of a two-stage business cycle is worth considering. In the normal course, notes Koo, businesses focus on profit maximization as is suggested by traditional economic theories. Following a highly leveraged boom, however, the power of debt-deflation dynamics drives companies to focus on deleveraging—even if at the expense of profit maximization. The result is a lack of demand for credit, and, as he observed in Japan, constant deleveraging despite interest rates of close to 0 percent.[17] This part of the business cycle is one that Koo labels a "balance sheet" recession.

The debt-deflation theory to some extent mixes the dynamics of leverage with reflexive tendencies. That is, selling begets more selling, and the self-fulfilling fear of lower prices is amplified by leverage. Debt-deflation theories emphasize what occurs after a bust—inadequate demand driving deflation, which becomes particularly toxic when compounded with debt. The next section describes the Austrian business cycle theory, a similar theory (different in its emphasis on events prior to the bust) suggesting that overinvestment and excess capacity create the bust.

The Austrian Business Cycle Theory

The Austrian School of Economics[18] uses the banking function of connecting savers with borrowers as the basis upon which it builds a theory of boom and bust cycles. At its root, the theory posits that excessive credit growth (driven by government intervention via interest rate policies, etc.) is the root of speculative booms and busts by generating unsustainable growth. The underlying belief is that "there is an economic and moral difference between legitimate ownership that comes from deferred consumption and premature ownership that is subsidized by the monetary system."[19]

The Austrian business cycle theory is similar in many respects to Minsky's financial instability hypothesis. According to the theory, artificially low interest rates result in bad investments and over-consumption, creating excess capacity and motivating businesses

---

Fractional Reserve Banking and Money Creation

Banking institutions serve many roles, the most important of which is the deployment of funds from savings into productive investments. To do this, many banks collect deposits from individuals and institutions (the savers), before lending those same funds on to other individuals and institutions (the borrowers).

Because savers may demand their money back from a bank at any time, banks need to keep cash on hand to meet this potential need. If the banks kept $100 on reserve for every $100 deposited with them, there would be no excess capital to lend out to the borrowers. Further, such a full-reserve approach would be inefficient in that very few savers ask for their capital to be returned in a short time. Fractional-reserve banking is a solution to these problems and is the dominant form of banking practiced today. In it, banks keep only a fraction of deposits on reserve and also maintain the commitment to meet the demands of any saver requesting a return of his capital. This process expands the supply of money in the system, primarily by allowing deposited capital to multiply.

To understand how money is created, let's use a simple example in which $1000 is deposited into Bank 1 and the mandated reserve requirement is 10 percent. This means that Bank 1 will keep $100 on reserve and will lend out $900. But that $900 is going to end up in other banks. Those other banks will keep $90 on reserve and lend out $810 . . . which ends up in other banks. If we assume this process stops after 10 cycles (it need not), then approximately $6500 will exist in bank deposits. After 25 cycles, the aggregate deposits will be more than $9250. Ultimately, total deposits will reach $10,000, or 10 times the initial deposit. To generalize, simple math will demonstrate that the money multiplier is exactly [1 / (Reserve Requirement)].Thus, if the reserve requirement is 25 percent, then total deposits will eventually reach 4× the initial deposit or $4000. Similarly, a 50 percent reserve requirement will result in 2× the initial deposit or $2000. The accompanying figure graphically demonstrates this process of money multiplication and how it varies by reserve requirement.

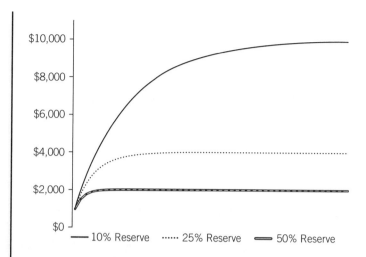

Money Multiplication via Fractional Reserve Banking

The use of fractional reserve banking creates a meaningful vulnerability for banks—the risk that many savers simultaneously may ask for their capital. Although in practice this happens quite rarely, a severe shock to confidence can result in bank runs in which the amount of money being demanded by savers exceeds the reserves held by the bank. For this reason, many governments have created a deposit insurance scheme, hoping to create the confidence needed to avoid bank runs.

Note: For a more complete description of the money-creation process via fractional reserve banking, the reader is encouraged to consult Modern Money Mechanics: A Workbook on Bank Reserves and Deposit Expansion published by the Federal Reserve Bank of Chicago. The publication was originally authored by Dorothy M. Nichols in 1961 and was later revised and updated by Anne Marie Gonczy in 1992.

and individuals to under-save. Because central banks monopolize money creation (see box on Fractional Reserve Banking and Money Creation) and therefore affect the credit cycle, Austrian economists suggest that central banks lie at the origin of financial bubbles.

Underlying Beliefs: Macroeconomics and Capital Structure

The Austrian school has three underlying beliefs that are particularly pertinent to our discussion of booms and busts: (1) equilibrium is a nonsensical construct, (2) aggregation is not possible, and (3) interest rates help determine preferences for consumption today vs. consumption in the future.[20] To begin, they reject the idea of equilibrium. Noble-prize winning Austrian economist Friedrich Hayek succinctly captured the perspective that equilibrium is the exception by stating "before we can even ask how things might go wrong, we must first explain how they could ever go right."[21]

Another Austrian tenet is that aggregates are nonsensical constructs because individuals have unique tastes and time horizons that cannot be summed into singular demand curves. Llewellyn Rockwell, founder of the Ludwig von Mises Institute, eloquently captures the spirit of this second point by noting that "every actor in the economy has a different set of values and preferences, different needs and desires, and different time schedules for the goals he intends to reach."[22]

Though there are many ways of interpreting this belief, the most popularized manner[23] of presenting the heterogeneity of capital decisions (the most relevant for our boom–bust focus) is the stages of production triangle, also known as the Hayekian triangle in honor of Hayek. Figure 2.1 presents a simplified version of it with five production stages.

Examples of production stages that might be early (i.e., stage 1) include basic research and development and other capital allocation decisions that might be years from impacting a firm's bottom line. These earlier stages are truly "investment" stages in which today's profits are foregone in return for the expectation of future profits. Likewise, examples of late-stage production functions include inventory and working capital management. These are production functions that are temporally proximate to consumption.

Because the dynamics that affect capital allocation decisions in early stages differ from the dynamics affecting later stages, Austrians believe that a simple aggregation is inappropriate. The

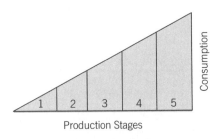

Production Stages

Figure 2.1   The Hayekian Triangle and Stages of Production

slope of the triangle's hypotenuse can be thought of as an indicator of the interest rate. Steep triangles imply high interest rates, and a corresponding minimization of long-run (i.e., stage 1) investments. Flat triangles imply low interest rates with corresponding emphasis on long-run investments. In many ways, the slope can be thought of as a proxy for the time value of money and therefore the hurdle rate for investment decisions.

The third Austrian belief of relevance to us is that consumption and investment trade off against each other (unlike the traditional economic interpretation that economic output is the result of consumption plus investment plus government spending plus net exports). Thus, investment is defined as foregone consumption, and likewise, consumption is foregone investment. Given that this consumption vs. investment framework necessitates a trade-off between the suppliers of funds and the demanders of funds, we are effectively talking about the market for money. The clearing price of the money is the interest rate.

Malinvestment and Overconsumption: Central Banks and Money Creation

Market-clearing interest rates, note the Austrians, allow for the optimal allocation of resources between consumption and investment. The following diagram summarizes how the interest rate (i.e., the price of money that allows the supply of saving and the demand for investment capital to be matched) drives the trade-off on the consumption/investment frontier. The various stages of production then align with the consumption for an appropriate allocation of corporate resources. Figure 2.2 summarizes these relationships.

The involvement of central banks in setting the price of money is confusing and causes problems, assert the Austrians. Central banks in democratic capitalist societies[24] are motivated to keep interest rates below their appropriate level, and the result on investment decisions is an inappropriate increase in long-run investments. By long-run, we are describing capital investments that do not provide a payback for a significant period of time. Research and development, plant expansions, and the like would be good examples of long-run investments. Increasing a sales force might be considered a short-run investment.

From the perspective of the corporate entity making investment decisions, it appears that the savings are greater than they in

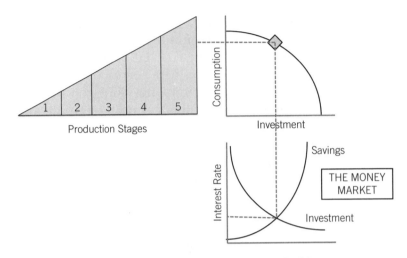

Figure 2.2   How Interest Rates Drive Investment and Consumption Decisions

fact are. This distorted perspective arises due to the primary mechanism through which central banks manipulate interest rates— management of the money supply. To reduce interest rates, central banks can "manufacture" money by either lowering the interest rate by mandate or lowering required reserve ratios.

Likewise, inappropriately low interest rates cause consumption to be higher than would be the case with an appropriate rate. From the perspective of the saver, it appears that there is less demand for capital than is actually the case. With a lower opportunity cost for consuming, entities choose to consume at a level above one that would naturally occur at an appropriate interest rate. The result of this higher consumption is that corporate investment decisions are shifted increasingly toward short-run production stages. Because demand is robust, inventories are built, and so on. Figure 2.3 summarizes how inappropriately low rates result in both malinvestment (top half) and overconsumption (bottom half).[25]

Eventually, bad investments and/or overconsumption must be addressed and an overly "consumed" society is found with too much debt (due to the low cost of money) and a need to increase savings. At this point, the bust portion of the cycle begins as savings increase (either via actual savings or via debt repayment), consumption slows, and profit maximization is deemed subservient to balance sheet repair typical of Koo's balance sheet recessions.[26] Significant excess capacity from overinvestment results in

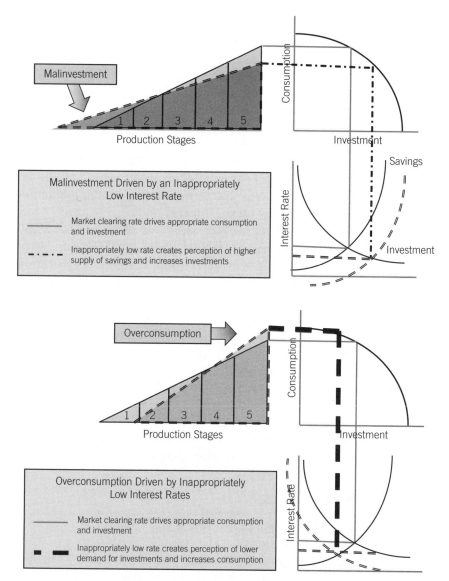

Figure 2.3   Overconsumption and Overinvestment Driven by Inappropriately Low Interest Rates

deflationary forces, which increases the real value of debt. Austrians believe that this process must be free to run its course, independent of bailouts and other government intervention, in order to purge the system.

As is clear from the above diagrams and descriptions of the relationships that result in malinvestment and overconsumption,

Austrians believe the root cause of the boom–bust cycle is inappropriately low interest rates. One mechanism through which central banks such as the Federal Reserve control interest rates is via deposits held at their member banks. So, the Federal Reserve creates money and then deposits it into banks. Through the money multiplier effect described above, these deposits are multiplied as banks lend capital to those seeking it. Simple supply and demand dynamics (i.e., more supply) drive the cost of money (i.e., the interest rate) down as a result of the money-creation process. The unlimited capability of the Federal Reserve's "printing press," combined with the multiplicative power of fractional reserve banking, enables the Fed to effectively set short-term interest rates.[27]

Austrians note the inherent contradiction of economists who claim the "market knows best" working at the Fed. In many ways, the Federal Reserve operates as a central planning organization more typically found in communist/socialist societies.[28] Austrians believe knowledge is inherently difficult to obtain (not unlike Soros's belief regarding social science) and that any intervention into markets is inherently distortive. This belief regarding the U.S. central bank is perhaps best captured by U.S. congressman and 2008 presidential candidate Ron Paul, who notes: "After decades of experience in grappling with Fed officials in committee meetings and of lunches and private discussions with Fed chairmen, a lifetime of reading serious economic literature, and a profound awareness of the dangers to liberty in our time, I know there is absolutely no hope for the Fed to conduct responsible monetary policy."[29]

Integrating the Macro Lenses

Although some of the lenses presented in this Chapter are not fully-accepted by economists, they provide powerful tools through which to recognize, evaluate, and understand booms and busts. Further, despite their seemingly disparate foci, the Austrian cycle, Financial Instability Hypothesis, and debt-deflation theory can be integrated into one coherent theoretical construct.

Figure 2.4 notes the interaction of these components into an integrated macroeconomic lens for the evaluation of financial extremes. As shown by the circular flow, the cyclical nature of debt is at the heart of the framework, with debt and its magnifying power as the primary drivers of the cycle.

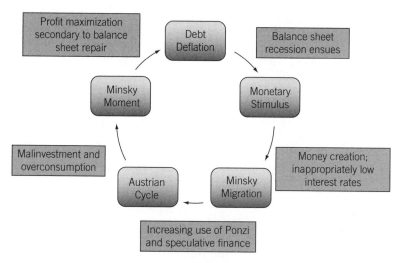

Figure 2.4   Credit Cycles Drive Constant Instability

As we turn to the next chapter, the focus of our lens-building efforts turns to psychology and the cognitive biases that often affect human decision-making processes.

CHAPTER

The Psychology Lens

HOMO ECONOMICUS MEETS *HOMO SAPIENS*

Investing is not a game where the guy with the 160 IQ beats the guy with the 130 IQ . . . Once you have ordinary intelligence, what you need is the temperament to control the urges that get other people into trouble in investing.

—Warren Buffett

The third discipline through which we evaluate financial booms and busts is psychology. We can gain a fresh perspective by focusing on actual, rather than theoretical, human behavior. One of the key underlying assumptions of most economic lenses is that humans are rational individuals. Although the term *rational* is one that might be interpreted in many ways, it generally refers to profit-maximizing, self-interested, and optimized decision making. According to such "rational choice" logic, humans accurately weigh costs and benefits to make the most economically rewarding decisions.

The framework of rational choice and rational action theories has had a dominating influence over most of the social sciences in recent years, stemming in large part from the success it achieved in influencing the economics discipline. According to John Scott at the University of Essex, "what distinguishes rational choice theory is that it denies the existence of any kinds of actions other than the purely rational and calculative."[1] In fact, rational choice logic goes further to describe individual preferences in terms of utility functions—functions that are transitive (i.e., if A is preferred to B and B is preferred to C, then A is preferred to C), complete (i.e., for any choice between options X and Y, an individual will either prefer X, prefer Y, or be indifferent between the two), and invariable (if L is preferred to M, then M is not preferred to L).[2]

To illustrate completeness, consider the choices made by a woman named Sara. If Sara is presented a choice between apples and oranges, she will choose an apple, an orange, or be happy with either. She will not answer, as a three-year-old might, with "I want strawberries." Suppose that Sara chooses the orange. But before she is able to peel the orange, she's given the option of strawberries. She can now choose the orange, the strawberries, or be indifferent between the two. She chooses the strawberries.

Sara has now revealed her preferences to us in a manner that means strawberries are preferred to oranges, and oranges are preferred to apples. According to rational choice theory, Sara has also revealed that strawberries are preferred to apples (even though she did not explicitly make such a choice). From an academic research perspective, these simplifying assumptions of completeness and transitivity provide a robust foundation for the application of scientific methods, regardless of their accuracy.[3] By enabling the modeling of human choice into equations and formulas, these assumptions enable physics-like "rigor."

It is only relatively recently that psychologists have demonstrated that humans may not be "rational" in the sense described above. In fact, according to one behavioral perspective, it seems that "human beings are motivated by cognitive biases of which they are largely unaware (a true invisible hand if ever there was one)."[4] Through hundreds of empirical studies, psychologists have found that people often make suboptimal decisions for a variety of reasons, including incomplete accounting of costs and benefits, partial risk understanding, and flawed assumptions regarding the probabilities of various outcomes. As psychologists and economists began to share ideas, a burgeoning new field of study was born: behavioral economics.

If ever an entire discipline and field can be traced back to the pioneering work of one or two people, then behavioral economics provides a great example. Princeton professor Daniel Kahneman and the late Amos Tversky are the original pioneers of research that has now become known as behavioral economics. In 2003, addressing the American Economic Association, Kahneman reflected on the original confusion that motivated his research:

> My first exposure to the psychological aspects of economics was in a report that Bruno Fey wrote on that subject in the early 1970s. Its first or second sentence stated that the agent of economic theory was rational and selfish, and that his tastes did not change. I found this list quite startling, because I had been professionally trained as a psychologist not to believe a word of it.[5]

This chapter uses findings from recent research in this new field to demonstrate that we are all plagued by predictable and consistent biases that affect our decision making in a manner that directly conflicts with our supposed rationality. In the study of booms and busts, it is essential to understand why people behave the way they do. Some of the research findings presented in this chapter helps us understand why irrationality may be the norm, rather than the exception, making booms and busts more likely than stability. This chapter connects the dots between the observation of booms and busts and the individual actors that create them.

The Study of Irrationality Is Born

Take a moment to complete the test shown in Table 3.1, as originally presented by J. Edward Russo and Paul Shoemaker in *Winning Decisions: Getting it Right the First Time*.[6] For each question, write your best estimate of the correct answer in column marked "Estimate."

Upon completion of this exercise, go back and use the next two columns to place a range around your point estimate. Don't modify your original estimate. Try to make the range as narrow as possible, but wide enough that you have 90 percent confidence that the correct answer lies within the range. To truly appreciate the value of this chapter, complete the exercise before proceeding any further.

Table 3.2 provides the correct answers. Check and see how many of the answers lie within the ranges you provided. Use the "?" column to mark an "X" for those you missed and a "✓" for those you got correct. Count the number of ✓s. Is it less than 9? A number of less than 9 indicates overconfidence, as the instruction was to state a range within which you believed with 90 percent confidence that the answer lay. This means you should be correct 9 times out of 10.

Table 3.1   A Simple Knowledge Test

Question	Estimate			?
1. What is the weight of an empty Airbus A340–600? (kg or tons)				
2. In what year did John Steinbeck win the Nobel Prize for Literature?				
3. What is the distance from the Earth to the Moon? (km or miles)				
4. What is the air distance from Madrid to Baghdad? (km or miles)				
5. In what year was the construction of the Roman Colosseum completed?				
6. What is the height of the Aswan High Dam? (meters or feet)				
7. In what year did Magellan's crew complete the first naval circumnavigation of the globe?				
8. In what year was Mohandas K. Gandhi born?				
9. What is the surface area of the Mediterranean Sea? (square km or miles)				
10. What is the gestation period of the great blue whale? (days)				

Source: From Winning Decisions by J. Edward Russo and Paul J.H. Schoemaker, copyright© 2002 by J. Edward Russo and Paul J.H. Schoemaker. Used with permission of Doubleday, a division of Random House, Inc.

Although many might argue that the exact questions are somewhat arbitrary and therefore only test random knowledge, the test has proven robust as a test of metaknowledge[7] and overconfidence. As noted by Russo and Shoemaker,

> Of the more than two thousand American, Asian and European managers to whom we have given a ten-question quiz like this one, less than 1 percent met the challenge. Most fail to be even in their range (not the point estimate) for four to seven questions out of ten.[8]

Few people are able to do well at this test. I have personally given this test to hundreds of undergraduates, MBA students, managers, colleagues, and others both inside and outside the United States. Most score between 3 and 6 correct answers. Although this may seem to be aberrational, it is actually quite reflective of a consistently biased human decision-making process. Humans appear to be routinely overconfident and unaware of their own knowledge limitations. As you might imagine, the inability to estimate accurately and other such behavioral biases throws quite a wrench into the study of "rational" individuals and their behavior during booms and busts. In addition to exploring how we make decisions, the rest of the chapter explores why we consistently produce less-than-optimal decisions.

Heuristics Gone Wild: How Rules of Thumb Lead Us Astray

Beginning in the early 1970s, Amos Tversky and Daniel Kahneman started empirically analyzing how people make decisions in uncertain situations. What they found was interesting, and at first glance, contradictory to the economic perspective of rational actors. Rather than accurately weighing the costs and benefits (including the probabilities of each) of each decision made (like a supercomputer might), humans tended to rely on a handful of heuristics or "rules of thumb" to simplify the complexity of a cost/benefit analysis for each decision. In most circumstances, "these heuristics are quite useful, but sometimes they lead to severe and systematic errors."[9]

The simple example used by Tversky and Kahneman does an excellent job of illustrating the power of a heuristic and its ability to mislead us in a consistent manner:

> The apparent distance of an object is determined in part by its clarity. The more sharply the object is seen, the closer it appears to be. This rule has some validity, because in any given scene the more distant objects are seen less sharply than nearer objects. However, the reliance on this rule leads to systematic errors in the estimation of distances . . .[10]

By employing a heuristic such as "sharpness = nearness," we find that we are prone to overestimate distances in conditions of poor visibility and underestimate distances when visibility is good. Thus, a normally useful rule of thumb (clarity as a measure of distance) can systematically mislead one into inaccurate estimation of distances.

Significant research over the past 40 years has focused on what might be deemed the two primary heuristics utilized by most human decision makers that tend to bias our decisions. Although we humans likely employ dozens, if not hundreds, of other heuristics, these two rules of thumb tend to be consistently problematic in terms of our ability to make good decisions. More specifically, they

Table 3.2   Answers to the Simple Knowledge Test

Question	Answer
1. What is the weight of an empty Airbus A340–600? (kg or tons)	218,000 kg or 240 tons
2. In what year did John Steinbeck win the Nobel Prize for Literature?	1962
3. What is the distance from the Earth to the Moon? (km or miles)	384,400 km or 238,850 miles
4. What is the air distance from Madrid to Baghdad? (km or miles)	4,308 km or 2,677 miles
5. In what year was the construction of the Roman Colosseum completed?	A.D. 80
6. What is the height of the Aswan High Dam? (meters or feet)	114 m or 375 ft
7. In what year did Magellan's crew complete the first naval circumnavigation of the globe?	1522
8. In what year was Mohandas K. Gandhi born?	1869
9. What is the surface area of the Mediterranean Sea? (square km or miles)	2,510,000 sq km or 970,000 sq miles
10. What is the gestation period of the great blue whale? (days)	335 days

Source: From Winning Decisions by J. Edward Russo and Paul J.H. Schoemaker, copyright © 2002 by J. Edward Russo and Paul J.H. Schoemaker. Used with permission of Doubleday, a division of Random House, Inc.

each result in biases to our decision-making processes that drive suboptimal outcomes due to consistently poor estimation of the probabilities and values needed for rational optimization.

We now turn to a discussion of the representativeness heuristic and the availability heuristic, as well as a brief exploration of the cognitive biases that they each cause. Although the implications of these findings for our study of booms and busts should be obvious, the chapter wraps up by highlighting several ramifications pertinent to our study of booms and busts.

Representativeness

The representativeness heuristic is a rule of thumb we all use to form a conclusion when presented data that looks like other data that we know to be true. Not dissimilar to the concept of stereotyping, in which we assume one member of a group must be like the image we have of the group, the representativeness rule of thumb is one in which we use identifiable clues to cognitively label an individual observation as *representative* of a class of observations.

For example, suppose you are walking down a street in Boston and meet a person who is thin, athletic looking, wearing sneakers, and is asking for directions. Suppose further that it happens to be two days before the Boston Marathon. It is highly likely that you will assume that this person is an athlete visiting Boston to run the marathon. Likewise, if you meet a disheveled-looking, absent-minded and poorly dressed older individual carrying a disorderly stack of papers near a college campus, you might hypothesize, with good reason, that the person is a professor.

Though these rapid conclusions drawn from limited data may be accurate, they need not always be. In fact, let's turn to an example (based upon Tversky and Kahneman's work) in which the representativeness heuristic might lead you astray. Suppose a colleague describes an individual (let's call him Stanley) as being "shy, withdrawn, extremely helpful, detail oriented, meek yet tidy, and extremely interested in structure."[11] Now suppose you are asked to guess what this person does for a living (farmer, car salesman, secretary, artist, physician, librarian, etc.) and to order the list of possibilities from most to least likely. For lots of people, Stanley is thought to be a librarian.

The process by which most people would order the list is based on the similarity of the description to their stereotyped image of each occupation. Although using this heuristic may be efficient in determining the identification of the person's occupation, it unfortunately creates numerous biases and may therefore generate incorrect conclusions. The biases emanating from this heuristic occur because representativeness allows little room for the necessary probability-affecting variables that should influence our thinking. Five primary cognitive biases[12] emerge from our extensive use of the representativeness rule of thumb. Let us now turn to each and discuss them in turn.

Inattention to Base Rates   The fact that Stanley resembles our image of a librarian absolutely overwhelms our awareness of base rates. Base rates are the frequency with which a type occurs in a population. In our example above, if we knew nothing about Stanley and were asked to rank his likely profession, we would probably turn to our knowledge of base rates to determine the ranking. So, given that not many individuals are actually librarians, the probability of Stanley being a librarian would likely fall. Likewise, the probability

Stanley is a physician would perhaps rise (given there are more physicians in the world than librarians).

Thus, it seems that our brains overweight representativeness (i.e., similarity of description) and underweight the generic probability of an occurrence. The result of our brain's reliance on the representativeness heuristic is that our decision-making processes suffer from a cognitive bias in which we underweight or even dismiss statistical likelihoods (e.g. the number of physicians is many times the number of librarians in America) that should inform our thinking.

Insensitivity to Sample Size   Tversky and Kahneman[13] asked undergraduates to answer the following question:

> A certain town is served by two hospitals. In the larger hospital about 45 babies are born each day and in the smaller hospital about 15 babies are born each day. As you know, about 50% of all babies are boys. However, the exact percentage varies from day to day. Sometimes it may be higher than 50%, sometimes lower.
>
> For a period of 1 year, each hospital recorded the days on which more than 60% of the babies born were boys. Which hospital do you think recorded more such days?
>
> A. The larger hospital
> B. The smaller hospital
> C. About the same (i.e., within 5%)

More than 50 percent of respondents indicated "C" was their choice, with the remaining respondents evenly split between "A" and "B." According to statistical theory, however, the larger the sample, the less likely it is to "stray" from an average. If this is not obvious, think about the probability of getting 75 percent "heads" while flipping a coin. Surely it must be easier to get 3 heads when flipping a coin 4 times than it would be to get 3,000 heads when flipping a coin 4,000 times, right? Tversky and Kahneman note that this "fundamental notion of statistics is evidently not part of people's repertoire of intuitions."[14]

Again, we find that our cognitive processes are biased in a manner that leads to suboptimal decision making. We tend to extrapolate our thinking across all scenarios, disregarding the likelihood of deviations that might exist due to limited sample sizes.

Misconceptions of Likelihood (The Gambler's Fallacy)   Consider the following question from Bazerman and Moore's spectacular review of the academic literature on behavioral decision making.[15]

> You and your spouse have had three children together, all of them girls. Now that you are expecting your fourth child, you wonder whether the odds favor having a boy this time. What is the best estimate of your probability of having another girl?
>   A. 6.25% (1 in 16), because the odds of getting four girls in a row is one out of 16
>   B. 50% (1 in 2), because there is roughly an equal chance of getting each gender
>   C. A percentage that falls between these two estimates (6.25% and 50%)

Most respondents chose either A or C, believing that the probability of having another girl must be low. Specifically, our brains want us to assume that random deviations will be offset over time. However, as noted by Bazerman and Moore, "the problem with this reasoning is that the gender determination of each new baby is a chance event; the sperm that determines the baby's gender does not know how many other girls the couple has."

The situation is not dissimilar to the thinking of a gambler at a roulette wheel. Having just witnessed 5 consecutive red numbers emerge, he is convinced that the probability of the next number being black is higher than it actually is. In fact, depending on the type of roulette wheel, the probability will always be either 18 out of 37 or 18 out of 38. These likelihoods do not change.

This miscalculation of chance is driven by our brain's desire for order, even when there may be randomness. Tversky and Kahneman correctly summarize: "Chance is commonly viewed as a self-correcting process in which a deviation in one direction induces a deviation in the opposite direction to restore the equilibrium. In fact, deviations are not 'corrected' as a chance process unfolds, they are merely diluted."[16]

Dismissing the Powers of Regression   Even though most humans believe that randomness from an underlying statistic is likely to be quickly corrected, for some reason we do not believe that performance regresses. When professional athletes do really well, we are willing to assume that it is due to skill. When one mutual fund does well while others falter, we are willing to assume that it is due to skill. A well-cited example is taken from Kahneman and Tversky's early work on the psychology of prediction in which poor performers were punished and good performers were rewarded. Despite these interventions, the poor performers improved, while the good performers deteriorated. The authors suggest that interventions may have had absolutely nothing to do with performance and that simple regression to the mean drove the outcomes.[17] By relying too greatly on a single data point (and believing it to be highly representative), our brains lead us to overestimate the capabilities of high performers and to underestimate the capabilities of low performers.

Conjunction Fallacy   One rule of statistics is that the probability of a subset cannot be more than the probability of the whole set. Thus, the probability of being a blond woman from Boston must necessarily be less than or equal to the probability of being a woman, the probability of being blond, and the probability of being from Boston. It is not possible that there is a 50 percent chance of being a blond woman from Boston and a 5 percent chance of being from Boston. Even if only 5 percent of the population is from Boston, then if all Bostonians are female and blond, the probability of being a blond woman from Boston will also equal 5 percent. However, if some portion of Bostonians is not female, or blond, then the probability of being (a) blond, (b) female, and (c) from Boston will be less than 5 percent.

The representativeness heuristic, however, plays games with our probabilistic assessments. If we went on to describe the woman just mentioned as having a heavy New England accent in which she pronounces words like *car* as "cah," our brains would act as if we placed a greater probability of the person being a Bostonian woman than being a woman. Consider the following example from Bazerman and Moore[18]:

> Linda is thirty-one years old, single, outspoken, and very smart. She majored in philosophy. As a student, she was deeply concerned with issues of discrimination and social justice, and she participated in antinuclear demonstrations. Rank the following eight descriptions in order of the probability (i.e., likelihood) that they describe Linda.

A. Linda is a school teacher in an elementary school.
B. Linda works in a bookstore and takes yoga classes.
C. Linda is active in the feminist movement.
D. Linda is a psychiatric social worker.
E. Linda is a member of the League of Women Voters.
F. Linda is a bank teller.
G. Linda is an insurance salesperson.
H. Linda is a bank teller who is active in the feminist movement.

Most respondents to this question ranked C as more likely than H and H as more likely than F. This means that people in this study believed it more likely that Linda was a feminist bank teller than a bank teller. Given that the feminist descriptor actually narrows the universe (as feminist bank tellers are a subset of feminists and a subset of bank tellers), it is impossible for the probability of being a feminist bank teller to exceed that of being a bank teller (or being a feminist).

Because the description of Linda is more representative of a feminist bank teller than that of a bank teller, use of the representative heuristic leads us to a logical inconsistency in that we place a higher likelihood on a less-likely occurrence.

Availability

The second primary bias-inducing rule of thumb is the availability heuristic. As eloquently summarized by Tversky and Kahneman, "there are situations in which people assess the frequency of a class or the probability of an event by the ease with which instances or occurrences can be brought to mind."[19] Thus, the availability heuristic is one in which personal experience and personal knowledge of events is more heavily weighted than an objective person might consider appropriate. Because our minds will more easily recall events of greater frequency, the availability heuristic is generally useful in that events with greater frequency are usually more likely. The breakdown occurs because "availability is affected by factors other than frequency and probability"[20] and is more heavily weighted toward events that are easily remembered or more memorable.

Thus, vividness and memorability (which are unrelated to frequency) are overweighted in terms of our assessment of probability. This results in a consistent and predictable set of cognitive biases. As succinctly summarized by Bazerman and Moore, "We too easily assume that our available recollections are truly representative of the larger pool of events that exists outside of our range of experience."[21] The two primary decision-making biases that emanate from use of the availability heuristic are biases due to the ease of recall and biases due to the retrievability of the image or event. We now turn to each of them.

Ease-of-Recall Bias Because recent and vivid experiences tend to be more prominent in our cognitive processing, we tend to believe they occur more frequently than they actually do. Consider the following problem, presented by Bazerman and Moore[22]:

> Please rank order the following causes of death in the United States between 1990 and 2000, placing a 1 next to the most common cause, a 2 next to the second most common cause, etc.
> __Tobacco
> __Poor diet/physical inactivity
> __Motor vehicle accidents
> __Firearms (guns)
> __Illicit drug use
>   Now please estimate the number of death caused by each of these five causes between 1990 and 2000.

According to the *Journal of the American Medical Association*,[23] the most common cause of death on the list is tobacco, followed by poor diet/physical inactivity. The next three causes of death are motor vehicle accidents, firearms, and illicit drug use. Although few respondents actually correctly ranked the frequency of these causes, even fewer were able to accurately describe the relative frequencies. The list below gives the raw data for actual deaths.

Tobacco	435,000
Poor diet	400,000
Motor vehicles	43,000
Firearms	29,000
Drugs	17,000

Because the last three causes are more vivid and easily recalled (perhaps due to media attention that increases their vividness in our memories), most of us tend to overestimate the frequency of their occurrence, while underestimating the likelihood of the less-vivid causes. The availability of memorable stories about drug, firearms, and motor accident–related deaths is driven by more prominent and vivid stories about them. Thus, we tend to believe our immediately recent experience is more reflective of reality than it may in fact be.

Retrievability-Based Biases   A retrievability bias occurs when we overestimate the probability of an event because our memory structures make it more retrievable. For instance, try to answer the following question relatively rapidly: Are there more words that begin with the letter "a" or words in which the letter "a" is the third letter?

Most people believe there are more words beginning with the letter "a" than words in which the third letter is "a." Reality, however, is quite different. Roughly 6 percent of English words begin with the letter "a" while almost 9 percent have the letter "a" as the third letter. For most people, it is easier to recall words that begin with the letter "a." Because our memory structures allow for greater retrievability of words beginning with the letter "a," we overestimate their frequency.[24]

An example used by Tversky and Kahneman concerns the relative fame of people:

> Subjects heard a list of well-known personalities of both sexes and were subsequently asked to judge whether the list contained more names of men than of women. Different lists were presented to different groups of subjects. In some of the lists, the men were relatively more famous than the women, and in others, the women were relatively more famous than the men. In each of the lists, the subjects erroneously judged that the class (sex) that had the more famous personalities was the more numerous.[25]

Thus, we tend to believe whatever is more retrievable from our experience set is more frequent, when actual frequency has very little to do with our ability to retrieve actual data. Unfortunately, the media tends to exacerbate this problem by highlighting events that either sell newspapers or generate loyal watchers, rather than statistically representative stories. Thus, despite the fact that very few graduate students become billionaires, the story of Google founders

Larry Page and Sergey Brin has received tremendous attention—likely leading to a perception that successful graduate student-turned-entrepreneurs are more likely than the data might suggest. Might this inspire graduate students to pursue riskier ventures than they should? Or perhaps venture capitalists are more likely to fund long shots because of such biases?

Our Flawed Brains: Other Cognitive Issues

In addition to these two primary rules of thumb and their numerous accompanying biases, there are a host of other cognitive issues that disrupt our ability to be economically rational in our optimization efforts. Several such issues are discussed below, with a brief mention of how they may each affect boom–bust cycles.

The Power of Irrelevance: Anchoring and Adjustment

Recall the 10 questions you answered in Table 3.1, ranging in topic from distances to years to areas. In most cases, you were asked to estimate an unknown number. Chances are high that after you came up with your best point estimate, the number you wrote in the "Estimate" column, you created an insufficiently wide range around that number. Such insufficient adjustment complicates our assessment of what we think we know. As you might guess, the ramifications of anchoring and adjustment have profound implications for the analysis of individual securities prices.

When attempting to estimate an unkown quantity, most of us usually begin with an initial guesstimate and then adjust the value appropriately to reflect modifications we deem appropriate. In most cases, we tend to "anchor" on our initial guesstimate and subsequently make insufficient or inadequate adjustments. The following example is taken from Tversky and Kahneman:

> In a demonstration of the anchoring effect, subjects were asked to estimate various quantities, stated in percentages (for example, the percentage of African countries in the United Nations). For each quantity, a number between 0 and 100 was determined by spinning a wheel of fortune in the subjects' presence. The subjects were instructed to indicate whether that number was higher or lower than the value of the quantity, and

then to estimate the value of the quantity by moving upward or downward from the given number. Different groups were given different numbers for each quantity, and these arbitrary numbers had a marked effect on estimates. For example, the median estimates for the percentage of African countries in the United Nations were 25 and 45 for groups that received 10 and 65, respectively, as starting points. Payoffs for accuracy did not reduce the anchoring effect.[26]

This is quite a profound finding. People are influenced by knowingly random numbers when asked to determine an unknown quantity. This is hardly the stuff of "rational" humans. If a stock were trading for $300 per share, despite what your own analysis might suggest, you're less likely to think it is worth $100 per share than if the stock were currently trading at $150. Why? Because the $300 price provides a powerful anchor that prevents us from placing an appropriately large range around possible values. It also creates a mindset that focuses on adjustments to current values, rather than the absolute values themselves. Think of how much attention is paid to the relative performance of mutual funds or other asset classes over time. Does it really matter if a stock fund was up 75 percent in 2009 if it were down 95 percent in 2008? Might such performance comparisons be counterproductive? In times of excess, such anchoring can be extremely powerful motivation for non-economic behavior.

Framing and Preference Reversal

Is how you ask a question more important than what you ask? Surely what you ask is more important than how you ask it, right? Perhaps not. Original research conducted by Kahneman and Tversky on prospect theory suggests otherwise. Some of their groundbreaking work on the topic demonstrated that how a question is asked can often impact the answer received. Consider the following example, taken from their 1981 article titled "The Framing of Decisions and the Psychology of Choice."[27]

Imagine that the United States is preparing for the outbreak of an unusual Asian disease, which is expected to kill 600 people. Two alternative programs have been proposed. Assume that the exact scientific estimates of the consequences of the programs are as follows:

If Program A is adopted, 200 people will be saved.

If Program B is adopted, there is a 1/3 probability that 600 people will be saved and a 2/3 probability that no people will be saved.

Which of the two programs would you favor?

For those who responded to this question, more than 70 percent were risk-averse enough to take the sure thing of saving 200 lives, despite the equivalent probability-weighted value. Tversky and Kahneman then rephrased the descriptions of the program consequences. For this second group, they were given the same preface and then the following options:

If Program 1 is adopted, 400 people will die.

If Program 2 is adopted, there is a 1/3 probability that nobody will die and a 2/3 probability that 600 people will die.

Which of the two programs would you favor?

For this set of options, almost 80 percent of respondents chose Program 2. Mathematically, Program A and Program 1 are equivalent, while Program B and Program 2 are equivalent. Despite these characteristics, a significant reversal of preference took place simply by changing the manner in which the question was asked. Why?

Cutting straight to the punch line, it turns out that most humans are risk averse when facing choices about gains and risk seeking when facing choices about losses. Basically, we're willing to lock in a sure gain (a win is a win, we don't necessarily need the largest win), but we hate the idea of a sure loss (so we're willing to gamble against larger possible losses).[28] Because Programs A and B were described in terms of gains, most respondents were risk averse and sought to lock in the gains of 200 saved lives. However, when faced with a different framing of the problem, one based on the sure loss of 400 lives, respondents were willing to risk a loss of 600 lives rather than lock in a sure loss of 400.

The fact that people are able to change their preferences between identical options depending on how the question is asked violates a fundamental belief of rational choice theory—the belief that preferences are invariable—because if preferences vary, it becomes extraordinarily difficult to model human behavior. Consider the following example, which notes the power of "free."

In a recent study, people were offered a choice of either buying a Hershey's Kiss for a penny or a Lindt chocolate truffle for 15 pennies. A large majority of respondents (greater than 70 percent) chose the Lindt truffle. However, when given the choice was between a free Hershey's Kiss or a 14-cent Lindt truffle, almost 70 percent of respondents chose the Hershey's Kiss.[29]

How "Fairness" Impacts Decisions

As I write this section of the book, a major water pipe break in Weston, Massachusetts has created a "boil water order" for all customers of the Massachusetts Water Resource Authority who live east of Weston. Emergency water supplies held in the Sudbury Aqueduct, the Chestnut Hill Reservoir, and the Spot Pond Reservoir were activated, so that much of the greater Boston area continued to have water for bathing, flushing, and fire protection. However, the water flowing to most of Boston was deemed unsafe for drinking unless boiled for at least one minute.

As might be expected, this resulted in a "run" on bottled water. Within hours of the warning notice, grocery stores in the greater Boston area were sold out of bottled water. With such a demand shock to the system, you might imagine that stores that did have water (or could get it quickly) would be able to raise prices quite dramatically (after all, more than 2 million Massachusetts residents were suddenly searching for bottled water). However, this did not happen. Why not? What might public reaction have been if Walmart, Costco, or BJ's had raised the price of water 500 percent in response to overwhelming demand? From a simple economically rational perspective, such a price increase is not unwarranted and would be a logical output of most supply and demand–driven models—yet it did not happen. Why not?

In a series of questions given to respondents in the mid-1980s, Kahneman, Knetsch, and Thaler demonstrated that fairness affects how we make decisions.[30] They posed a series of questions to various respondents on the topic of price changes. Two categories of questions were presented, one reflecting a need on the part of the companies to protect their profits (i.e., a situation in which costs had risen) and the other in which companies were exploiting increased market power due to a shift in demand. The findings were remarkably consistent in acknowledging the need for a return on capital (i.e., it is acceptable to protect profits) and the non-necessity of exploitation due to a supply or demand shock (i.e., profiteering).

One of the more interesting types of questions asked in the academic research on fairness is an "ultimatum" question.[31] It goes something like this. You and a random person are greeted by a third person seeking to give away money (let's just say $10,000). The person indicates that your newfound friend will propose a split, and that you will have to agree to the split in order for the two of you to receive the money. If you disagree, then neither of you will receive anything and he will move on to two other random people. You and your "friend" agree to play, and she then proposes the following split: $9,900 for her, $100 for you. Do you accept?

Most people reject the offer. From a strictly economically rational perspective, $100 is more than $0 so you would be better off accepting the offer. Why reject this offer? There are two primary ways to consider this action: You have agreed to pay $100 to punish your "friend" for being unfair, or you are unwilling to accept an unfair deal. If humans exhibit even some desire for fairness (as appears to be the case), the microeconomic assumption of self-interested individuals falls apart. The ramifications of fairness on the formation and subsequent deflation of asset bubbles is likely to be quite high.

Mental Accounting: Why a Dollar Is Not a Dollar

A dollar in one's wallet is valued the same as a dollar on one's dresser and a dollar in one's car, correct? Recent research suggests this may not be the case. A phenomenon called mental accounting is humorously (and accurately) depicted in the following story, taken from Belesky and Gilovich.[32]

> By the third day of their honeymoon in Vegas, the newlyweds had lost their $1,000 gambling allowance. That night in bed, the groom noticed a glowing object on the dresser. Upon closer inspection, it was a $5 chip they had saved as a souvenir. Strangely, the number 17 was flashing on the chip's face. Taking this as an omen, he donned his green bathrobe and rushed down to the roulette tables, where he placed the $5 chip on the square marked 17. Sure enough, the ball hit 17 and the

35–1 bet paid $175. He let his winnings ride, and once again the ball landed on 17, paying $6,125. And so it went, until the lucky groom was about to wager $7.5 million. Unfortunately, the floor manager intervened, claiming that the casino didn't have the money to pay should 17 hit again. Undaunted, the groom taxied to a better-financed casino downtown. Once again he bet it all on 17—and once again it hit, paying more than $262 million. Ecstatic, he let his millions ride—only to lose it all when the ball fell on 18. Broke and dejected, the groom walked the several miles back to his hotel.

"Where were you?" asked his bride as he entered their room.

"Playing roulette."

"How did you do?"

"Not bad. I lost five dollars."

This story, which highlights the issue of mental accounting better than any other I've heard, illustrates one of the many behavioral biases that affect gamblers. The truly rational person will treat each dollar she has in her pocket as her dollar, not to be trivially disposed of or imprudently risked. Surely then it wouldn't matter how the dollar got into her pocket, would it? As the story above illustrates, however, the idea of "house money" contradicts this concept. Economist Richard Thaler has demonstrated several other similar mental accounts that fundamentally violate the concept that money should be thought of as fungible.[33]

The classic and most commonly utilized demonstration of mental accounting is visible in the following questions. Answer them as honestly as possible. Suppose you arrive at a concert and realize that you lost your ticket, which had cost $200. Fortunately, similar seats are available for $200. Do you buy another ticket? Now for the second question: Suppose you arrive at a concert to buy a ticket, but realize that you lost $200 in the parking lot on the way to the ticket booth. Fortunately, you happen to have enough money to still buy the ticket. Do you go ahead and buy it?

Most people answering questions like this tend to answer no to the first question and yes to the second question. Why is that? Well, it seems that individuals consider the first scenario (buying two tickets) to be equivalent to spending $400 on entertainment, which may exceed one's budget. The second scenario, however, is treated differently because there is a $200 loss and a $200 entertainment expense. Although related and unfortunate, they fall in separate mental accounts.

Such mental accounts create massive complications in the study of booms and busts if investors have made a great deal of money in the bubble formation stage. Might investors be less logical/rational if they are playing with "house money"? What if you had purchased a stock for $5 and it was now trading for $50. Would you sell your whole position, or perhaps only 10 percent of it? By selling 10 percent of your position, you are now effectively playing with "house money" and might be more willing to let it ride than rational decision making might suggest.

The Endowment Effect: Why It's Worth More to You if You Already Have It

Another effect that has been repeatedly demonstrated among behavioral studies of decision making is called the endowment effect. This label is used to describe the impact that ownership has on perceived value, or more specifically, the difference between our willingness to pay (WTP) and our willingness to accept (WTA) a price for a good. Rational agents do not suffer from a difference between these two prices, something noted by the use of the term *indifference* to describe the curves that graphically illustrate trade-offs.

In actuality, however, people value what they have more highly than if they did not have it. Consider the following example, taken from Kahneman, Knetsch, & Thaler, in which the professors conducted a now-famous study using coffee mugs.[34] They presented mugs to members of a Cornell undergraduate class and asked them each to evaluate the mug. Then they told some students that the mug was theirs to keep. Finally, they asked everyone in the class to place a price on the mug. Those who owned the mug would decide the price at which they would sell the mug (WTA) and those who did not own the mug would decide the price at which they would buy the mug (WTP). The average WTA was over $5 and the average WTP was slightly more than $2. This difference between the WTA and the WTP illustrates the endowment effect.[35] In numerous studies, the ratio between selling prices and buying prices has been demonstrated to be between 2 and 5 times.[36]

The ramifications of the endowment effect, particularly when combined with other biases and cognitive effects, can have dramatic impacts on the financial markets. If people value what they own at up to 5× the price they would willingly buy the same good, you can imagine how severe the bust phase of a boom–bust cycle might be once forced selling results in prices falling dramatically. How likely are you to part with an asset when willing buyers are offering prices that are well below your perceived value of the asset?

The Congruence Heuristic and the Confirmatory Bias

The congruence heuristic[37], also known among academic psychologists as the positive hypothesis testing heuristic, is one in which our thinking process is systematically skewed in a manner to validate hypotheses as true, rather than testing them.

Consider the approach most people take to a question asking if something about a group of people is true. The first step (usually) is to recall individuals you may know who are in the group. The second step is to ask if those individuals fit the criteria being asked. Based on your answer to the second question, you conclude you have a reasonable answer. For example, think about how you might answer the question of "Are couples living in rural settings more likely to have bigger families than couples living in urban settings?"

Optimal decision-making processes, however, have to do with evaluating four separate groups: rural couples with big families, rural couples with small families, urban couples with big families, and urban couples with small families. Only after considering all four sets can we accurately assess the frequency of each occurrence relative to each other. However, most people seeking to answer the question will immediately attempt to think about rural families they know and compare them with urban families they know (actually also falling prey to the availability bias in the process).

Again, it is easy to see how this limited "research" process that our brains conduct leads us astray in financial markets. Particularly when combined with other cognitive effects (the endowment effect, anchoring, etc.), we can easily imagine situations in which we are too slow to acknowledge evidence that contradicts our own views regarding a stock or bond, and it is only reluctantly that we would alter our assessments of its value. On an aggregated basis, this effect can have a massive impact when applied to millions of participants simultaneously.

The Certainty of Uncertainty

Given that making decisions in uncertain environments is a certainty of life, it is critical that we understand the ways that our brains miscalculate and misinterpret data. For the purposes of studying booms and busts, however, the primary insights of this chapter are summarized in Table 3.3.

As highlighted in the table, the numerous biases that plague human decision-making processes have the potential to severely distort the rationality of individual actors. Although all of these biases (and others) are important in seeking a better understanding of financial extremes, the cases presented in Part II will show a greater emphasis on the concept of overconfidence. In many ways, the idea of "this time is different" (a phrase that often typifies the boom phase of a cycle) is the ultimate manifestation of overconfidence. As we shall see in later chapters, however, the availability bias, anchoring and insufficient adjustment, and other decision-making flaws also rear their ugly heads in ways that consistently lead to

Table 3.3   Human Irrationality and Financial Booms and Busts

Bias/Effect	Investment Implication/Example
Base Rate Insensitivity	Google as representative of startup success
Sample Size Insensitivity	"Couldn't have been random"
Likelihood Misestimation	Patterns must correct; "odds now in my favor"
Regression Dismissal	Belief in trend, "grow to the moon"
Conjunction Fallacy	Misextrapolation of small to big
Recall	College dropout entrepreneurs = Bill Gates, Mark Zuckerberg
Retrievability	False belief in rarity of an occurrence
Anchoring/Adjustment	Stock is $300, surely correct value can't be $100.
Framing	Upside/downside confusion
Mental Accounting	"House money" effect; reluctance to sell; "Let it ride"
Fairness	Righteousness versus profit-maximization
Endowment	Reluctance to sell; illiquidity
Congruence	Self-validation of conclusions, misinterpreted as "testing"

nonrational decisions. It is this consistency of the biases that proves problematic, for if humans were inconsistently irrational, individual irrationality would offset other individual irrationality, resulting in a population that was rational.

Let us now turn to the political lens to understand how property rights and the price mechanism can lay the very basic foundations on which booms and busts thrive.

CHAPTER 4

Political Foundations

EVALUATING PROPERTY RIGHTS, PRICE
MECHANISMS, AND POLITICAL DISTORTIONS

*If you put the government in charge of the Sahara Desert, in five
years there'd be a shortage of sand.*

—Milton Friedman

When a collection of individuals agrees to form a society, they
have many options in determining how to organize themselves. The
political philosophy of the group will be manifested in its political-
economic systems and the range of possible solutions is wide. This
chapter focuses on two key decisions that relate to a society's vulnerability to boom and bust cycles. First, we evaluate the different
philosophies relating to property rights. A society's choice to allow
private property to exist and to protect such property with corresponding rights is an essential prerequisite for market-determined
prices to be "discovered" via supply and demand dynamics. Further,
without private property rights, the idea of booms and busts may be
moot, as the state owns everything.[1]

The chapter evaluates the mechanism through which a society chooses to determine the prices of goods, and the roles that
those prices play in the allocation of scarce resources. Although significant gradations exist between the extremes, two primary price
determination methodologies are considered: first, supply and

demand–driven price "discovery" processes that take place through the interaction of buyers and sellers, and second, central planning–driven price dictation in which the prices of goods and services are set or influenced by government bureaucrats. Again, the political choice of determining a pricing methodology has significant ramifications for the relative fertility of booms and busts. Market-determined prices are inherently more volatile than state-mandated prices; as such, they create the conditions in which economic dislocations have the potential to snowball into extreme price movements. Societies that have state-mandated prices are unlikely to have extreme price volatility; rather, they may suffer from extreme fluctuations in the availability of goods.

Respected property rights and market-determined prices are two essential ingredients for booms and busts to take place. Political processes in societies having these preconditions are likely to exacerbate financial extremes. Specifically, politically determined price floors and price ceilings can confuse price discovery processes, and tax policies are prone to either inflate or depress the demand (and supply) for certain goods, sometimes quite dramatically. Let us now turn to the issues of property and prices.

Can Anyone Own Anything?

According to the *Concise Encyclopedia of Economics*, property rights are defined as:

> the exclusive authority to determine how a resource is used, whether that resource is owned by the government or by individuals. . . . *Private* property rights have two other attributes in addition to determining the use of a resource. One is the exclusive right to services of the resource . . . [and the other is] the right to delegate, rent, or sell any portion of the rights by exchange or gift at whatever price the owner determines (provided someone is willing to pay that price).[2]

Private property rights thus have three primary characteristics: exclusive rights to determine how the property is used, exclusive rights to the services of such property, and exclusive rights to sell or exchange the property.

The spectrum of possible property rights ranges from complete and total state ownership of all property to complete and total private ownership of all property. Private property rights are a hallmark of capitalism, and the lack of private property rights (i.e., state ownership of all assets) is typified by communism. In fact, Karl Marx succinctly captured the essence of communism in the Communist Manifesto when he wrote "The theory of the Communists may be summed up in the single sentence: Abolition of private property."[3]

At the root of this objective was a belief that private property rights enabled the accumulation of inequality to compound over time, ultimately leading to disparities of wealth so large as to threaten systemic collapse. Without private property rights, and in a society in which everything was owned by the state, it would be possible to achieve another socialist ideal: a harmonious society in which everyone worked hard to make sure that everyone had what they needed. As noted by Marx and Engels, such an ideal state would be summarized by the slogan, "From each according to his ability, to each according to his needs!"[4]

Although the complete lack of property rights characterizes one extreme of the property rights spectrum, the other extreme is one in which laissez faire capitalism provides for complete private property rights. Property rights are essential for a market mechanism to work. Without property rights, the incentive to drive profits or generate economic returns relies not on economic self-interest, but rather on psychological factors—if it exists at all. If such an economic incentive did not exist, prices would not be determined by market forces—thereby negating the powerful information content they might otherwise contain. Let's consider how political decisions to restrict or remove property rights have affected the price mechanism by examining recent nationalization efforts in Venezuela.

Tenaris, the world's leading producer of steel tubes and pipes for the oil and gas industry, had a facility in Venezuela in which they had invested substantial capital. The facility had been performing relatively well economically, and its prospects for future profits were bright. Then, on May 22, 2009, the Venezuelan government informed the management of Tenaris that they would be nationalizing the company's assets and they would belong to the state.[5] What impact might nationalization have on the price mechanism for steel assets in Venezuela? By establishing that private property rights were not respected, the government of Venezuela sent a very clear message to the global investment community. Would a reasonable person or company invest in a country where the rights to their investment might not be respected? Not surprisingly, global investors seem to have lost their appetite to invest in Venezuela.

Lest we think that nationalizations only take place in countries controlled by commodity-enriched dictators, Table 4.1 highlights a handful of nationalizations that have taken place since the year 2000, excluding those nationalizations that might be better characterized as bailouts in which the company or industry might have gone bust without the bailout.

Although nationalization is the most extreme form of a change to property rights once granted, equally problematic approaches might include poorly defined property rights, or property rights that are subject to some limitations. A good example of poorly defined property rights might exist in areas of territorial ambiguity. For instance, the Spratly Islands in Southeast Asia are a collection of islands that were claimed by no fewer than six nations. Vietnam, the Philippines, Brunei, Malaysia, China, and Taiwan all claimed ownership of the territorial waters. In the mid-1990s, when it was believed the islands might be sitting on top of significant oil reserves, gunboats actually exchanged fire. Crestone Energy, a Denver-based energy company, had secured what they believed were legitimate rights to drill for oil from the Chinese government. The Vietnamese government disputed this right, claiming territorial sovereignty over the area. When Vietnam later sent a rig into the area, the Chinese responded with a gunship and a naval blockade of the rig to prevent it from receiving needed supplies.

Likewise, fishing rights in the Grand Banks were not clearly delineated, resulting in competitive overfishing by both U.S. and Canadian fishermen that ultimately made fishing in the region commercially unviable.

Table 4.1   Selected Nationalizations since 2000

Country	Year	Target
Bolivia	2006	Natural gas industry
Germany	2008	Federal print office
New Zealand	2001, 2008	Rail networks
United Kingdom	2001	Rail networks
United States	2001	Airport security services

Property rights with limitations are another case of distortion by government interference. Consider the fate of Unocal, a U.S. oil and gas company that tried to sell itself to CNOOC, one of the Chinese national oil companies. The U.S. government effectively blocked the transaction. Consider also the fate of London-based port operator Peninsular & Oriental Steam Navigation Company (P&O) in the sale[6] of their assets (which included U.S. port operations) to DP World, an investment company controlled by the government of Dubai in the United Arab Emirates. Political forces and public uproar resulted in the Emiraties agreeing to divest of the U.S. ports in order to get the transaction completed.

These three property rights "modifiers" (nationalization, ambiguity, and limitation) have a dramatic impact on the likelihood of booms and busts. By mitigating investor desires to participate in markets that lack clearly defined and well-respected property rights, it appears that all modifications to property rights in fact dampen the possibility of booms and busts. It seems extraordinarily unlikely that frenzied buying of companies will take place in Venezuela after Hugo Chavez nationalized various industries. Likewise, areas of territorial disputes and property rights ambiguity are likely to deter many investors and limit the risks they are willing to bear. Finally, the ability to exit from investments free and clear of last-minute modification of terms by the government appears a necessary condition for the formation of bubbles. Without this ability, open-ended, believable stories of justified price extremes would meet resistance.

There is also the possibility that financial booms and busts can be enabled via the granting of property rights where they were previously absent. A glance at prices in the privatized housing markets of (former) communist nations (i.e. China, Russia) begins to demonstrate the possibilities.

Prices: To Guide or Be Guided?

If property rights are present (and respected), the next logical question for a society might be "How should we determine the price of an item and who should be involved in the process?" Although a seemingly trivial and innocuous question, this question strikes at the heart of different political philosophies ranging from laissez faire capitalism to communism (and everything in between).

Surely it makes sense that an intricate, hand-woven sweater made of cotton that has been spun into yarn, dyed various colors through inks generated by finding and squeezing appropriate fruits and vegetables that have proven to generate such pigments, and finally woven into a wonderfully attractive pattern is worth more than a couple of leaves that have been picked up off the ground and stuck together with the sap of local, readily available trees, right? The intricate sweater has taken a great deal of time to construct, thereby embodying a great deal of labor. Such logic implies the leaf clothing is easier to make, and should therefore have a lower price. The earliest theories of price and value were based on calculations of the amount of labor that went into the good or service. This approach to thinking about prices dates back at least to Adam Smith, who wrote:

> The real price of every thing, what every thing costs to the man who wants to acquire it, is the toil and trouble of acquiring it. What every thing is really worth to the man who has acquired it, and who wants to dispose of it or exchange it for something else, is the toil and trouble which it can save to himself, and which it can impose upon other people.[7]

Adam Smith goes on to further distinguish between "value in use" and "value in exchange," noting the seeming paradox between the value of water and the value of a diamond:

> Nothing is more useful than water, but it will purchase scarce any thing; scarce any thing can be had in exchange for it. A diamond, on the contrary, has scarce any value in use; but a very great quantity of other goods may frequently be had in exchange for it.[8]

It turns out that supply–demand dynamics do a reasonably good job of explaining this paradox. By focusing on the marginal value (i.e., what would one additional unit be worth) of each good, it becomes easier to understand why each good is priced the way it is. How much would you consider paying for one additional cup of water in your life each year? Most people would not pay very much because, in most parts of the world, water is plentiful. In commenting on the water–diamond paradox presented in *The Wealth of Nations,* Nobel prize–winning economist Joseph Stiglitz noted "water has a low price not because the total value of water is low—it is obviously high, since we could not live without it—but because the marginal value. . .is not very high."[9]

There are two fundamentally different methods through which society can generate prices for its goods and services: market mechanisms through which supply-and-demand dynamics determine a price, or central planning in which prices are dictated by government bureaucrats. These two methods generate different perspectives on the role of prices in a society's allocation of scarce resources. The market-oriented approach to price determination is generally utilized in societies that seek to have prices guide investment and consumption decisions. The central planning approach has historically been used by societies in which the government guides prices in a quest to maintain social or economic stability.

The Market-Oriented Approach

Let us first turn to the market-oriented approach to price determination. In addition to being deemed efficient and effective, an important argument made in favor of market-determined prices is that prices contain tremendous information about the appropriate allocation of scarce property: "Market prices condense, in as objective a form as possible, information on the value of alternative uses of. . .property."[10]

Suppose an entire block of central midtown Manhattan suddenly became available for sale today. For simplicity's sake, let's say it's between 53rd and 54th Street, and between 5th and 6th Avenue. There is no skyscraper on it, no pavement, just some overgrown grass and a rickety old fence. The price at which this block will sell is a reflection of all the alternative uses for the block and is therefore "informationally rich" and useful in guiding the appropriate investment decisions related to the block's use. Should a pig farmer purchase the block and arrange to construct the world's most modern pig-slaughtering facility on it? Perhaps an entrepreneur should buy it and build an underwater basket-weaving training facility on the block?

Though there is nothing wrong with investing to create a pig-slaughtering or underwater basket-weaving facility on this block, we might agree that neither of those uses for the land is the "best" use of the land. Surely a commercial real estate developer will recognize the value he might create through the building of an office tower or residential condominium building and outbid our prospective pig farmer. In fact, it is highly likely that the person or firm that sees the highest value for the land (perhaps a hotelier enters the scene and outbids our residential condo developer) will bid the price up to a point where the land will be used in an economically optimal manner.

If the land sale takes place as an auction, with the opening bid starting at $1.00, it is easy to see how the rising price will eliminate inappropriate investments on the land and effectively select the investment on the land that will maximize its value or use. Ten-year-old Johnnie takes the bus in from New Jersey to attend the auction and believes a lemonade stand would thrive on that block. He bids $9.28, the amount of money in his piggy bank. He is outbid by a young couple from a third-world country thinking that this plot of land might suit them to build a small house for themselves in which they could start a family (with a bid of $25,000). Next comes along an entrepreneurial college student who wants to convert the block into a training center for the homeless. Believing learning is most effective in an environment similar to one's home, he proposes to not build anything (with a bid of $100,000). After him comes a parking lot company that believes a shortage of parking lots would justify high prices to park on this block, and proposes an investment to create a three-story parking garage (it bids $500,000). Our underwater basket-weaving school builder is next, bidding a cool $1 million, beaming with confidence that she will be addressing one of Manhattan's largest unmet needs.

Next come the folks from the pork industry, armed with projections of the sausage revival that is expected to imminently displace chicken breasts on grocery shelves. They limit their bid to $10 million, knowing that the facility will cost a pretty penny to construct in such an inconvenient location. Following our pig farmers are the executives of Cheapo Motel, Inc. They see the global economic recession driving more and more travelers (business and leisure alike) to seek "clean beds, by the hour if necessary." Their projections justify a bid of $50 million. The penultimate bidder is a commercial office developer. He thinks he can build a 30-floor tower and fill it with office tenants. After estimating construction and operating costs, he believes he can pay $250 million for the land

and still generate a profit. The final bidder is a hotel development company that believes it can build the city's finest six-star hotel and convince Seasons Carlton (one of the world's best hospitality companies) to manage it. At an estimated occupancy rate of 97 percent and average daily rate assumption of $750 per night, the company justifies a bid of $1 billion. The gavel falls: "Sold."

As this process demonstrated, the price of the property informed bidders of potential uses. It ensured that a pig-slaughtering facility did not end up in midtown Manhattan, and channeled our underwater basket-weaving school to the suburbs. Ultimately, it was the price of the property that resulted in the allocation of the scarce land to its most "valuable" use. Because market-determined prices are dynamic, it is conceivable that the property may in time find a more valued use.

Suppose for a moment that scientists at the Massachusetts Institute of Technology, in close cooperation with the National Institutes of Health and the Centers for Disease Control and Prevention, determine that natural pork, if cooked within four hours of slaughtering, has meaningful life-extending health qualities by materially reducing cholesterol, lowering blood pressure, improving metabolism, generating muscle mass, and increasing memory and overall brainpower. Upon completion of this research, professors at Johns Hopkins Medical School determine that such pork, when combined with a diet of hummus and red wine, removes the need for any and all pharmaceutical treatments for cholesterol, high blood pressure, diabetes, and a host of other common ailments. Not surprisingly, the price of "local pork" skyrockets from $5 to $1,000 per pound—supported by its qualification for health insurance reimbursements. Most consumers (depending on their medical coverage) are now entitled to three servings of local pork a week for the cost of their medical co-payment (typically between $10 and $20).

Given these dynamics, our aforementioned pork-slaughtering executives return to Manhattan and present an offer to our real-estate developer. Perhaps due in part to the lack of local pork offerings in New York City, many businesses had moved to New Jersey to improve employee welfare. As a result, rents in Manhattan are down materially. These new market conditions enable our pig men to buy the block from our real-estate developer, knock down the building, and build their pork-slaughtering facility. Within two years, the facility is recognized as the most profitable pork slaughterhouse in the world by the Global "Local Pork for Health" Slaughterhouse Federation.

The dynamics described above would not have been possible without informationally rich price signals. The higher pork prices provided a valuable incentive for our pork men to invest in Manhattan. The lower rents led our real-estate developer to sell. These decisions were informed and facilitated by the knowledge and information embedded in prices. In a nutshell, this is the basic argument in favor of market-determined prices.

The Price-Dictation Method

The argument against market-derived prices is one that fundamentally believes prices are fickle and subject to irrational whims. As such, interpreting information that is supposedly embedded in prices is a fool's game. For this reason, centrally planned economies that generate prices from government decisions do not look to markets or supply–demand dynamics for price generation.

In the former Soviet Union and other socialist economies, prices were set by decree. In some cases, governments attempted to model out what an appropriate market-determined price might be and then dictated that as the price. Stiglitz notes the futility of such an approach:

> Even if the government was successful in deciding on an appropriate price, it could do so only after a lengthy bureaucratic process. But economic conditions were changing while the bureaucrats were deliberating, which means the government-announced price was rarely the same as the market price.[11]

By setting prices that were either too high or too low, government interference with market-determined prices resulted in both shortages (when prices were set too low, resulting in excess demand or inadequate supply) and oversupply (when prices were too high, resulting in inadequate demand or excess supply). Not surprisingly, government interference tended to also produce black markets in which illegal transactions were taking place at prices negotiated between sellers and buyers. Despite these problems, the political process of setting prices via central planning was adopted by many countries in the twentieth century.

Government Meddling with the Price Mechanism

Representative governments are often beholden to popular sentiment in a manner that makes them highly likely to respond to outcries relating to unfair prices. There are many ways to deal with seemingly unfair prices, the most rapid of which is to simply apply a price ceiling (or floor) on the price of the good or service and require all citizens to adhere to the mandated price. Not unlike the communist approach, such a method is prone to creating excess supply or excess demand and inadequate demand or inadequate supply. If one thinks of prices as the symptoms and underlying supply and demand fundamentals as the cause, mandating a price is addressing the symptom but not acknowledging its cause.

Price Floors and Price Ceilings Governments tend to utilize price controls and price ceilings because they provide an easy-to-implement method of assuring citizens that they will be able to afford goods and services, or that an important supplier/constituent will be given a fair price for his production. Rather than addressing the issues that may be driving the price to be higher or lower than their constituents might like (i.e., too much production or supply in the case of low prices or too much demand or inadequate supply in the case of high prices), governments find it easier to simply mandate a price via decree. When prices in a society are generally free to move (and interpreted as providing valuable resource allocation information), but certain prices are constrained from moving completely freely, however, unintended consequences arise with respect to both the supply and demand. In short, as governments interfere with the price mechanism, both producers and consumers react to the artificial price signals. The end result is suboptimal resource allocation and a higher likelihood of booms and busts.

Perhaps the most common example of a price floor that adversely affects price discovery is the policy of mandating minimum wages. Although the labor market is generally one that utilizes supply and demand fundamentals to determine prices (i.e., wages), government intervention constrains the free movement of prices. By setting a price for unskilled labor that is higher than the price justified by supply and demand fundamentals, the policy of minimum wages incentivizes more workers to enter the workforce while simultaneously discouraging companies from hiring as many workers as they may in fact seek at a market price. The result is higher unemployment than might exist without such a policy. This perverse outcome is unfortunately often exacerbated at times of economic hardship when the political expediency of raising the minimum wage generates short-term political gain at the expense of employment.

In terms of price ceilings, the most often cited example is rent control. Although price ceilings are able to ensure that consumers can afford to rent a home, the unintended consequence of such a policy is a shortage of available rental units. This is the simple result of having more people trying to rent apartments than there are apartment owners willing to rent their units. Owners have no incentive to increase the supply of rental units because they are not compensated for doing so. Rent control is a particularly intractable problem to overcome because the political value in the short run (citizens pay less for housing) is accompanied by a long-term cost (the supply of rental apartments is not increased). Thus, although well intended, rent control actually creates artificial scarcity and magnifies (rather than mitigates) the problem. Might this policy then result in more home buyers than might otherwise be the case as the supply of rental units becomes inadequate? What impact does such a policy have for the likelihood of housing booms and busts?

Tax Policies The section of the U.S. Tax Code titled "Election to expense certain depreciable business assets" (Title 26, Subtitle A, Chapter 1, Subchapter B, Part VI, Section 179) effectively paid for a portion of my 2004 purchase of a BMW X5. Why is it that the U.S. government paid for a portion of my vehicle purchase?

As it turns out, Section 179 is commonly known among tax accountants as the "SUV deduction." Originally intended to help farmers needing to purchase expensive vehicles, the deduction applied to vehicles with a gross weight above 6000 lbs. Global automobile manufacturers studied these laws and, surprise surprise, my BMW X5 had a gross vehicle weight of 6005 lbs. I guess the Germans were nervous enough to add a bit of an extra weight to accommodate those who might opt not to have a CD player and such. Because I was running my own business at the time, I was able to expense virtually the entire amount of the vehicle against my income for that year. This was equivalent to the federal government paying approximately 40 percent of my car's cost.

When speaking with the sales representatives at various dealerships during my car search process, I learned of what various salesmen had termed the "mad December dash" in which all sorts of business-owning executives come into the showroom and are willing to pay full price for 6000lb+ SUVs. Virtually every year, dealerships sell out of these cars during the last week of the year. As you might imagine, such a policy artificially inflates demand for certain cars by effectively subsidizing their purchase. What might these cars cost if such a deduction did not exist? What is the real demand for a $100,000 Hummer?

Are Booms and Busts a Capitalist Phenomenon?

Given the fact that asset booms and busts are driven by prices that rise and fall more rapidly than might otherwise be expected, it should come as no surprise that booms and busts appear to be a phenomenon more frequently found in democratic capitalist economies. Alan Greenspan succinctly captured the essence of this distinction in noting the absence of boom and bust sequences in the most socialist of all economic systems in the twentieth century—the Soviet Union: "I do not recall bubbles emerging in the former Soviet Union."[*]

Does this imply that booms and busts are a solely capitalist event? Is it possible to have booms and busts in socialist economies? Given the apparent necessity of two basic political constructs (property rights and unconstrained market prices) for the enablement of booms and busts, and the fact that fully socialist states prevent these two constructs from existing, it indeed appears that booms and busts are a capitalist phenomenon.

The fact that many capitalist societies have also adopted representative governments such as democracies provides a further complication to our political analysis. Myopic representatives often place short-term political objectives in front of more-prudent longer-term-oriented policies. The result is often a distortion of the basic price mechanism that guides production and consumption decisions. This distortion, in turn, exacerbates the tendency of the system to swing between extreme states.

The case of democratic socialism—and hybrids between the traditional extremes of authoritarian socialism (communism) and democratic capitalism—is more interesting and complicated. As demonstrated by the recent cases of Greece, Italy, Spain, and Portugal, states that fall toward the middle of the spectrum (i.e., democratic socialists) appear equally prone to booms and busts. Might this be because socialist tendencies create entitlements that eventually outstrip the ability of the state and its citizens to generate the resources needed to support those same entitlements?

[*]*Alan* Greenspan, "We Need a Better Cushion against Risk." *Financial Times* supplement on "The Future of Capitalism" (March 27, 2009).

This example is just one illustration of how government tax policies can dramatically affect supply and demand dynamics. Similar influences can be found with tax breaks for hybrid automobiles, as well as the much-discussed mortgage interest deduction (which we shall discuss in a case study of the housing boom in a later chapter). Hundreds of examples exist (electric vehicles, window replacements, solar energy installations, biofuel facilities, etc.), and unlike property rights interferences, which tend to dampen the likelihood of booms and busts, government interference with the price mechanism tends to amplify the likelihood of booms and busts.

Political Distortions of Property and Price

Political decisions regarding property rights and prices are at the foundation of a market's receptivity to boom and bust cycles. Without private property rights, the incentives to profit are less obvious, thereby tempering—if not eliminating—financial extremes. Just as the removal of property rights (think of Venezuela's nationalizations) dampens investor enthusiasm and decreases, if not eliminates, the likelihood of bubbles forming, the introduction of property rights where they previously did not exist (think of China's housing reform program of the late 1990s) creates a particularly fertile ground on which bubbles may grow. In many ways, private property rights are a measure of a society's willingness to allow successful investors and speculators to keep their winnings.

Modifying or constraining property rights through price ceilings and floors has a ripple-through effect on the market dynamics (i.e., supply and demand) that determine prices. As described previously through the example of minimum wages, price floors tend to keep prices artificially high and therefore incentivize supply and dis-incentivize demand. Likewise, price ceilings such as rent control tend to keep prices artificially low and incentivize demand and dis-incentivize supply. The result is that politically motivated or mandated price distortions usually exacerbate, rather than mitigate, the problems they seek to address.

It is easy to see how these policies can increase the likelihood of booms and busts occurring. Might consistent underinvestment due to price ceilings result in an eventual supply shortage that is too large to ignore? Could the genuine supply shortage create hoarding mentalities that further exacerbate the problem? How might prices react in such an environment? Likewise, might price floors drive overinvestment that generates excess supply? Might overproduction result in bloated inventory levels that will eventually become too large to ignore? What might happen to prices then?

Just as price ceilings and floors distort supply and demand drivers, so too do taxes have a confounding effect. By effectively subsidizing or penalizing particular consumption and investment behavior, taxes alter underlying demand or supply. One of the most well-known tax policies to do that is the mortgage-interest deduction in the United States. By effectively paying a portion of the interest owed on a mortgage, the U.S. government has lowered the cost of home ownership and increased demand for homes. Although Chapter 10 will address this specific topic in greater depth, the bottom line is obvious: by increasing demand for housing, the policy has the potential to magnify booms (and therefore busts) in the U.S. housing market.

In the next chapter, we turn to biology as a lens through which we might gain some insights for our study of booms and busts. In particular, two biologically inspired constructs are emphasized as specifically helpful: the use of an epidemic lens to understand a boom's relative maturity, and the application of an emergence lens to comprehend the processes through which uninformed individuals might form a consensus.

Biological Frameworks

EPIDEMIOLOGY AND EMERGENCE

Even completely rational people can participate in herd behavior when they take into account the judgment of others, and even if they know that everyone else is behaving in herdlike manner. The behavior, although individually rational, produces group behavior that is, in a well-defined sense, irrational.

—Robert Shiller

This chapter provides two biological lenses through which to study booms and busts: an epidemic lens and an emergence lens. The epidemic lens, as described next, has use in helping us to determine the relative maturity of a boom and the potential imminence of a bust. The emergence lens provides a powerful explanatory framework through which to understand how groups can be misled into an uninformed consensus.

Scientists and medical professionals alike have been studying the dynamics of epidemics for hundreds of years. The basic framework utilized by these practitioners has been one focusing on infection rates. Many variables complement this focus, but if we recognize human behavior typical of a boom as "feverish," then the analogy becomes more obvious. Although the "infection rate" (for example, how quickly people believe the world is different) is not very useful by itself, combining it with the rate at which people are either "cured" of their disease or die from it, exponentially increases its value to us. The chapter briefly touches on these dynamics before turning to the idea of emergence.

Emergence is the study of seemingly chaotic efforts by large groups of animals that tends to produce extremely robust and adaptive order. Herds and swarms are among the most prominent of such phenomena in the biological arena, but examples exist in urban planning and other domains. This chapter briefly discusses herd and swarm behavior in social insects and animals before evaluating these dynamics in humans. We close the chapter by considering the ramifications of these tendencies for financial markets.

Revealing the Maturity of an Unsustainable Boom

Epidemiology is the study of diseases and their transmission across a population. If we think about markets as being composed of individuals who are either affected or not affected by a particular "disease" (i.e., infatuation with the new thing), the basic terminology of epidemics has a striking pertinence to the study of booms and busts.

Epidemiologists have developed extraordinarily complex and intricate models of disease transmission. The most basic elements of all these models, however, are the infection rate and the removal rate. The infection rate is the rate at which the disease is transmitted from infected individuals to those who are susceptible to infection. The removal rate is the rate at which infected people are removed from the population of transmitters, either because they die or because they have recovered and are now immune to the disease. Although relapses may prove possible, for purposes of our discussion, we assume that those who contract the disease either die or recover into an immune state.

To better understand how these two rates interact, let us consider three primary scenarios: (1) infection rate > removal rate = 0, (2) infection rate > removal rate > 0, and (3) removal rate > infection rate > 0.

Our first scenario, in which the infection rate is greater than the removal rate and the removal rate is 0 percent, produces an epidemic that eventually infects 100 percent of the population. The pace at which the disease spreads will depend on the infection rate. Graphically, any scenario that involves a removal rate of 0 percent will follow a logistic curve, as in Figure 5.1. As can be seen in the

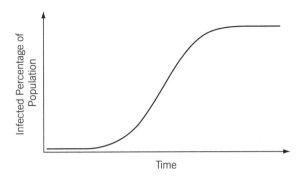

Figure 5.1   Infection Rate > Removal Rate = 0%

graph, the initial percentage of the population that is infected rises slowly at first. Because the removal rate is set to 0 percent, the population is infected at the infection rate. As summarized by Robert Shiller in *Irrational Exuberance*:

> Although the rate is nearly constant at first, the absolute number of people recorded as contracting the disease rises faster and faster: as more and more people become contagious, more and more people become infected . . . but the rate of increase starts to decline as the pool of yet-to-be-infected susceptible individuals begins to be depleted.[1]

Eventually, 100 percent of the population is infected, as seen by the flat line at the upper right of the graph.

The second scenario is one in which the infection rate is greater than the removal rate, but the removal rate is greater than zero. In this case, the cumulative distribution of the infected population will resemble a bell curve. The graphical depiction of the infected population will rise from zero slowly and then accelerate before peaking and returning to zero. Although 100 percent of the population might still get infected in reality due to random factors, it is highly likely the peak will occur before 100 percent of the population is affected. Figure 5.2 below summarizes this scenario.

The third scenario in which the removal rate is greater than the infection rate which is greater than 0 percent is particularly uninteresting as it provides for no epidemic. People are cured more quickly than the disease is spread, resulting in no cumulative

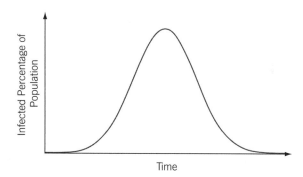

Figure 5.2   Infection Rate > Removal Rate > 0%

infection of the population. The best analogy for this situation is a noncontagious disease.

Though the formal academic application of epidemic models to financial markets has not gained significant traction, there has been some research conducted on word-of-mouth dissemination of ideas. Ideas, however, are not nearly as consistent as biological diseases and are subject to transmission errors via what Shiller calls a "mutation rate."[2] Shiller goes on to note that the transmission of ideas is similar to the children's game of telephone in which an original idea is so distorted via transmission as to be laughable after several transmissions. Further, alternative newsworthy items (such as a murder, car crash, or death of a major celebrity) may in fact affect the infection rate in a manner that deflects attention from the idea being transmitted. Thus, the relative prominence of an idea and the attention it therefore receives will affect its transmission rate.

Despite these concerns, the overarching objective of presenting this lens is to provide a vocabulary for thinking about the spread of ideas through a population during speculative bubbles. The framework of infection, removal, and mutation rates provides a useful conceptual method of understanding. Although Shiller is clear in describing the limitations of applying an epidemic model to idea diffusion through a population, he highlights the usefulness of the framework for thinking about speculative manias, emphasizing the need for a transmittable story:

> Word of mouth may function to amplify public reaction to news events or to media accounts of such events. It is still necessary to

consider the infection rate relative to the removal rate in order to understand the public impact of any new idea or concept, since most people's awareness of any of these is still socially mediated. Thus the likelihood of any event affecting market prices is enhanced if there is a good, vivid, *tellable* story about the event. . . . Word-of-mouth communications, either positive or negative, are an essential part of the propagation of speculative bubbles.[3]

Ultimately, the usefulness of an epidemic lens is its ability to help gauge the approximate maturity of an unsustainable boom. Just as a bubble that is relatively more progressed (i.e., closer to the point of bursting) will have more of its population infected, so too will an earlier stage bubble have a large "yet-to-be-infected" and susceptible population. Because it is very difficult to gauge with any precision the percentage of the population that is infectable or that has been infected, red flags or indicators that reveal approximations are useful. For example, a growth in amateur or beginner investors into a particular asset class is very telling. After all, we must assume that expert investors have already been infected, and if amateur investors are now infected, who is left to infect? Thus, by gauging the prevalence of newcomers to an asset party, one can get an approximate sense of the bust's imminence.

How Micro Simplicity Drives Macro Complexity

In many biological examples, group actions that appear ordered and deliberate emanate from uncoordinated individuals. How is it that these collections of social animals appear to operate in a seamless manner typical of a single organism? The study of complex biological systems has been the focus of significant research and has spawned a niche industry of "emergence" scholars. Despite being a relatively new area of rigorous research, early studies on the topic were taking place in the 1970s, albeit without the label of *emergence*. One of the first studies on this topic involved the behavior of Atlantic pollock.[4] University of Miami biologist Brian Partridge took it upon himself to gather schools of 20–30 fish (each about 3 feet long and weighing 40–50 pounds) and have them swim in a circular tank (33 feet in diameter) while he observed them from above, while spinning himself in a manner that kept him geospatially above the moving fish. Each fish was labeled in a manner that allowed him to track individual behavior.

The movement of each individual fish was then analyzed by reviewing more than 10,000 frames of film and Partridge's real time observations. After completing such painstaking research, Partridge and his research team concluded that individual pollock followed two simple rules to move as if they were a single unit: it was as if they were being told to "swim behind the fish directly in front of you" and "swim at a speed that keeps pace with the fish next to you." As simplistic as these two rules seem, they appear adequate to explain how the school manages to react when threatened by a predator or seeking to avoid an obstacle in the water.

During the summer of 2010, I decided (don't ask me why because I'm not sure I know the answer!) to compete in an international distance triathlon. In an effort to provide a "unique experience" to the athletes, the race director decided to send hundreds of swimmers into the ocean at once. Over the course of the roughly 1-mile swim, I found myself often stuck in a group of swimmers. If I sped up, I found I ran into other athletes. If I slowed down, others were running into me. When I tried to move to the left, I hit another swimmer. The same occurred while trying to move right. Eventually, I decided to settle into following the rules that Partridge and his team found drove the fish in a school . . . and was shocked by the overwhelming sense of peace that overcame my efforts when this occurred. Not surprisingly, several observing friends noted that "it looked like a school of fish were swimming together. . . . The whole group of you managed to turn and zigzag for no apparent reason, but almost as if someone were directing you all to do so." Knowing full well that none of us were coordinating anything, I was impressed by the sense of group order that came out of what I knew was utter chaos at the individual level.

As it turns out, swarms are examples of emergent complexity that originates from the following of simple rules on the part of its members. No group consciousness that forces the subservience of individual action is required. As an example of how simple rules exercised by individuals might create group behavior that appears complex to external observers, consider the popular human wave at a ballgame. As noted in *The Perfect Swarm*, "The wave might look to a visiting Martian like a complicated exercise in logistics, but its dynamic pattern emerges from a simple rule: Stand up and put your hands in the air (and put them down again) as soon as you see your neighbor doing it."[5]

To better understand how such emergent order occurs, we turn to the behavior of several social insects[6]—locusts, bees, and ants— that have demonstrated the ability to generate coherent, organized, methodical group behavior, despite the seeming improbability of doing so with billions of individual members. After discussing how group complexity emerges from individual simplicity in insects, we consider the manifestation of this phenomenon in human behavior. Let us now begin by understanding locust behavior.

Locusts

Of the more than 12,000 known species of grasshoppers, fewer than 20 are classified as locusts.[7] Nevertheless, locust plagues—written about since biblical times—continue to affect more than 10 percent of the world's population.[8] For this reason (as well as scientific curiosity), scientists have been very interested in understanding their behavior.

Locusts are different from other grasshoppers in one major and very important way: Their behavior changes radically when placed into crowded situations. Grasshoppers tend to disperse if placed in close proximity to each other, but locusts tend to synchronize their movements. The conversion from chaotic crowd to orchestrated swarm occurs as the locusts find themselves in dense quarters. Research has shown that young locusts will move chaotically until the density of their crowd approaches seven locusts per square foot, at which point they begin marching in sync with each other.[9]

As it turns out, most marching is a quest for food, and given the extraordinary volumes of food—daily intake equivalent to their body weight—that locusts consume,[10] cannibalism is not uncommon.[11] This desire not to be eaten provides the motivation to keep moving. Although this might have seemed obvious to our pollock-watching biologist, it is a useful third rule to explicitly articulate: "Avoid hitting the member directly in front of you or being hit by the member behind you." Given this avoidance desire, why don't the locusts simply disperse? The best way to avoid being eaten is to avoid your fellow hungry locusts, right?

As noted by Len Fisher,

> Normally shy and solitary, the close proximity of other locusts... stimulates them to produce the neuro-modulator serotonin, which not only makes them gregarious, but also stimulates other nearby locusts to generate serotonin as well. The ensuing chain reaction soon has all the locusts in the vicinity seeking each other's company.[12]

Literal party animals! A physiological response then creates more mobile locusts that begin moving in swarms, initially on the ground and then in the air. Just as the serotonin, which is released in escalating amounts as the serotonin in close-by locusts rises,[13] drives the desire to be with each other, so too does such intense partying make the locusts hungry—thereby assuring some healthy distance between each of them. As the party progresses, it gathers more members, until dense swarms of around one hundred billion (100,000,000,000!) locusts cover areas of up to 500 square miles.[14]

Although locusts are helpful in demonstrating how group behavior emerges from seeming chaos through the individual member's application of three simple rules (avoidance, alignment, and attraction), they fail to show us how a swarm makes decisions and develops a group logic that is different from an individual's logic. To see how decision making in swarms takes place, let us now turn to bees.

Bees

Bees are social insects that tend to follow the three simple swarm rules as they travel in groups. Where they differ, however, is in the group's ability to head directly for a particular target (for a new hive, or a food source) identified by scout bees. How is it that a group of uninformed bees in a swarm are able to efficiently find their way to a target? Although much has been written about the famous "waggle dance"[15] that scout bees conduct in their hives to communicate the direction and distance to a target,[16] recent evidence suggests this communication is not sufficient to explain the swarm's behavior. Fisher notes:

> The dance is performed in a hive that is almost as dark as some discos, so only those bees nearby (about 5 percent of the total) see the dance. The majority doesn't see it, so most bees begin

flying in complete ignorance. Those that have seen the dance aren't even out in front, showing the others the way. They are in the middle of the swarm, flying with the rest.[17]

Given the lack of obvious leadership in the swarm, efficient direction of the group toward a target seems a highly unlikely outcome. To better understand what might be going on, scientists used cameras to capture individual bee movement behavior to see if they might identify some possible explanation for the group's flight pattern.[18] By photographing the bees from below and leaving the camera's aperture open for a short time, researchers were able to produce a "map" of a bee swarm in motion in which each bee's movement was a short line. Most of the lines were short and curved, but a handful of the tracks were a bit longer (indicating greater relative speed) and pointed straight at the target. Those speedy bees heading straight for the target were labeled "streakers" by the scientists and provide the answer to our question.

It turns out that if a group is following the three simple rules of swarm behavior (avoidance, alignment, and attraction), these informed bees are able to take an unsuspecting group of ignorant bees rapidly and efficiently to their target. By moving a bit faster than the group, the informed bees exert a silent leadership that the uninformed bees follow.[19]

Fisher eloquently summarizes this finding:

> In other words, it needs only a few anonymous individuals who have a definite goal in mind, and definite knowledge of how to reach it, for the rest of the group to follow them to that goal, unaware that they are following. The only requirements are that the other individuals have a conscious or unconscious desire to stay with the group and that they do not have conflicting goals.[20]

Ants

This methodology of the few informed animals leading a group directly toward a target is not the only form of emergent swarm intelligence that has been observed in social insects. Ants have proven to be equally effective at finding direct routes to food sources and other targets, yet their methodology is entirely different from that pursued by the bees.

Research conducted on a colony of Argentine ants at the University of Brussels specifically sought to understand why it was that ants were able to efficiently and directly travel to their targets.[21] Scientists working in the Department of Behavioral Ecology created a forked path between the ant colony and a source of food. One path was approximately twice as long as the other path. They found that although the initial ants chose randomly, within a few minutes the whole colony was utilizing the shorter route. How and why did that happen?

The answer is actually quite simple, and once understood, the efficiency of ants makes a great deal of sense. Ants emit a chemical substance called a pheromone, which attracts other ants. More pheromone attracts more ants more intensely, and pheromone dissipates with time. Thus, the ant that took the short path ended up getting back quicker and producing an option for other ants that has at least twice[22] the pheromone of the longer path. Because of the greater pheromone on that trail, the next ant is highly likely to choose the shorter path. Even ants that take the longer trail to the food will be more likely, again due to the higher pheromone levels, to return via the shorter route and to further increase the pheromone levels on that route. Within minutes, the pheromone levels on the shorter trail overwhelm those on the longer trail to the point that the entire colony begins using the shorter path to the food. Here again, we find that individual adherence to basic rules lies at the root of this collective behavior: "The colony's efficient behavior emerges from the collective activity of individuals following two very basic rules: lay pheromone and follow the trails of others."[23]

The other interesting finding from the study of ants is that emergent behavior with silent leadership (even if random or unintended) was able to efficiently guide the swarm of ants to a target. Thus, the idea of the queen bee or queen ant has been refuted by research in favor of group-driven behavior, with significant implications for group decision making in animal groups.[24]

Emergent Behavior in Human Swarms

We now turn to the study of a particularly social and group-oriented animal, the human being. Historically, animal decision-making processes have been studied from a "simple rules" perspective whereas human decision-making processes have been focused on complex utility functions. Unfortunately, the two disciplines have not cross-pollinated their research efforts until very recently. The next section provides highlights emerging from this multidisciplinary research.

Swarm Processes and Group Dynamics

As we transition from social insects to humans, swarm logic is more robust and transferable than most might believe. Although the case studies later in the book will illustrate how swarm logic among investors might exacerbate booms and busts, this section of the chapter will briefly touch on the research that has been conducted on humans as social animals and in which group decision-making processes are the focus. Unlike Chapter 3, which focused on how individuals make decisions, this section will focus on how groups make decisions and how individuals within them affect and are affected by group dynamics.

We begin by reviewing some recent research conducted by biologists, zoologists, and ecologists, and mostly published in journals not typically read by economists, financiers, or social scientists. Several of these studies were conducted to determine if humans act similarly to social insects in their approach to making group decisions. A recent issue of the *Philosophical Transactions of the Royal Society of London* was dedicated to the topic of "Group Decision Making in Humans and Animals."[25] The findings, though not entirely shocking, have profound implications for our study of booms and busts.

One particularly interesting piece of research[26] published as part of this collection of papers was about an experiment conducted on groups of college volunteers. Several students were told to walk anywhere in the room, as long as they stayed within one arm's length of another student, which effectively created both the avoidance and the attraction criteria needed for swarm conditions. Communication was prohibited, but around the room were several targets in the form of uniformly placed letters. Prior to the experiments, one or two students in the group were given secret instructions to head toward one of the targets. By the time the experiment was stopped, most groups had ended up at the target letters given to the informed students. The unsuspecting students had been "led" there by a small minority of focused and informed leaders.

Although it is interesting to learn that uninformed human groups can be led by covert but informed leaders, the world is often filled with multiple leaders often targeting different objectives. Because of this fact, researchers began investigating the behavior of uninformed groups in situations including multiple leaders with conflicting targets. A recent article in the scientific journal *Animal Behavior* summarizes the research (which is based on a similar research design to the one just mentioned, but utilizing two informed students who were given differing objectives): "When conflicting directional information was given to different group members, the time taken to reach the target was not significantly increased; suggesting that consensus decision making in conflict situations is possible, and highly efficient."[27]

Basically, the same experiments were conducted with two individuals given differing objectives. The groups were no slower in reaching the targets, and quite rapidly made decisions about the appropriate course to be pursued. The implications of this finding on the study of booms and busts are enormous. If unsuspecting group members (think ordinary investors) can be led in any direction by a relatively small number of confident (regardless of whether such confidence is merited) members, one can imagine how such confidence might feed upon itself to generate a boom-like scenario.

Famous research conducted by Stanley Milgram[28] in the late 1960s demonstrated the power of silent leadership in groups.[29] Professor Milgram arranged to have people on the street stop and stare up at a window on the sixth floor of a tall building. Len Fisher eloquently summarizes the findings of the research: "With just one person staring up, 40 percent of passers-by stopped to stare with them. With two people, the proportion rose to 60 percent, and with five it was up to 90 percent."[30]

If nothing else, the research confirms the ability of a few people to guide the behavior of a much larger mass. Note that this experiment actually demonstrated the ability of a few to *mislead* the many, an outcome that has significant pertinence to the study of booms and busts.

Intentional misleading may not even be a motivation of the group's pioneers, but the idea that initial decisions matter is significant. Consider the following informal experiment I ran after having read a great deal about bee logic and the ability of silent leaders to generate consensus. After landing at the Las Vegas airport (an airport with which I have a bit too much familiarity), I was the first person to get off the plane. I decided to get off the plane and head right (the opposite direction of the main terminal), walking briskly and with the conviction of a knowledgeable passenger. Despite signs pointing in the opposite direction, I was amused to see that the next 10–15 passengers that got off the plane immediately turned right and followed the "crowd." I repeated this experiment on eight other flights over the next six months in various airports, all with similar results. It definitely seemed that bee logic applied to humans! The key lesson of this ad hoc research was that humans have a tendency to conform to the behavior of the seemingly knowledgeable group member.

The next section demonstrates how initial decisions made without meaningful reason might be interpreted by later deciders to have been based on careful analysis and contemplation. By placing greater weight on early decisions made during a chain of decisions, information cascades may develop and create outcomes that seem to defy explanation.

Information Cascades and Herd Behavior

Imagine, for example, that two equally good restaurants open on the same street adjacent to each other.[31] They are very similar in every way, including cuisine, price, and ambience. Suppose now a young couple comes by and must decide on which restaurant to choose. Given that both restaurants are empty at this point, they have very limited information with which to make a choice. After perusing both menus, they flip a coin. Heads they go to restaurant A, tails they go to Restaurant B. They flip the coin and end up in Restaurant A. The second couple that comes by now has the same information as the first, as well as the fact that it appears the first couple chose Restaurant A. Unable to decide based on the restaurants' menus and atmospheres, they opt for Restaurant A, assuming the first couple must have chosen for a good reason. Likewise, a family of five comes by, and seeing Restaurant A fuller than Restaurant B, they choose Restaurant A. This process might continue until Restaurant A is full, while Restaurant B remains empty.

As stated at the outset, the two restaurants are virtually identical, so how is it that one received all the business, and the other remained empty the whole night? Given customers made their

Career Risk, Herd Behavior, and Client-Driven Bubbles

John Maynard Keynes noted in Chapter 12 of his *General Theory of Employment, Interest and Money* that "worldly wisdom teaches us that it is better for reputation to fail conventionally than to succeed unconventionally." Boston-based money manager Jeremy Grantham of GMO has built on this logic to replace the word "reputation" with "your career." Describing the phenomenon as "career risk," Grantham notes that herd behavior and consensus investing is the norm not because professional investors do not recognize financial extremes, but rather that the risks to their careers for unconventional decisions are asymmetric. Failing with the crowd is accepted and succeeding with a crowd is expected, but failing on your own is likely to lead to termination. Succeeding on your own is likely to allow you to keep your job, perhaps with a promotion. In short, the likelihood of losing your job is small while sticking with the crowd and significant when deviating from the crowd. Why take such unnecessary career risks?

Might such behavior create investor herds that fuel bubbles? What are the costs of being a contrarian investor? Consider the fate of Grantham's firm GMO during the bull market of the late 1990s. While many crowd-followers accumulated assets, GMO stuck to their belief that markets were overvalued. They invested assets accordingly. Although eventually proven right, the firm watched assets in its International Intrinsic Value strategy fall by more than 75 percent (from ~$2.8bn to ~$650mm) between 1996 and 2001 as clients fired GMO.*

Andrew Smithers, author of *Valuing Wall Street: Protecting Wealth in Turbulent Times*, eloquently summarized the dilemma facing fund managers in a short piece he wrote on March 13, 2000, near the absolute peak of the technology bubble, in which he highlights the role of clients:

> Most fund managers are aware the market has gone bananas. What they do not and cannot know is when the madness will end. If they are going to stand out for sanity, they must have stalwart clients who will back their judgment even if the result is poor performance over a number of years. Unfortunately, such clients are rare. It is, therefore, more reasonable to blame the clients than the fund managers.**

* David Swensen, *Pioneering Portfolio Management: An Unconventional Approach to Institutional Investment*. Revised and Updated Edition (New York, NY: The Free Press, 2009).
** Andrew Smithers, "Lemming Like Fund Managers and Dotty Markets." *The Evening Standard (London)* (March 13, 2000).

decisions based on the decisions of those prior to them, an information cascade took place through which information—relevant or not, but embedded in the choices made by others—influenced the actions of those who followed.

It is believed that such information cascades serve as the basis of herd behavior and have deep evolutionary value. If the leading buffalo in a herd suddenly stops and moves right, it may be because he has seen a lion. If 50 buffalos do that, it would likely be unwise for the 51st buffalo to dismiss this data. When it comes to the rationality of markets, however, such herd behavior can be quite distortive of market prices.

The Blind Leading the Blind

The biological lenses presented in this chapter have broad applicability to the study of booms and busts. Although the epidemic framework is a useful tool for evaluating the relative maturity of a boom and the corresponding imminence of a bust, it is only valuable in providing an approximate sense of timing. By no means can it generate the precision needed by active risk managers. It yields virtually no insight on a day-to-day basis and is unlikely to prove useful in timing the bursting of a bubble with precision. Nevertheless, thinking about financial euphoria as a disease that has the potential to spread through an entire population proves quite useful in gauging the relative maturity of a boom. The most telling signs of a mature boom that is rapidly approaching the bust phase are a rapid growth in the number and type of participants, as well as the increasingly prevalent participation of unsophisticated or amateur investors.

The implications of the emergence phenomenon for our study of booms and busts are quite dramatic. The applicability of information cascades and the restaurant example discussed above are easily understood: Seemingly irrelevant decisions take on greater meaning than originally anticipated and have the potential to snowball into herdlike behavior of uninformed individuals. If everybody else is making money investing in housing, why shouldn't I? Clearly they've done the analysis and everyone can't be wrong, can they? Yet everyone relying on the fact that everyone else has "done their homework" can create a dynamic in which random decisions made earlier in the chain acquire unwarranted and unintended significance.

The jump to silent leadership from information cascades is not a particularly large leap. The connection occurs via the (seemingly) informed individuals, and just as actually informed individuals like our streaker bees can accurately lead a group of uninformed individuals, so too can silent leadership by seemingly informed (but actually uninformed) individuals lead groups astray. Recall my ad hoc experiment at the Las Vegas airport. Not only did my seemingly informed status (likely conveyed by the definitiveness of my direction and focus of my efforts) lead others astray, this silent leadership snowballed in a small cascade. Like ant pheromone, each additional person that followed me provided "guidance" to exiting passengers to follow the crowd. Surely not everyone would be walking in the wrong direction, would they?

The fact that many uninformed individuals can be so easily misled by other uninformed (but acting as if informed) individuals is a powerful finding. Suddenly, irrational group behavior is more understandable. If random events (such as the selection of a restaurant) have the potential to snowball into information cascades that create (without reason) completely lopsided outcomes, the implications become quite clear and important: Efficiency and stability can easily be replaced by positive feedback dynamics that drive instability and tipping away (rather than toward) an equilibrium point.

This chapter concludes Part I of the book and the presentation of the five lenses that we will use in our case studies that begin in Part II. Let us now turn to Tulipomania and the first demonstration of the lenses in action.

PART

II

Historical Case Studies

Each of the five lenses presented in Part One—microeconomic, macroeconomic, psychological, political, and biological—might be used on its own to solve puzzles. But the application of the five lenses in concert is suited to addressing mysteries. Part Two illustrates the power of a multilens approach through five short case studies. From tulips in Holland to financial crises in Asia to McMansions in America, there is no part of the world that has proven exempt from financial turmoil. Part Two demonstrates how a multilens perspective might have helped observers to understand these bubbles before they burst.

Tulipomania

A BUBBLE IN SEVENTEENTH-CENTURY HOLLAND

Speculation, it has been noted, comes when popular imagination settles on something seemingly new in the field of commerce or finance. The tulip, beautiful and varied in its colors, was one of the first things so to serve.

—John Kenneth Galbraith

During the 1630s in the Netherlands, a series of events occurred that have been popularized as one of the first recorded financial bubbles. Tulip bulbs escalated in price to the point that particularly rare bulbs traded for sums equivalent to several decades of an average salary.[1] More concerning than this rapid rise in the prices of rare bulbs, however, was a similarly rapid—albeit less dramatic—rise in the price of common tulip bulbs for which there were no meaningful supply constraints. Between November 1636 and January 1637, many tulip prices rose by a factor of 10.

After providing a basic overview of tulips and what made them particularly unique in seventeenth-century Holland, the chapter discusses the social, political, and economic context of the times. Finally, the chapter evaluates Tulipomania via the microeconomic, macroeconomic, psychological, political, and biological lenses—illustrating how the multilens approach presented in Part I can be used to evaluate the likelihood of financial bubbles forming and bursting.

The Uniqueness of Tulips

The tulip is not native to Western Europe. The first noteworthy shipment of tulips from the eastern Mediterranean (where they had been growing in the wild) to western Europe arrived in 1562 on a ship that had arrived in Antwerp from Constantinople.[2] A year later, in 1563, tulips were brought to Holland by a botanist.[3] Cultivation of tulips is believed to have begun in earnest in 1593 when Flemish botanist Charles de l'Ecluse accepted a position at the University of Leiden to establish the Hortus Academicus.[4]

Tulips grow from bulbs, but can reproduce by either seeds in the flower or buds that form on the mother bulb. If handled with the appropriate care, buds can directly produce another bulb. After a flower blooms, usually for a week or two in April or May, the original mother bulb disappears. In its place will be the primary bud, in the form of a functioning bulb. Other buds may also be on this new bulb. It is estimated that bulb-based reproduction is able to generate a replacement rate of between 100–150 percent, implying that meaningful supply growth is severely constrained. Reproduction via seed is a longer and slower process, but one likely to produce greater volume given the high seed count per flower. Seed-based reproduction takes 7–12 years to produce a bulb.[5]

According to Michael Dash, author of *Tulipomania,* one of the most thorough histories written of the bubble and its context,

> It is impossible to comprehend the tulip mania without understanding just how different tulips were from every other flower known to horticulturalists in the 17th century. . . . The colors they exhibited were more intense and more concentrated than those of ordinary plants . . .[6]

The vivid colors, unique patterns, and unusual flames on the petals of a tulip are generated when a mosaic virus "breaks" the flower. This is an important fact because the virus (and corresponding flower coloration and design pattern) is only reproduced via bud-based reproduction. Seed-based reproduction does not reproduce the virus, and hence results in bulbs that may or may not later be broken into a pattern and color scheme that may or may not be deemed desirable. The virus also impacts the bulb's health. Although it may improve the visual appeal of the flower, the virus adversely affects the bulb's ability to reproduce.[7]

As the popularity of the tulips began to rise, they were classified into four primary categories, based on their coloration[8]:

- *Colouren* – solid red, yellow, or white
- *Rosen* – red or pink on a white background
- *Violetten* – purple or lilac on a white background
- *Bizarden* – red, brown, or purple on a yellow background

Further, many tulips were given grandiose names, often prefixed with *Admirael* or *Generael*. The most famous and sought-after variety was known as *Semper Augustus*.

Because of the tulip bulb's need to be in the ground for much of the year, physical tulip bulbs could only be uprooted and exchanged between May and September. To accommodate the need for speculators to trade these bulbs throughout the year, contracts were developed and notarized for purchasers to commit to buying (and sellers to commit to selling) bulbs at an arranged price at the end of the growing season. Because these futures contracts did not require full payment, they effectively enabled purchasers to obtain economic and financial exposure to tulip prices with leverage. According to bubbleologist Don Rapp,

> Many sales were made on contracts in which the buyers put up little cash, but paid a down payment in kind, with personal goods, and promised to pay the seller a large cash payment after the buyer took possession (based on the expectation that he could sell the bulbs to another buyer at a higher price). . . . Thus, buyers were highly leveraged.[9]

Until 1630 or so, most bulbs were sold by the pound. By the 1630s, the rapid price escalation was drawing the attention of financial investors and the bulbs became desirable not only for their rare beauty, but for their ability to increase in value and be sold for a profit. By offering the prospect of rapid riches, the tulips became an excellent mechanism through which to speculate. As noted by British journalist Charles Mackay in 1841,

> It was deemed a proof of bad taste in any man of fortune to be without a collection of them. . . . The rage for possessing them soon caught the middle classes of society, and merchants and

shopkeepers, even of moderate means, began to vie with each other in the rarity of these flowers and the preposterous prices paid for them.[10]

Although data is quite limited on the actual trading activity in the bulbs, several of the recorded transactions are noteworthy. In 1633, three rare bulbs were purchased for the equivalent of a farmhouse. The frenetic pace of trading escalated for approximately four years more, when, possibly representing the peak, a rare *Violetten Admirael van Enkhuizen* bulb sold for 5,200 guilders, an all-time record. A bill of sale from one transaction indicated that one *Viceroy* bulb was exchanged for "two lasts of wheat, two lasts of rye, four fat oxen, eight fat swine, twelve fat sheep, two hogsheads wine, four tuns beer, two tons butter, one thousand pounds cheese, one bed (complete), one suit clothes, and one silver cup."[11] Quite the exchange for a single tulip bulb! During the 1636–1637 period, some bulbs were changing hands 10 times a day.

Eventually, the bubble burst "at a routine bulb auction, when, for the first time, the greater fool refused to show up and pay. Within days, panic spread across the country. Despite the efforts of traders to prop up demand, the market for tulips evaporated. Flowers that had commanded 5,000 guilders a few weeks before now fetched one-hundredth that amount."[12]

Fertile Soil for Bubble Formation

The 1630s were an extremely unique time in Holland. The country was embarking on its own golden age of peace and prosperity having just won itself independence from Spain. Much of the effort and many of the resources that had been channeled into the military struggle for independence were now being productively deployed for commercial and economic purposes. The lucrative East Indies trade was dominated by Amsterdam, where it was thought that per-voyage profits of 400 percent were not uncommon. According to economist Peter Garber,

> From 1620 to 1645, the Dutch established near monopolies on trade with the East Indies and Japan, conquered most of Brazil, took possession of the Dutch Caribbean islands, and founded New York. . . . Spain ceased to be the dominating power in Europe,

and the Netherlands, though small in population and resources, became a major power center because of its complete control over international trade and international finance. The Dutch were to seventeenth century trade and finance as the British were to nineteenth century trade and finance. . . . At the time of the tulip speculation, the Netherlands was a highly commercialized country with well-developed and innovative financial markets and a large population of sophisticated traders.[13]

To celebrate this new era of prosperity, grand estates were erected across Amsterdam, most of which were surrounded by flower gardens. According to Mark Frankel, in his review of *Tulipomania,* "the Dutch population seemed torn by two contradictory impulses: a horror of living beyond one's means and the love of a long shot."[14]

This bifurcated approach to thinking of prosperity was a direct result of the unprecedented commercial success the country had experienced following its war with Spain, as well as its recent experience with the bubonic plague. From 1635 to 1637, contemporaneous with the formation of the tulip bubble, the Netherlands was ravaged by the plague.[15] Although data from the period is not complete, the following data points illustrate the magnitude of the problem:

- Almost 18,000 people (more than one-seventh of the population) were killed in Amsterdam in 1636.
- More than 14,500 people died in Leiden (more than a third of the last available population estimate from 1622)
- Between August 1636 and November 1636, more than 14 percent of Haarlem died from the plague.

This context of tremendously good times (and corresponding financial innovations) with an ominous overlay of disease, uncertainty, and death proved a potent mixture for speculative desire among the Dutch. Mackay captures the spirit of speculation in the air, highlighting the social mood on both the boom and subsequent bust phases of Tulipomania:

The demand for tulips of a rare species increased so much in the year 1636 that regular marts for their sale were established on the Stock Exchange of Amsterdam, in Rotterdam, Harlaem, Leyden, Alkmar, Hoorn, and other towns. . . . Many individuals were suddenly rich. . . . Every one imagined that the passion for tulips would last forever, and that the wealthy from every part of the world would send to Holland, and pay whatever prices were asked of them. . . . Nobles, citizens, farmers, mechanics, seamen, footmen, mid-servants, even chimney-sweeps and old clotheswomen, dabbled in tulips. People of all grades converted their property into cash and invested it in flowers . . .

At last, however, the more prudent began to see that his folly could not last forever. Rich people no longer bought the flowers to keep them in their gardens, but to sell them again at cent per cent profit. It was seen that somebody must lose fearfully in the end. As this conviction spread, prices fell, and never rose again. Confidence was destroyed, and a universal panic seized upon the dealers. . . . Defaulters were announced day after day in all the towns of Holland. Hundreds who, a few months previously had begun to doubt that there was such a thing as poverty in the land suddenly found themselves the possessor of a few bulbs, which nobody would buy, even though they offered them for one-quarter of the sums they had paid for them. . . . Many who, for a brief season, had emerged from the humbler walks of life, were cast back into their original obscurity. Substantial merchants were reduced almost to beggary, and many a representative of a noble line saw the fortunes of his house ruined beyond redemption.[16]

There are lots of theorized reasons for the bust phase of Tulipomania, ranging from regulatory intervention to a simple exhaustion of "greater fools." Professor Earl Thompson at the University of California has suggested that the primary reason for the boom and subsequent bust was due to regulatory changes that effectively converted futures contracts into option contracts and thereby created asymmetric reward for limited risk.[17]

To understand why such a change might have a dramatic difference in the price purchasers might be willing to pay, it is best to think of tulip futures as actually paying full price today for a tulip bulb to be delivered in the future. At the time of delivery, the owner of the future contract will be entitled to the gain or loss from his original purchase price. For instance, if I agree to buy a *Semper*

Augustus bulb from you today at a price of $25,000 for delivery in nine months, I effectively own the bulb today at that price. If the price of the bulb goes up, I do not have to pay more and the gains are mine to keep. Likewise, if the price falls, I suffer the losses of having paid the higher price. I have indeed bought the bulb (to be delivered in the future) for $25,000 and am subject to both the gains and losses that emanate from price movements.

If, instead, I choose to purchase an option contract on the bulb with a price of $25,000, then I have acquired the right—but not the obligation—to purchase the bulb in the future. If the price is above $25,000, I am likely to purchase the bulb. If however, the price falls, then I can simply walk away from the deal and forfeit the money I paid to acquire the option. Given that options offer disproportionate (in theory, unlimited) gain with limited loss potential (your maximum loss is the price you paid to get the option), it is easy to understand why—particularly in a rapidly rising price environment—options might prove a more attractive manner through which to speculate.

Thompson argues that regulatory changes that effectively converted futures contracts into option contracts in November 1636 account for the massive upward surge, while the February 1637 revision to this change accounts for the bust: "The contract price of tulips in early February 1637 reached a level that was about 20 times higher than in both early November 1636 and early May 1637 . . . and it was simply a period during which the prices in futures contracts had been legally, albeit temporarily, converted into options exercise prices."

The Boombustology of Tulipomania

Having briefly described Tulipomania, we now turn to evaluating the events of the time through the five primary lenses presented in Part I of the book. Each lens considers relevant facets of Tulipomania. The objective of this section is to paint a multidisciplinary picture of the boom and bust sequence that characterized this bubble.

Microeconomics

The primary focus of the microeconomic lens discussed in Chapter 1 was the tendency of a financial phenomenon to move toward or away from an equilibrium price. Though we have limited data from the time, the price action of tulips over the 1636–1637 period does not suggest a tendency toward equilibrium. Rather, the fact that prices rose 10× for rare bulbs over a period of several weeks at the peak of the mania suggests that a reflexive process with positive feedback loops may have been at work. In fact, this may even have been the case as early as 1630.

According to George Soros, a reflexive situation is one in which perception not only reflects the so-called fundamentals but also *affects* the fundamentals. Was this the case in the tulip markets of 1630s Holland? Although data is limited, the evidence we do have suggests that it might have been the case. Consider the fact that "a trader at Harlaem paid one half of his fortune for a single root, not with the design of selling it again at a profit, but to keep in his own conservatory for admiration of his acquaintance."[18] Is this a case of prices reflecting or affecting demand?

Even economist Peter Garber, who has suggested that the price behavior of rare tulip bulbs resembles the price behavior of other rare bulbs and is inherently a reflection of supply and demand fundamentals, concedes that the price behavior of common bulbs "defies explanation."[19] By definition, any situation in which the laws of supply and demand are suspended (even temporarily) may be deemed one that does not tend toward equilibrium. Further, although it is clear that an excess of buyers drove prices higher, it seems conceivable that the higher prices generated additional demand, a dynamic that usually indicates the presence of a bubble.

Holland's Liquidity and Money

In an interesting article titled "The Dutch Monetary Environment during Tulipomania," Doug French described the impact of increased money supplies on tulip prices.[20] Because of its global economic dominance, the Netherlands became the recipient of massive capital inflows. The stability of banking systems in Amsterdam, notes French, created "the impetus that channeled large amounts of precious metals being discovered in the Americas, and to a lesser degree in Japan, toward Amsterdam."[21] In addition to these voluntary flows of precious metals toward Holland, precious metals also came to Amsterdam as a result of Dutch seizure of Spanish vessels possessing wealth en route from the Western Hemisphere.

Data from French's article tells the story. Table 6.1 is the best proxy we have for the growth of money supply that was occurring in the Netherlands—mint output. Table 6.2 demonstrates the balances and metal stock at the Bank of Amsterdam. Given the importance of reserves in the money creation process, the noticeable growth in mint output helps explain the increase in the Bank of Amsterdam's total balances. Might this increase of money in circulation have found its way into the supply and demand equation of tulips, thereby affecting their prices?

Table 6.1   Total Mint Output in Seventeenth-Century Southern Netherlands (Guilders)

Years	Gold	Silver	Copper	Total	% Change
1628–1629	153,010	2,643,732	4,109	2,800,851	
1630–1632	364,414	8,838,411	6,679	9,209,503	228%
1633–1635	476,996	16,554,079		17,031,075	84%
1636–1638	2,917,826	20,172,257		23,090,083	36%
1639–1641	2,950,150	8,102,988		11,053,138	−52%
1642–1644	2,763,979	1,215,645	47,834	4,027,458	−63%

Source: Jan a Van Houtte and Leon Van Buyten (1977), as quoted in "The Dutch Monetary Environment during Tulipomania" by Doug French.

Table 6.2   The Bank of Amsterdam's Balance Sheet Balloons (currency: Florins)

Year	Total Balances	% change	Metal Stock	% change
1630	4,166,159		3,105,449	
1631	3,784,047	−9%	2,976,742	−4%
1632	3,636,079	−4%	3,281,113	10%
1633	4,272,224	17%	3,866,890	18%
1634	3,995,666	−6%	3,474,527	−10%
1635	3,860,342	−3%	3,416,112	−2%
1636	3,992,338	3%	3,486,306	2%
1637	5,680,522	42%	5,315,576	52%
1638	5,593,750	−2%	5,256,606	−1%
1639	5,802,729	4%	5,446,002	4%

Source: J. G. Van Dillen, *History of the Principal Public Banks.* New York NY: Augustus Kelley, 1964, as quoted in Doug French, "The Dutch Monetary Environment during Tulip Mania." *The Quarterly Journal of Austrian Economics*, Vol 9, No 1, Spring 2006.

Although it is extremely difficult, given data constraints, to accurately identify the destination of this new money, it seems possible that the increase in money at least partially affected the demand for tulips and their prices. Similarly, it is also possible that the rapid gains in tulip prices generated additional deposits that increased the money supply.

Further, because many of the tulips were traded via early derivative contracts resembling today's futures contracts (due to the growing season constraints), the entire system was built on a precarious foundation of leverage. Data to confirm this hypothesis is lacking, but the fact that most of the transactions required speculators to put a fraction of their purchase price down led to significant embedded leverage. Further, if speculators were buying bulbs (on leverage) with the intention of selling them at higher prices, and not having the financial ability to service or repay the amount that they were basically borrowing, they were effectively engaging in a form of Ponzi finance. Such arrangements, as highlighted by Minsky's financial instability hypothesis in Chapter 2, are inherently destabilizing and highlight an increasingly imminent correction.

The Psychological State of Tulipjobbers

Given the end of the war with Spain and the impact of the bubonic plague on the residents of seventeenth-century Holland, residents were likely in a particularly vulnerable psychological state. The uncertainty of life due to rampant disease generated a short-term orientation and focus on the present and immediate future. Longer-term thinking was considered wasted thought. Alongside these reminders of mortality, however, overconfidence was ubiquitous during this golden age of the Netherlands' economic history. In short, economic optimism combined with the heightened uncertainty of life to generate and strengthen a gambling tendency, thereby magnifying bubble possibilities.

Might the financial extremes have taken place without these conditions? Although such counterfactuals are mere intellectual speculation and there is no way to actually know what might have occurred under such "what if" scenarios, it seems unlikely that the bubble would have formed and ballooned as rapidly and as dramatically as it did in the absence of economic overconfidence or disease-inspired fatalism.

Mackay's account of the events captures the psychological conditions that prevailed among the general population: "Everyone imagined that the passion for the tulips would last forever."[22] Given recent economic successes in the country, participants in the tulip market were likely affected by many of the psychological biases discussed in Chapter 3, including anchoring on the last price, insufficient adjusting of a range around the anchor, and believing regression in prices was unlikely. Might it have been possible that newfound riches from the East Indies were being treated as house money and gambled in the tulip market? Perhaps gains from tulips were themselves considered house money. Finally, the illiquidity that arose in the market for tulip bulbs might have been an expression of the endowment effect in action. Is it conceivable that sellers were over-valuing what they owned, thereby preventing market-clearing transactions from taking place?

Political and Regulatory Considerations

A large part of the confidence generated among the Dutch was driven by the political and economic successes they had been experiencing as a country. The winning of independence from the Spanish, combined with massive innovation and virtual domination of world trade, made the population extremely confident: perhaps overconfident.

A counterfactual scenario is again worth considering. If the Dutch had still been fighting a war with Spain and resources that were channeled toward economic progress were instead being channeled toward military actions, would the Dutch have been as confident as they were? Although it is impossible to tell, it does not seem that they would have been *as* confident.

Perhaps most pertinent to our study of Tulipomania, however, is the regulatory and political dynamics that drove individual speculators. Specifically, the conversion of futures contracts into option contracts is the most significant feature. Such a policy change is a modification of property rights, and as noted in Chapter 4, such meddling by governments dramatically impacts the supply and demand dynamics that drive price determination.

Underlying the conversion was a political process in which many of Holland's influential elites, speculators who included politicians, had lost a great deal of money in the October–November 1636 tulip price correction. Because the losses were borne by leveraged (professional) speculators, tulip growers—many of whom had made a fortune during the prior price surge—became the object of resentment. Not surprisingly, politicians (many of whom had personally lost money) met with the enraged public to help address the issue. The solution discussed: Convert the futures contracts into call option contracts.

These efforts to support prices instead created a buying frenzy. The debate that ensued between tulip growers and speculators focused almost exclusively on the option premium to be paid. Although public officials and speculators (often one and the same) had initially suggested the option premium be priced at 0 percent of the original futures contract price, the growers pushed back. Thompson summarizes the political dynamic between planters and buyers with respect to the option price:

> The public officials were suggesting 0%. However, the planters were not totally lacking in political power. Although, after lengthy deliberations, the planters subsequently announced that they would, as accepted, accede to the conversion of their contracts and accept a price equal to a mere 10% of the contract price, they demanded a later conversion date than the October date that had been publicly supported by most of the government officials. In particular, the planters announced, again on February 24th, that they would convert only those contracts that had originated after November 30th, a date by which virtually all traders knew that the ostensible futures prices would be converted into option exercise prices, with a 0–10% price for the option to be subsequently determined by Holland's legislatures and courts.[23]

By effectively fiddling with the supply and demand–driven price discovery process, regulators exacerbated the boom by encouraging more "swing for the fences" style speculation. Not surprisingly, this is precisely what seems to have occurred when they considered converting futures contracts to options contracts.

More than Botanical Biology

The two key insights from a biological perspective relate quite well to the Tulipomania phenomenon: The epidemic lens provides an interesting framework through which to gauge the maturity of the boom, and the swarm logic of leadership by example provides an explanation of how so many people could be misled into such inappropriate pricing.

Let's begin with the epidemic logic. A key lesson from Chapter 5 was that the participation of amateur investors heralded the beginning of the end. Just as the involvement of professional financiers in a market is rarely alarming as it represents their normal course of activities, the involvement of amateurs and historical nonparticipants is very concerning as it indicates the pool of vulnerable and potentially infectable individuals is dwindling. Thus, the involvement of "nobles, citizens, farmers, mechanics, seamen, footmen, maid-servants, even chimney sweeps and old clotheswomen"[24] in the tulip markets is particularly troublesome and indicates a significantly advanced (perhaps peaking?) stage of the boom.

The second biological lens of relevance to Tulipomania is emergence, or more specifically, the impact of seemingly informed leadership on group behavior. Here again, Mackay's account of the events is informative. In particular, references to the participation in Tulipomania of "Councellor Herwart, a man very famous in his day for his collection of rare exotics"[25] indicated a willingness on the part of uninformed members of the speculative swarm to follow the movement of such informed individuals. Further, the fact that "many learned men, including Pompeius de Angelis, and the celebrated Lypsius of Leydan, the author of the treatise 'De Constantia,' were passionately fond of tulips"[26] further validates the view that silent leadership of seemingly informed individuals contributed to the development of a group consensus. (Given limited data from the time, there is no better gauge of seemingly informed status than fame, and these descriptions imply fame.)

The Multilens Look

The purpose of this chapter was not to be exhaustive in its treatment of Tulipomania or any facet of the period. Rather, it was to

Table 6.3   The Five-Lens Approach to Tulipomania

Lens	Notes
Microeconomics	Higher prices induced buyers Lower prices induced sellers
Macroeconomics	Hot money inflows provided cheap capital Financial innovation (leverage via futures contracts)
Psychology	Political-economic inspired overconfidence Conspicuous consumption / trophy bulbs "New era" thinking (golden age)
Politics	End of war Government meddling in property rights, distorting price mechanism
Biology	Amateur investors Silent leadership

demonstrate the power of a multidisciplinary framework through which to analyze bubbles. A summary of the Tulipomania discussion is listed in Table 6.3. The next chapter will similarly illustrate the power of the five-lens framework during the Great Depression.

The Great Depression

FROM ROARING TWENTIES TO YAWNING THIRTIES

*Optimism built on optimism to drive prices up. Then came the
crash and the eventual discovery of the severe mental and moral
deficiencies of those once thought endowed with genius and their
consignment, at best, to oblivion, but, more grimly, to public
obloquy, jail, or suicide.*

—John Kenneth Galbraith

The Great Depression began in October 1929 with the U.S. stock
market crash and quickly became a severe worldwide economic contraction.[1] Before the Great Crash, however, a significant boom and
bust sequence took place in Florida, one that revealed the speculative tendencies of the time. In this chapter, we'll discuss the Florida
land boom that took place during the mid-1920s and the rapid
ascent of the stock market in the late 1920s before evaluating the
events via the five lenses presented in Part I of the book.

Castles in the Sand

The great Florida real estate bubble of the 1920s was a revelatory
manifestation of the speculative tendencies that were sweeping
through America following World War I. Confidence was running
high, and by the mid 1920s, an unsustainable boom in Florida land
was underway. In fact, to many, the rapid boom and bust of Florida

real estate was thought to be like castles built in sand. It only took high tide to wash them away. One of the most prominent developers of the times, Carl Graham Fisher, was also a promoter of the Indy 500 and helped create some of the first transcontinental roads. Fisher was one of the primary reasons that Florida transformed into the hottest market during a great bull market. Fisher successfully converted portions of South Florida into a heavenly combination of golf, polo, deep sea fishing, luxury hotels, and glamour.

Although property fever spread throughout Florida, migrating up the state's east coast and west coast, Miami represented ground zero of the speculative tendency. Consider the following passage from a chapter titled "Home, Sweet Florida" in the book *Only Yesterday*, written in 1931:

> There was nothing languorous about the atmosphere of tropical Miami during the memorable summer and autumn of 1925. Miami had become one frenzied real estate exchange. There were said to be 2,000 real estate offices and 25,000 agents marketing house-lots or acreage.... The city fathers had been forced to pass an ordinance forbidding the sale of property in the street, or even the showing of a map, to prevent inordinate traffic congestion.... A traveler caught in a traffic jam counted the license-plates of eighteen states among the sedans and flivvers waiting in line. Hotels were overcrowded. People were sleeping wherever they could lay their heads, in station waiting-rooms or in automobiles. The railroads had been forced to place an embargo on imperishable freight in order to avert the danger of famine; building materials were now being imported by water and the harbor bristled with shipping. Fresh vegetables were a rarity, the public utilities of the city were trying desperately to meet the suddenly multiplied demand for electricity and gas and telephone service, and there were recurrent shortages of ice.[2]

Not exactly a description of sparsely attended Sunday afternoon open houses in suburban settings! As the description reveals, there was an intense flurry of activity that had drawn many from near and far and swirled them into a speculative frenzy. The other prevalent component of the times was the effective use of leverage via the 10 percent down payments made to "buy" land. This facilitated sales and postponed the tiresome formalities of recording deeds, etc. An executive of the Retail Credit Company of Atlanta described the sales process quite succinctly:

> Lots are bought from blueprints, they look better that way. . . . Reservations are accepted. This requires a check for 10 per cent of the price of the lot the buyer expects to select. On the first day of sale, at the promoter's office in town, the reservations are called out in order, and the buyer steps up and, from a beautifully drawn blueprint, with lots of dimensions and prices clearly shown, selects a lot or lots, get a receipt in the form of a "binder" describing it, and has the thrill of seeing "SOLD" stamped on the blue-lined square which represents his lot, a space usually fifty by a hundred feet of Florida soil or swamp.[3]

Allen continues his description of the speculative frenzy, noting that few actually intended to purchase the land:

> The binder, of course, did not complete the transaction. But few people worried much about the further payments which were to come. Nine buyers out of ten bought their lots with only one idea, to resell, and hoped to pass along their binders to other people at a neat profit before even the first payment fell due at the end of thirty days.[4]

Allen cites seven primary causes for the speculative land boom that took place in Florida during the mid-1920s: (1) the climate, (2) accessibility to the populous northeast United States, (3) the automobile, which Allen notes "was making America into a nation of nomads, teaching all manner of men and women to explore their country . . ." (4) abounding national confidence inspired by years of economic prosperity under the Coolidge administration, (5) the backlash against "the very routine and smoke and congestion and twentieth century standardization of living" that created a desire for country club living, (6) the success of Southern California's resort-image developments, and (7) the belief that Florida offered a chance to develop sudden wealth (i.e., one could get rich quick!).

Eventually, however, the greater fools stopped showing up and the boom turned into a bust. The land boom began to collapse during the late spring and summer of 1926 when binder-holders began defaulting on the payments they were supposed to make. Rapp notes how the embedded leverage combined with other developments, including two hurricanes, to put the finishing touches on the bust:

> Many of those with paper profits found that the properties they owned were preceded by a series of purchases and sales, all at 10% down, and as many of these defaulted, the only options were to either hold onto the land at a great loss, or default. The land was often burdened with taxes and assessments that amounted to more than the cash received for it, and much of the land was blighted with a partly constructed development. As the deflation expanded, two hurricanes added the finishing touches to the bursting bubble. The hurricanes left four hundred dead, sixty-three hundred injured, and fifty thousand homeless.[5]

Following the bust, Henry Villard described the images he saw as he drove into Miami in *The Nation*:

> Dead subdivisions line the highway, their pompous names half-obliterated on crumbling stucco gates. Lonely white-way lights stand guard over miles of cement sidewalks, where grass and palmetto take the place of homes that were to be. . . . Whole sections of outlying subdivisions are composed of unoccupied houses, past which one speeds on broad thoroughfares as if traversing a city in the grip of death.[6]

Allen highlights the economic impact on Miami by citing bank clearings data (see Table 7.1). After rising steadily during the early 1920s and crossing $1bn in 1925, bank clearings steadily fell.

Table 7.1   Miami Bank Clearings

Year	Bank Clearings
1925	$1,066,528,000
1926	$632,867,000
1927	$260,039,000
1928	$143,364,000
1929	$142,316,000

Noting that this economic distress took place during "the very years when elsewhere in the country prosperity was triumphant," Allen eloquently summarizes the Florida land bust: "Most of the millions piled up in paper profits had melted away, many of the millions sunk in developments had been sunk for good and all, the vast inverted pyramid of credit had toppled to earth, and the lesson of the economic falsity of a scheme of land values based upon grandiose plans, preposterous expectations, and hot air had been taught in a long agony of deflation."[7]

From Booming Twenties to Busted Thirties

It is impossible to understand the Great Depression without understanding the Roaring Twenties. The economic boom of the 1920s is perhaps as significant a development in the history of booms as the Great Depression is in the history of busts. While lots of attention has been given to the Great Depression, it seems unlikely that it would have been as significant without the less-addressed boom of the 1920s.

There are numerous factors that help explain the 1920s boom. To begin, not unlike the Dutch military successes, the United States and its allies had just won the First World War, and not unlike the Dutch following their victory over Spain, American confidence was running high. WWI had helped the country accelerate its transition from an agricultural economy to an industrial nation. The Federal Reserve system, which had been created in 1913, was seen by many as the solution to the business cycle problem (i.e., the Federal Reserve would be able to steer the economy with such precision that booms, busts, and blowups would never again occur).

Mass production had been gaining prominence and reduced the costs of many goods, productivity soared[8] while unit costs sank, and several industries appeared poised to change the world. In particular, cars and radios were the "new thing" of the day, and there seemed to be limitless demand for these goods. Automobiles were increasingly commonplace, and by the 1920s, more than 50 percent of Americans owned cars.[9] Transportation was being revolutionized, and trains and cars provided the means for domestic commerce to boom with increasingly lower frictional costs. Taxes were low, consumer optimism ran high, and electricity distribution was now so

widespread that most Americans were "on the grid." Most industries (agriculture being a primary exception) were booming as consumption and investment were supported by a massive tailwind of
hope and optimism.

According to John Kenneth Galbraith, the real economic gains in
the 1925–1929 period were substantial. GNP was up 13 percent
in five years, auto production was up 23 percent in three years,
industrial production was up 64 percent in seven years. He says,
"Throughout the twenties, production and productivity per worker
in manufacturing industries increased by about 43 percent. Wages,
salaries, and prices all remained relatively stable."[10]

Although economic progress was indeed substantial and based
on genuine increases in productivity, asset prices—specifically, the
stock market—eagerly reflected these developments and likely
more. It is hard to know when exactly the stock market began to distance itself from the extraordinary fundamental developments and
entered the realm of speculative excess, but Galbraith eloquently
notes that "early in 1928, the nature of the boom changed. The
mass escape into make-believe, so much a part of the true speculative orgy, started in earnest. . . . The time had come, as in all peri-
ods of speculation, when men sought not to be persuaded of the
reality of things but to find excuses for escaping into the new world
of fantasy."[11]

Galbraith goes on to note how the market's quiet winter months
of 1928 were followed by stock prices rising "not by slow, steady
steps, but by great vaulting leaps."[12] Figure 7.1 demonstrates the
magnitude of the leaps by plotting the real S&P Composite Index
divided by the 10-year moving average of real earnings. By using
inflation-adjusted numbers and a 10-year earnings period, the data
measure how expensive the market is relative to corporate profit-
generating abilities and is not subject to single year surges (or
depressions) in profits. Note the chart goes back to 1881 and stops
in October 1929, right before the market crash.

Lest you think that the index was the only manifestation of
the market's upward jaunt, Table 7.2 summarizes the movement
in share price of 12 very popular and widely held stocks between
March 3, 1928 and September 3, 1929.

The beginning of the economic bust is widely believed to be the
October 1929 crash of the stock market. Although most students of
the Great Depression focus on the events of Tuesday, October 29,

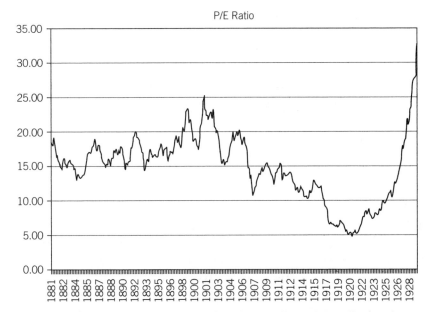

Figure 7.1   Real S&P Composite Index as a Multiple of 10-Year Moving Average Earnings, January 1881–October 1929

Source: Robert Shiller. Data accessed via www.econ.yale.edu/~shiller/data

Table 7.2 The Big Bull Market

Company	Opening Price (3/3/28)	High Price* (9/3/29)	% Change
American Can	77	181 $^7/_8$	136.2%
AT&T	179 ½	335 $^5/_8$	86.9%
Anaconda Copper	54 ½	162	197.3%
Electric Bond & Share	89 ¾	203 $^5/_8$	126.9%
General Electric	128 ¾	396 ¾	208.2%
Montgomery Ward	132 ¾	466 ½	251.4%
New York Central	160 ½	256	59.5%
Radio (RCA)	94 ½	505	434.4%
Union Carbide	145	413 $^5/_8$	185.3%
US Steel	138 $^1/_8$	279 $^1/_8$	102.1%
Westinghouse	91 $^5/_8$	313	241.6%
Woolworth	180 ¾	251	38.9%

Source: Frederick Lewis Allen, *Only Yesterday: An Informal History of the 1920s* (New York, NY: Harper & Row, 1931).
* Adjusted to reflect the effects of stock splits and rights issues.

1929, much can be learned by studying the three prior trading sessions—back to and including the prior Thursday.

On Black Thursday, as October 24, 1929 has since been known, the market entered a serious state of panic—with no immediate or palpable cause. Historian Edward Chancellor notes, "Unlike former stock market panics, it was not preceded by tightness in the money market. No banking, brokerage, or industrial failures served as a trigger—and yet panic there was."[13] Many stocks were dropping more than several percentage points between trades, and the market appeared to be in the midst of a complete meltdown—until calm was restored by JP Morgan and others who jointly entered the market and began publicly buying to support share prices. By the end of the day, the Dow Jones Industrial Average had recovered most of its losses and closed down 6 points to 299. Nearly 13 million shares had been traded on the NYSE, which was almost triple the "normal" volume.

Friday was a relatively calm day, and many brokers worked through the weekend to catch up on trades and to calculate margin calls that needed to be sent out to clients. The market fell 38 points to 260 on Monday, and by Tuesday, the market was in complete panic. Chancellor describes the events as follows: "On the floor of the Stock Exchange, a broker grabbed a messenger by his hair, another fled the floor screaming like a madman, jackets were torn, collars dislodged, and clerks in their frenzy lashed out at each other. . ... On Black Tuesday, the glamour stocks of the bull market suffered the worst damage."[14] Table 7.3 summarizes the magnitude of the one-day fall among these glamour stocks.

The slide into depression that followed the stock market crash was likely caused by numerous factors, including (but definitely not

Table 7.3   The Rapid Fall of Glamour Stocks

Stock	10/28/29	10/29/29	% Change
Radio (RCA)*	40.25	26.00	−35.4%
GSTC	60	35	−41.7%
Blue Ridge	10	3	−70.0%
United Corp	26	19.30	−25.8%
First National	$5,200	$1,600	−69.3%
National City	$455	$300	−34.1%

* Adjusted for splits

limited to) the presence of bank failures[15], "sticky wages,"[16] adherence to the gold standard[17], the unsustainable growth of consumer credit,[18] and high leverage levels among consumers, corporations and other organizations.[19]

Allen cites seven economic diseases that plagued businesses around the world and contributed to the conversion of the Great Crash in America into the global Great Depression: (1) overproduction of capital and goods, (2) artificial commodity prices, (3) collapse of silver prices and the corresponding drop in purchasing power of Asian consumers, (4) the international financial derangement caused by the shifting of gold to France and the United States, (5) unrest in foreign countries, (6) the self-generating and vicious feedback loops of confidence that affected the economy, and (7) "the profound psychological reaction from the exuberance of 1929" and corresponding destruction of consumer and corporate confidence.

The full impact of the Great Depression that followed the stock market crash of 1929 is hard to understand for Americans born and raised following the end of World War II. Robert Samuelson summarized the massive impact it had on the American economy, the world economy, and the world that emerged after the Great Depression:

> The Great Depression of the thirties remains the most important economic event in American history. It caused enormous hardship for tens of millions of people and the failure of a large fraction of the nation's banks, businesses, and farms. It transformed national politics by vastly expanding government, which was increasingly expected to stabilize the economy and to prevent suffering. Democrats became the majority party. In 1929 the Republicans controlled the White House and Congress. By 1933, the Democrats had the presidency and, with huge margins, Congress (310–117 in the House, and 60–35 in the Senate). President Franklin Roosevelt's New Deal gave birth to the American version of the welfare state. Social Security, unemployment insurance, and federal family assistance all began in the thirties.
>
> It is hard for those who did not live through it to grasp the full force of the worldwide depression. Between 1930 and 1939 U.S. unemployment averaged 18.2 percent. The economy's output of goods and services (gross national product) declined

30 percent between 1929 and 1933 and recovered to the 1929 level only in 1939. Prices of almost everything (farm products, raw materials, industrial goods, stocks) fell dramatically. Farm prices, for instance, dropped 51 percent from 1929 to 1933. World trade shriveled: between 1929 and 1933 it shrank 65 percent in dollar value and 25 percent in unit volume. Most nations suffered. In 1932 Britain's unemployment was 17.6 percent. Germany's depression hastened the rise of Hitler and, thereby, contributed to World War II.[20]

The Boombustology of the Great Depression

Applying the five disciplinary lenses developed in Part I of the book proves fruitful in trying to understand the 1920s and 1930s from a bubble-spotting perspective. Let us now begin by evaluating the (lack of) equilibrium tendencies during the Florida real estate boom and the Roaring Twenties, as well as the subsequent Great Depression.

Disequilibrium Tendencies

How is it that individuals and institutions that found it logical and rational to pay one price for a security one day would not be willing to pay 50 percent of that price the next day? Surely, such developments do not occur in a totally "efficient" market. In fact, the tendency toward equilibrium is one of the major tenets of microeconomics that seems to have broken down during both the booming 1920s and the busted 1930s.

The procyclical nature of leverage enabled consumers to buy more during good times as credit was easily obtained in a rising market. Financial innovations such as installment purchases (i.e., buy now, pay later) effectively increased consumer demand as the market boomed. When such credit contracted, not only did such credit-fueled buying slow, but so too did normal buying demand disappear as it had been "brought forward" into the 1920s by access to this credit.

Perhaps the most obvious example of the self-reinforcing nature of the times is found in Florida. Allen captures the essence of the dynamic quite eloquently in describing the fate of an individual who experienced both the boom and bust as well as the accompanying joy and pain: "One man who had sold acreage early in 1925 for twelve dollars an acre, and had cursed himself for his situation when it was resold later in the year for seventeen dollars, and then thirty dollars, and finally sixty dollars an acre, was surprised a year or two afterward to find that the entire series of subsequent purchases was in default, that he could not recover the money still due him, and that his only redress was to take his land back again."[21] Thus, just as higher prices induced more buyers, so too did lower prices generate more sellers. Not surprisingly, this dynamic generally failed to produce an equilibrium.

The economic bust that followed the Great Crash had a very reflexive component to it, with a very self-reinforcing element to the dynamics of business during the 1930s. As described in *Only Yesterday*, "each bankruptcy, each suspension of payments, and each reduction of operating schedules affected other concerns, until it seemed almost as if the business world were a set of tenpins ready to knock one another over as they fell; each employee thrown out of work decreased the potential buying power of the country."[22] Again, the snowballing effect here seems to resemble a reflexive dynamic connected by confidence.

Inappropriate Interest Rates

Recall that one of the primary beliefs of the Austrian school of economics is that inappropriately cheap money results in malinvestment and overcapacity, which must be "cured" via capital destruction, deflation, and a general working-through of the excesses. Austrian economists believe that the meddling of central banks in setting the price of money distorts the economy and exacerbates the likelihood of booms and busts. Could this criticism be applied to the Great Depression? What role did the price of money play during the 1920s and 1930s?

According to Chancellor, "The Federal Reserve in Washington— the institution that had supposedly abolished panics—had inadvertently ignited the stock market boom by lowering rates in 1925." This was explicitly intended to help Britain manage the accelerating outflows of gold after their return to the prewar gold standard. Although this action might have been useful to the Brits, it had an extraordinary effect (i.e., increasing it) on the American appetite for risk.

Although such low-priced money found its way into increased corporate capital expenditures and increased consumer purchasing of both durable and consumable goods, one of its most powerful outlets was via margin loans used to enable the purchase of additional securities. Margin loans, which enable the purchase of financial securities with borrowed money, had grown concomitantly with the stock market's climb. By October 1928, credit extended by banks, brokerage firms, and other financing sources to investors had risen to nearly $16 billion, which equated to approximately 18 percent of the total stock market capitalization of the entire market.[23]

If inappropriately low rates had created the boom that manifested itself most evidently in the stock market, might more "normal" but higher rates be responsible for the bust that immediately followed the Great Crash? According to Shiller, "On February 14, 1929, the Federal Reserve Board raised the rediscount rate from 5 percent to 6 percent for the ostensible purpose of checking speculation. In the 1930s, the Fed continued the tight monetary policy and saw the initial stock market downturn evolve into the deepest stock market decline ever, and a recession into the most serious U.S. depression ever."[24]

Perhaps the supply of money might help account for the boom–bust sequence. Figure 7.2 summarizes total money supply from June 1921 through June 1929. Might some of this money have found its way into asset markets?

Although it is very difficult to establish causality, it does appear that money supply was correlated with asset prices. These procyclical liquidity conditions likely exacerbated underlying boom and bust tendencies as asset prices correlated with the money supply.

The Psychological State of the Time

The psychological state of market participants during the 1920s was characterized by optimism and confidence inspired by self-reinforcing virtuous market developments. Might some of this optimism and confidence have translated into a sense of overconfidence and investor invincibility? Consider the following passage from Only Yesterday:

> As people in the summer of 1929 looked back for precedents, they were comforted by the recollection that every crash of the past few years had been followed by a recovery, and that every recovery had ultimately brought prices to a new high point. Two steps up, one step down, two steps up again—that

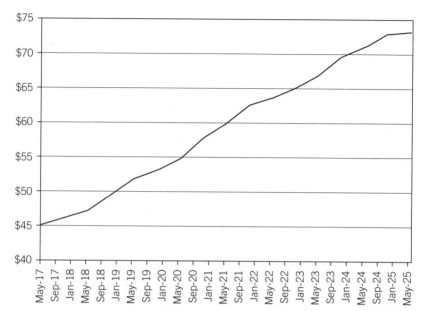

Figure 7.2   Total Money Supply during the 1920s

Source: Murray Rothbard, *America's Great Depression* (Auburn, AL: Ludwig von Mises Institute, 2000) Table 1, 92.

was how the market went. If you sold, you had only to wait for the next crash (they came every few months) and buy in again. And there was really no reason to sell at all: you were bound to win in the end if your stock was sound. The really wise man, it appeared, was he who 'bought and held on.'[25]

"New era" thinking was clearly present, as noted by the prominent emergence of the automobile and radio industries. Aerospace and movie production played supporting roles among investors' foci. The automobile soon replaced the railroads as the engine of commerce and "it transformed the culture and geography of the nation; roads were surfaced, highways built, and garages erected to accommodate the increasing number of passenger cars, which rose from seven million to twenty-three million during the 1920s."[26] Not surprisingly in this climate, General Motors' share price increased by more than 10 times between 1925 and 1928.

The radio, launched by Westinghouse in 1920, also began to fascinate the investor with unlimited possibilities of information dissemination. The industry was dominated by Radio Corporation of America (RCA), often referred to by investors of the time as "Radio." Known as the "General Motors of the Air" by investors,[27] Radio climbed from under $2 per share in 1921 to over $110 by 1929. In 1929, it was the most heavily traded stock on the New York Stock Exchange.

Aerospace also provided a believability to the new era thinking of the times, spurred in large part by Charles Lindbergh's solo crossing of the Atlantic in 1927, and the replacement of silent movies with "talkies" captured investor imagination.

The vision of the future held by most Americans in 1929 was one of unbridled optimism, a vision that likely generated and validated the (over)confidence that permeated investor sentiment. In describing the average American, Allen said he

> visioned an America set free from poverty and toil. He saw a magical order built on the new science and new prosperity: roads swarming with millions upon millions of automobiles, airplanes darkening the skies, lines of high-tension wire carrying from hilltop to hilltop the power to give life to a thousand labor-saving machines, skyscrapers thrusting above one-time villages, vast cities rising in great geometrical masses of stone and concrete roaring with perfectly mechanized traffic—and smartly dressed men and women spending, spending with the money they had won by being far-sighted enough to foresee, way back in 1929, what was going to happen.[28]

As an additional manifestation of the (over)confidence of the times, 40 Wall Street reigned as the tallest building in the world in 1929, only to be outdone by the Chrysler Building in 1930, which itself was unseated from the throne by the Empire State Building eleven months later. Chapter 11 will develop this "tallest building" indicator a bit further. John Kenneth Galbraith succinctly and eloquently summarized the spirit (and literal construction activity!) of the times and the dynamic it imposed on prices: "Optimism built on optimism to drive prices up."[29]

Political and Regulatory Conditions

A large part of consumer, business, and national confidence sprang from the ending of WWI and the redeployment of industrial efforts toward commercial, rather than military, ends. The Coolidge administration was particularly hands-off in its approach to handling markets, and prosperity was widespread.

Prohibition also played a role in the Florida land boom. Although unintended, the government's prohibition of the manufacture and sale of intoxicating beverages led money to flow to Florida, what William Johnson Frazer called "one of the countries leakiest spots on the country's dry border." The result was a surge in revenue that was deposited in Florida banks, which, due to banking regulation at the time (i.e., banks had been granted state charters and mandated to conduct business only within the state), effectively mandated that they lend this money out within Florida.

Every aspiring politician yearns for an opportunity to blame incumbents and the existing system for the ills faced by society, and the Great Crash and economic slowdown that followed provided such an opportunity. The early 1930s typify this spirit, and Roosevelt's 1932 campaign for the presidency touted the failure of market economics and Wall Street's self-seeking greed. In fact, his inaugural address captures this spirit:

> Let me assert my firm belief that the only thing we have to fear is fear itself—nameless, unreasoning, unjustified terror which paralyzes needed efforts to convert retreat into advance. . . . In such a spirit on my part and on yours we face our common difficulties. They concern, thank God, only material things. Values have shrunken to fantastic levels; taxes have risen; our ability to pay has fallen; government of all kinds is faced by serious curtailment of income; the means of exchange are frozen in the currents of trade; the withered leaves of industrial enterprise lie on every side; farmers find no markets for their produce; the savings of many years in thousands of families are gone. More important, a host of unemployed citizens face the grim problem of existence, and an equally great number toil with little return. Only a foolish optimist can deny the dark realities of the moment.
>
> Yet our distress comes from no failure of substance. We are stricken by no plague of locusts. Compared with the perils which our forefathers conquered because they believed and were not afraid, we have still much to be thankful for. Nature still offers her bounty and human efforts have multiplied it. Plenty is at our doorstep, but a generous use of it languishes in

the very sight of the supply. Primarily this is because the rulers of the exchange of mankind's goods have failed, through their own stubbornness and their own incompetence, have admitted their failure, and abdicated. Practices of the unscrupulous money changers stand indicted in the court of public opinion, rejected by the hearts and minds of men.

True they have tried, but their efforts have been cast in the pattern of an outworn tradition. Faced by failure of credit they have proposed only the lending of more money. Stripped of the lure of profit by which to induce our people to follow their false leadership, they have resorted to exhortations, pleading tearfully for restored confidence. They know only the rules of a generation of self-seekers. They have no vision, and when there is no vision the people perish.

The money changers have fled from their high seats in the temple of our civilization. We may now restore that temple to the ancient truths. The measure of the restoration lies in the extent to which we apply social values more noble than mere monetary profit.

Happiness lies not in the mere possession of money; it lies in the joy of achievement, in the thrill of creative effort. The joy and moral stimulation of work no longer must be forgotten in the mad chase of evanescent profits. These dark days will be worth all they cost us if they teach us that our true destiny is not to be ministered unto but to minister to ourselves and to our fellow men.

Consider the biblical overtones invoked by using "money changers" rather than "speculators" and the overwhelming sense that someone must be blamed. Chancellor notes that "in place of market forces came federal welfare, housing and work programmes, bank deposit insurance, prices and incomes policies, minimum wage legislation, and a number of other measures. Speculation, whether in stocks, bonds, land, or commodities, was no longer to play such a key role in economic life."[30]

The sweeping set of government programs were organized around the three Rs of relief, recovery, and reform. The economic policies of the Roosevelt administration were based on getting Americans back to work and alleviating economic hardships (i.e., relief), helping the American economy to recover toward full potential, and providing a new regulatory framework, complete with appropriate government authorities, to oversee the economy and prevent a repeat of the Great Depression. The New Deal policies produced a plethora of new government programs and agencies, including major programs such as Social Security and the Federal Deposit Insurance Corporation (FDIC) as well as the creation of the Securities and Exchange Commission (SEC).

Although such regulatory reform was designed to promote stability and prevent future hardships, it laid the roots of future troubles by creating issues of moral hazard through deposit insurance, a potentially unsustainable program of entitlements such as Social Security, labor market distortion via price floors (i.e., minimum wages), and the general growth of the government. The magnitude and impact of these programs by themselves suggest the 1920s and 1930s boom–bust sequence threatened the very fabric of the U.S. capitalist system. Though property rights were never directly threatened, the intention of Social Security and other programs was to redistribute from those who had, to those who needed.

Epidemic Thinking, Silent Leadership

One of the most important elements of a boom–bust sequence that helps one identify where in the cycle one might be is, to use language from epidemiology, the population of unaffected or unexposed individuals. When one hears that everyone, including those not traditionally active or invested in the market, is "in the market," then one might naturally (and accurately) assume that the boom cycle is far along and very mature (perhaps approaching expiration), with a limited population of infectable participants.

Consider Allen's description of the market in 1929:

> Grocers, motormen, plumbers, seamstresses and speakeasy waiters were in the market. Even the rebellious intellectuals were there: loudly as they might lament the depressing effects of standardization and mass production upon American life, they found themselves quite ready to reap the fruits thereof. . . . The Big Bull Market had become a national mania. . . . The speculative fever was infecting the whole country. Stories of fortunes being made overnight were on everybody's lips.[31]

Table 7.4   The Five-Lens Approach to the Great Depression

Lens	Notes
Microeconomics	Reflexive credit/collateral tendencies Higher prices induced buyers Lower prices induced sellers
Macroeconomics	Inappropriately cheap money Financial innovation (leverage via "binders")
Psychology	New era thinking (new industries) World's tallest skyscrapers (40 Wall, Chrysler, Empire State Building)
Politics	End of war Prohibition inspired money flows Re-regulation, blame game
Biology	Amateur Investors ("national mania") Silent Leadership (Florida governor, JP Morgan)

Further, the development of financial products such as investment trusts to meet the desires of ordinary individuals to get involved in the market boomed: "During the first nine months of 1929, a new investment trust appeared for every working day and the industry issued over two and a half billion dollars worth of securities to the public."[32] These two elements—namely the broad involvement in the market and the tremendous boom in products designed to meet the needs of the previously uninvested—clearly tip the scales in favor of a very mature boom.

The epidemic lens also yields some insight into the aftermath of the Great Depression and subsequent speculative tendencies. The magnitude of the bust was such that a large percentage of the American population was negatively affected (some might say scarred) by the economic and financial implosion. Perhaps this "immunized" most citizens from the speculative fever that drives booms and busts? Might this be the reason that the United States did not have any major financial bubbles for decades after the Great Depression?

The logic of swarm leadership described in Chapter 5 is also helpful in understanding the 1920s and 1930s. For instance, the Florida land boom had lots of "informed" investors that drew the attention of the uninformed masses. John Martin, then governor of Florida, was quoted as having said "marvelous as is the wonder-story of Florida's recent achievements, these are but heralds of the dawn. . ." and S. Davies Warfield, president of the Seaboard Air Line Railway, supposedly talked of Miami's population exceeding 1 million within the next ten years.[33] Such informed members were able to lead the swarm of uniformed investors into the mid 1920s Florida land boom.

The list of similarly informed individuals that led the uninformed into the Great Crash is too long to mention, but the most famous quote is from Yale University professor Irving Fisher, who stated, "Stock prices have reached what looks like a permanently high plateau" just weeks before the stock market crash in 1929.

The Multilens Look

This discussion of the Great Depression was intended to demonstrate the power of a multidisciplinary framework through which to analyze financial extremes. A summary of the discussion is listed in Table 7.4. The next chapter will similarly illustrate the power of this five-lens framework during the Japanese boom and bust.

CHAPTER 8

The Japanese Boom and Bust

A CREDIT-FUELED BUBBLE ECONOMY

The militaristic hubris that took Japan blindly into the Second World War found its counterpart in the speculative hubris of the Bubble Economy. History was repeating itself, except this time a stock market farce replaced the tragedy of war.

—Edward Chancellor

During the 1980s, Japan experienced an extraordinary speculative boom that resulted in a bust that has plagued the island nation for the last 20 years. This chapter describes the events that transpired during the 1980s and some of the resulting extremes witnessed in the course of unbridled speculation. The impact of the bust, which continues as this book is being written, is briefly considered as well, and the boom and bust are then evaluated via the five lenses presented in Part I.

Japan(ese) as Different

Japanese society emphasizes harmony. The primary religions in Japan, Buddhism and Shintoism, are heavily oriented toward collectivism. The heavy influence of Confucian ideals also strengthens the primacy of group harmony over individual success. Further, the Japanese, not unlike many other homogenous groups, genuinely think of themselves as unique and different from other societies and cultures. The Japanese hold a deep belief that they are unlike other races, religions, or frankly, humans. This belief is not one restricted to behavior, for as noted in *Devil Take the Hindmost: A History of Financial Speculation*, it actually begins with a notion that Japanese physiology is unique:

> Japanese intestines were said to be different from those of Westerners and therefore unsuited to foreign beef and rice. It was even claimed that American skis were useless in Japan because the snow was different. At other times, pointing out such differences became a barely concealed expression of Japanese cultural nationalism and xenophobia: the Japanese brain was said to have a heightened sensitivity to the sounds of nature and a more intricate understanding of social relationships. The Japanese distrusted Western-style rationalism as being incompatible with the preservation of social harmony. . . . Japanese reason was described as "wet," like the cloying rice of the national diet (which formed the glue of the community), while Western reason was "dry" and individualistic. Even in the ethical sphere, the Japanese were said to be different. They did not feel guilt, only shame on public revelation of misdeeds. At the root of all these differences, both real and spurious, lay a profound distrust of individualism, which found its counterpart in a strong attachment to community and deference to authority.[1]

This deep cultural focus on community (relative to the Western focus on individuals) manifests itself throughout Japan's political-economic systems. Although the West has historically[2] focused on a limited role for government in business, markets, and industry, the Japanese believed in an active role for government in delivering administrative guidance to companies and industries. Likewise, although Westerners distrust monopolies, Japanese seek industrial champions. Finally, Western distinctions between business matters and individual relationships have no counterpart among the Japanese. In Japan, relationships and social harmony supersede virtually all else.

Many Japanese assert that their society is less selfish and more long-term-oriented than the West. Perhaps due to their feudal roots[3] and collectivist culture, hierarchy reigned supreme. Samurai values emphasized frugality, and savings rates were high. Administrative guidance helped channel these savings into the most appropriate investments. Market share was deemed a better objective than profits as it aligned the organization toward long-term success.

Given the limited individual role in virtually all matters economic, a long-term orientation, cultural values oriented around frugality and thrift, and a system designed around governmental guidance, Japan was a highly unlikely place for a speculative bubble to form. Yet a speculative bubble driven by individualistic short-term pursuit of profits is exactly what Japan experienced in the mid- to late 1980s. The collective shock to Japan of the bubble and its subsequent bursting was monumental and continues to be felt today.

An Overview of the Bubble Economy

Japan had been absolutely devastated by the Second World War. In the aftermath, during which the United States and other nations provided meaningful economic support, Japan implemented numerous policies to promote savings. These savings, it can be argued, ultimately enabled banks to feel more "flush" and therefore effectively encouraged the expansion of credit—credit that fueled much of Japan's economic growth after the war.

The massive economic transformation that transpired between 1953 and 1973 generated tremendous confidence in the country. According to Paul Krugman, "in the space of two decades a largely agricultural nation became the world's largest exporter of steels and automobiles, greater Tokyo became the world's largest and arguably most vibrant metropolitan area, and the standard of living made a quantum leap."[4] As a further illustration (albeit less direct) of the resignation that "Japan had won," Krugman went on to author *The Age of Diminished Expectations* in which he effectively stated the United States was potentially losing the economic race to government/private partnerships like Japan.

The Land Boom and Trophy Properties

During the 1980s, Japan's economy grew by leaps and bounds. The period was characterized by fast growth, low unemployment, and big profits. Although these conditions were highly supportive of rising asset prices, the property market raced ahead at unsustainable rates. The property bubble reached truly extraordinary heights, particularly when compared with America, and ultimately served as the foundation of the entire "Bubble Economy," as it has since been known. Consider the following facts, as summarized by journalist-turned-strategist Christopher Wood:[5]

> America is twenty-five times bigger than Japan in terms of its physical area. Yet Japan's property market at the end of 1989 was still reckoned by sober people in the government's Management and Coordination Agency to be worth over ¥2,000 trillion, or four times the estimated ¥500 trillion value of American property. This is truly history's greatest accumulation of wealth in one country. It creates ludicrous anomalies. In early 1990 Japan in theory was able to buy the whole of America by selling off metropolitan Tokyo, or all of Canada by hawking the grounds of the Imperial Palace.[6]

Crazy as the absolute land valuations might seem, the actively traded market that developed for golf course memberships is perhaps more noteworthy as another extreme of the land bubble. Wood's commentary captures the spirit of the times better than any other:

> Not surprisingly, given the national obsession with golf, this became a ludicrously overheated market in the late 1980s. An estimated 1.8 million people own golf club memberships in Japan; the prices of these memberships, which are traded like securities, range from a few million yen up to the ¥250 million range. At the peak, Japan's 1,700 golf courses were estimated to have a total membership market value of some $200 billion.[7]

There are three primary reasons that land values in Japan were so high: physical scarcity, feudal tradition, and government policies. The following discussion will examine these three causal factors of the property bubble in greater detail, but for now, it is important to note that they created a market that was not particularly liquid.

Very few transactions (compared to what one might expect from such a highly valued market) actually took place. Although this might mean such high property values were meaningless, the fact that they served as collateral for a significant portion of bank lending meant that prices, regardless of their true "accuracy," were very meaningful. In addition to supporting loans, much of the credit created through and supported by Japanese property price gains ultimately found its way into various assets and foreign property investments.

Trophy properties in the United States soon dominated the attention of the Japanese. New York's Rockefeller Center and the Exxon Building were two prized properties for which the Japanese paid handsomely. Japan's Mitsui Real Estate Company paid $625 million for the Exxon building on Sixth Avenue, well above Exxon's $310 million asking price, solely to be listed in the *Guinness Book of World Records*.[8] In 1990, a medium-sized Japanese company purchased America's most famous golf course, Pebble Beach, for $831 million. Hawaii also became a target for Japanese investor interest. Between 1985 and early 1991, Japanese investors purchased or financed the building of all but two of the main hotel resorts in Hawaii.[9] The Grand Hyatt Wailea Resort and Spa on Maui (which opened its doors in 1991) was built for a total cost of over $600 million, which equated to a per room investment of over $760,000. According to Anthony Downs, former chairman of the Real Estate Research Corporation and a current Senior Fellow at the Brookings Institution, the hotel needed to charge over $700 per room per night (in the 1990s) and maintain occupancy of at least 75 percent in order to just break even.

The Art Market Meets the Bubble Economy

As the Japanese infatuation with property was bubbling to ever-higher heights, their interest in art gained tremendous momentum. Edward Chancellor's description summarizes the phenomenon extraordinarily well: "In the 1980s, the combination of ambitious Western auctioneers, promoting art with every trick in the book, and Japanese speculators, their wallets swollen with bubble profits, created the most extravagant art market on record."[10] Peter Watson, in his book *From Manet to Manhattan: The Rise of the Modern Art Market*, described the 1988–1990 period, driven primarily by Japanese buyers, as "the most sensational that the art world has ever seen."

The *New York Times* reported on the results of a Christie's art auction that took place in late March 1987 in London.[11] In the highest price ever paid for a painting, van Gogh's *Still Life: Vase with Fifteen Sunflowers* had been sold to an unidentified foreign buyer for $39.9 million, well above the previous auction record for a painting of $10.4 million for Andrea Mantegna's *Adoration of the Magi.* The foreign buyer was later identified as Yasuo Goto of Yasuda Fire & Marine, a Japanese insurance company.

On November 30, 1989, Tomonori Tsurumaki, a Japanese real estate developer, won an auction for Picasso's *Pierrette's Wedding* (*Les*

Sotheby's Stock as a Bubble Indicator?

As one of the world's leading art auction houses, Sotheby's has been a beneficiary of booms in the art market. Might the stock serve as a useful indicator of bubble conditions? Take a look at the following chart, noting that it has experienced four peaks in an otherwise generally flat line. The first peak represents the Japanese bubble economy. The next peak occurred when Internet wealth exploded, and the 2007 boom was one in which hedge fund managers, Russian billionaires, and others participated. The current peak is one being dominated by Chinese art buyers. Is China in bubble terrain?

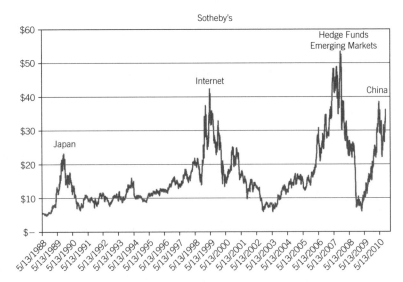

Sotheby's Stock Price as a Bubble Indicator

Source: Bloomberg Finance L.P.

Noces de Pierrette) that took place at the Paris auction house Drouot. Tsurumaki was bidding from the New Otani hotel in Tokyo while he was hosting a party launching his newest real estate development project—a $500 million auto racing resort to be called "Nippon Autopolis." After winning the Picasso, Tsurumaki noted that "One highlight of Autopolis will be a museum featuring works by such famous artists as Monet, Renoir, Chagall, and Magritte—and now, of course, this world famous Picasso."[12] The height of the Japanese art craze was reached when Ryoei Saito, chairman of Daishowa Paper Manufacturing, paid $82.5 million for van Gogh's *Portrait of Dr. Gachet* and over $78 million for Renoir's *Le Moulin de la Galette* in May 1990. He then proceeded to shock the art world by stating he would cremate the paintings along with his body upon his death.[13]

The Stock Market Goes Vertical

Not surprisingly, Japanese investors found a receptive and fertile opportunity to speculate in the stock market. In attempting to summarize the magnitude of the stock market bubble, Krugman noted that "at the beginning of 1990, the market capitalization of Japan— the total value of all the stocks of all the nation's companies—was larger than that of the United States, which had twice Japan's population and more than twice its gross domestic product."

Before describing the phenomenon in greater depth, a quick glance at Figure 8.1 demonstrates the tremendous boom the Japanese stock market experienced during the 1980s.

As is clear from the increasingly vertical move in share prices in the late 1980s in Japan, speculative juices were flowing rapidly. One stock that captures the spirit of the times perhaps better than any other is Nippon Telegraph and Telephone (NTT), the national telephone company. After being privatized in 1985 to encourage competition, NTT shares were floated to the public in several tranches. By November 1987, when the company did a further listing of shares valued at over $38 billion, the company had a total market valuation of approximately $300 billion. To provide some context for this figure, the *New York Times* suggested at the time that NTT was worth more than the stock markets of Switzerland and France *combined*.[14] Incidentally, Chancellor noted that NTT was worth more than the entire value of the West German and Hong

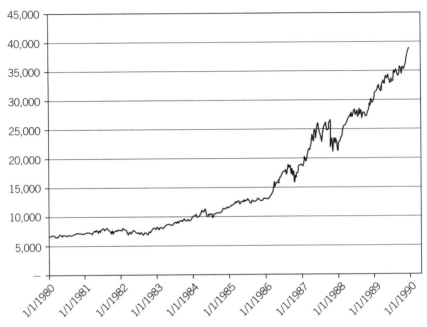

Figure 8.1   Japan's Nikkei 225 Index in the 1980s
Source: Bloomberg Finance L.P.

Kong stock markets, combined. Suffice it to say, NTT was a very highly valued company!

On top of this already ebullient market, the fact that most Japanese companies owned land provided justification for highly priced shares as professional and amateur analysts alike highlighted the "hidden" real estate values that were not fully reflected in official financial statements. Such land and property valuation was common-place. Chancellor notes "even NTT was valued primarily for its land assets rather than as a telecommunications company. Propelled by its extensive landholdings, the market value of Tokyo Electric Power increased by a greater value than that of all the stocks listed on the Hong Kong Stock Exchange."[15] Even airlines were considered land plays, with All Nippon Airways rising to 1,200 times earnings and Japan Airlines at 400 times (it was thought to have less land).

To eliminate the noise originating from individual extremes, let us take a look at some of the valuations placed by the market on various sectors. Table 8.1 highlights the heights to which several sectors rose.

Table 8.1   Selected Sector Valuations

Sector	Average P/E
Textiles	103×
Fishery & Forestry	319×
Services	112×
Marine Transportation	176×

Source: Robert Zielinski and Nigel Holloway, *Unequal Equities: Power and Risk in Japan's Stock Market* (New York, NY: McGraw Hill, 1992).

Bursting of the Bubble

In aggregate, the asset price boom that took place in Japan during the late 1980s was perhaps the world's most spectacular (and ephemeral) wealth creation event (up to that date).[16] As asset markets sprinted to unsustainable levels, Japanese authorities grew increasingly concerned and attempted to dampen speculative behavior. The Bank of Japan's incoming governor feared high housing prices might erode social harmony. (Separately, it is interesting to note that such social harmony was so highly valued by society that banks began designing products to allow such harmony to coexist with lofty valuations. One such product, according to Kindelberger and Aliber, was a hundred-year, three-generation mortgage!) In 1989, the Bank of Japan issued new regulations limiting the growth of real estate loans to the growth rate of total loans and began raising rates. The Bank of Japan raised the interest rate from 2.5 percent in May 1989 to 6.0 percent in August 1990 over the course of five incremental policy actions—undoing the reduction of interest rates from 5 percent in January 1986 to 2.5 percent by February 1987.[17]

Figure 8.2 below, taken from Richard Koo's *The Holy Grail of Macroeconomics: Lessons from Japan's Great Recession,* visually demonstrates the magnitude of the correction in the stock market, land market, and even the golf course market.

Given the magnitude of the wealth created and the unsustainable heights to which asset prices had risen, the bursting of the bubble economy was inevitably going to have a massive financial and economic impact on corporations, investors, consumers, and perhaps most importantly, the banks that had fueled the surge

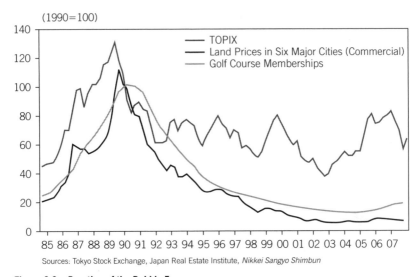

Sources: Tokyo Stock Exchange, Japan Real Estate Institute, *Nikkei Sangyo Shimbun*

Figure 8.2   Bursting of the Bubble Economy

Source: Richard Koo, *The Holy Grail of Macroeconomics* (Singapore: John Wiley & Sons, 2009). Reprinted with permission of John Wiley & Sons, Inc.

and accepted inflated assets as collateral. Kindelberger and Aliber eloquently summarize the bust:

> Once the rate of growth of bank loans slowed, some recent buyers of real estate developed a cash bind; their rental income was still smaller than the interest payments on their mortgages, but they could no longer obtain the cash needed . . . from new loans. Some of these investors then became distress sellers. The combination of the sharp reduction in the rate of growth of credit for real estate and these distress sales caused real estate prices to decline; the cliché that the price of land always rises was tested and found to be false.
>
> Stock prices and real estate prices began to decline at the beginning of 1990; stock prices declined by 30% in 1990 and an additional 30% in 1991. The stock price trend in Japan was downward . . . and at the beginning of 2003, stock prices in Japan were at the same level they had been 20 years earlier, even though the real economy was much larger. . .
>
> Now the perpetual motion machine began to work in reverse. Property sales led to declines in property prices. The decline in real estate prices and stock prices meant that bank

capital was declining; banks were now much more constrained in making loans. . . .

Bankruptcies increased, and the banks and other financial institutions incurred large loan losses. Those nonbank financial institutions that specialized in making real estate loans were in great distress.[18]

The Boombustology of the Japanese Boom and Bust

The Japanese boom and bust sequence exhibited many unique elements and took place in the most unlikely of locations—an administratively guided economy in which thrift and long-term thinking combined with market share prioritization over profits and the desire for social harmony at the expense of individual success. The application of the five lenses in this context will build the framework's relevance across the cultural spectrum and will help with the formulation of a generic framework through which to think about booms and busts.

The Reflexive Foundation of the Asset Boom: Land as Collateral

At the very root of the bubble economy was a tremendous boom and bust sequence in the property market. Land was, simply put, the foundation upon which the entire rickety system was built. By lowering rates to 2.5 percent in 1986, the Bank of Japan threw fuel on the already-burning speculative fire. Consider the reflexive dynamic eloquently described by Wood:

> This sparked a liquidity boom to beat all others. At its center lay the economy's main engine of credit creation, the banks. They were able to use a rising stock market to literally create bank capital and thus boost their lending. That extra credit was funneled back into two main markets (shares and property), boosting the value of banks' favored collateral (shares and property) against which to lend still more money.[19]

Further, the utter dominance of property as a source of collateral (some estimates indicate that real estate may have served as the backing for around 80 percent of all loans outstanding in Japan[20]) virtually assured that any dynamic that transpired (boom in the case of rising prices or bust in the case of falling prices) was surely going to tend *away* from any equilibrium condition that might theoretically exist.

Nevertheless, one might argue that the origin of the boom was a sound economic success story in which corporate Japan began growing profits as they took market share from global competitors. Over time, however, this initial fundamental development transformed into a reflexive, self-fulfilling and self-sustaining asset boom that ultimately exceeded its own capabilities and imploded upon itself.

The Effects of Macroeconomic Policy

Because of a savings-oriented culture and the Bank of Japan's decision to lower the official discount rate from 5 percent to 2.5 percent between January 1986 and February 1987, banks were flush with cash and money was close to free. As noted in the previous section, this reduction of rates ignited a liquidity boom that fed upon itself in an unrivaled manner.

Another factor that proved to be quite important was the deregulation and liberalization of the financial sector that enabled Japanese banks to increase the amount of loans guaranteed by property. Although this was initially a result of international lobbying to enable foreign banks to compete for Japanese business, the largest beneficiaries of the liberalization process were probably the Japanese banks.

A third factor was the Japanese yen. Because of external influences on the Japanese government to moderate the rate of Japanese currency appreciation, the Bank of Japan was active in the foreign exchange markets by constantly selling yen. Although the direct result of these efforts was a slower appreciation in the yen, the indirect result of it was a flooding of the system with yen. According to Kindelberger and Aliber:

> The result of extensive intervention was that money supply in Japan began to increase at an exceptional rate—that is, the monetary base was increasing. The increase in reserves of the Japanese banks meant that they were able to increase their loans at a rapid rate.[21]

Was the Japanese government's desire to control the currency the ultimate reason for many of these boom–bust oriented policies? Though it is not clear, it does seem stopping and/or slowing a rising yen, and the pressure that it puts on export industries in the country, was the target of policy efforts. Might the government have sought to induce speculation in a quest to get asset markets to support real economic activity?

The following quote, attributed to an unnamed executive at the Bank of Japan, suggests that asset price inflation may in fact have been the Bank of Japan's goal:

> We intended first to boost the stock and property markets. Supported by this safety net—rising markets—export-oriented industries were supposed to reshape themselves so they could adapt to a domestic-led economy. This step was then supposed to bring about an enormous growth of assets over every economic sector. This wealth effect would in turn touch off personal consumption and residential investment, followed by an increase of investment in plant and equipment. In the end, loosened monetary policy would boost real economic growth.[22]

The Psychology of Conformity

In discussing the observation made by Charles Mackay in *Extraordinary Popular Delusions and the Madness of Crowds* that "men think in herds, go mad in herds, but only recover their senses one by one,"[23] Wood notes that "as a group culture that discourages individualistic thinking, the Japanese are even more vulnerable than most to this decidedly human trait."[24] The cultural values that dominated pre-1980s Japan were uniquely communal in that social harmony was valued more highly than individual happiness. In a society focused on conformity and not being different, the mere introduction of the slightest differences can be quite destabilizing.

An analogy with preschool appears apt here. My daughter goes to a Montessori school in Boston. Virtually all the kids in her class (they're mostly 3-, 4-, and 5-year-olds) simply go with the flow. With the exception of the random tantrum that inevitably arises among children of this age, the group is quite harmonious. However, there are some key moments during the day when an individual opinion snowballs rapidly into group thinking. Arriving one afternoon shortly before snack time to pick up my daughter, I patiently (and covertly) observed the classroom dynamic. The teacher was about to put out some fruit and crackers when one young boy yelled, "I don't like crackers." In an almost comical sequence of events that left the teacher confused, probably frustrated, and definitely busy, all the other kids started agreeing. Nobody wanted crackers, despite the fact that I have seen virtually all of the kids voraciously eating crackers on other afternoons. It was as if a domino had fallen, knocking over all other opinions.

Not unlike this pre-primary classroom, Japan—a consensus-oriented, thrifty society focused on long-term economic development—found itself rapidly pursuing conspicuous consumption (in the form of art and trophy properties) and short-term individual gain despite harmful long-term implications.

Just as this harmonious society found itself drifting rapidly toward overconfidence and economic hubris during the boom phase of the cycle, so too did the bust phase of the cycle lead to a consensus of dejection, underconfidence, and utter despair. In referencing the dishonor that spread among Japan's financial services employees during the 1990s and onward, Wood notes that "this demoralization matters because it can become self-feeding. In a consensus society where there are few contrarians, yesterday's collective euphoria can too easily degenerate into tomorrow's collective panic."[25]

As this collectivist, consensus-oriented approach to life combined with the extraordinary confidence that emerged as a result of Japan's postwar economic success, textbook versions of cognitive biases soon emerged and were clearly recognizable. Might a society that had experienced great economic success (such success that books such as *Japan as Number One* were published) develop a collective sense of overconfidence? Would the availability bias lead to the extrapolation of most recent trends (land prices have been rising for a long time) into future projections (land prices will continue rising for a long time)? Might the public stories of grandiose global accomplishment such as the purchase of Rockefeller Center or prized Picasso paintings be seen as representative of Japanese society's new global economic status more than as examples of conspicuous consumption? In thinking about contractions, might anchoring and insufficient adjustment lead to the belief that a multiyear asset price deflation was particularly unlikely?

Political and Regulatory Conditions

Although the number of political and regulatory factors that influenced the boom and subsequent bust are too numerous to fully describe here, there are several policies that seem vital to under-standing the bubble economy. Given the root cause of the bubble economy was an unsustainable, credit-fueled rise in property prices, this section will focus on two main types of political and regulatory considerations that directly affected property prices: tax policies and financial de-regulation and credit controls.

In terms of tax policies, two taxes likely influenced the incen-tives to own property. The first tax, which might be deemed penal property taxation, was designed to discourage short-term trading of properties. The policy was straightforward, albeit very distortionary: "If land is sold within two years of its purchase, then 150 percent of the capital gain is added to the seller's annual income and taxed accordingly. If sold within five years, then 100 percent of the gain is added to income and taxed."[26] What effect might this have on purchasers who owned real estate that appreciated rapidly in the first five years of ownership? What might such taxes do to the trad-ing volume and liquidity of these assets? By distorting the supply of housing that was available for purchase each year, these policies cre-ated a false sense of scarcity, resulting rapidly rising prices. Further, this impact might also have created "house money" effects in which owners were not as disturbed or concerned about initial housing losses.

Another Japanese tax that seemed to affect real estate prices by artificially increasing the demand for property was the inherit-ance tax. The tax had a marginal rate structure in which mortgages were fully deductible from assessed property values, and property assessments (for tax purposes) were often well below market values (as is the case in much of America). Thus, it was possible to create negative asset value by purchasing a property with significant lev-erage. This negative value could offset other positive asset values and thereby reduce the tax burden. Citing this as a "well-known bequest strategy," Takatoshi Ito described the process as follows: "Those who were planning a bequest to their heirs were alarmed as their real estate values went up. In order to avoid high taxes, they purchased more real estate with high leverage, so that they could lessen the bequest tax burden. The higher prices generated more demand. . .[which may] have created an upward spiral in prices."[27]

Financial deregulation might also have contributed to the upward property price spiral, and its subsequent reversal. Initially due to pressure to open up the banking sector to foreign competition (the Americans wanted the ability to compete for business in Tokyo on comparable terms to the Japanese ability to compete for business in New York), Japanese financial deregulation was ultimately about decreasing administrative guidance.

As noted by Kindelberger and Aliber, "interest rate ceilings on deposits and loans were raised. Window guidance became much less extensive. The restrictions on the foreign investments of Japanese firms were relaxed."[28] The overarching philosophy is best summarized as follows: "Traditional banks were safe, but also very conservative; arguably, they failed to direct capital to its most productive uses. The cure, argued reformers, was both more freedom and more competition: let banks lend where they thought best, and allow more players to compete for public savings."[29] As a result of this deregulation wave, banks began increasing the amount of money they lent against property.

Eventually, the rapid rise in asset prices caught the attention of policy makers. In an effort to deflate the bubble, the government began reversing some of these pro-compeititon policies. Credit policies were reconsidered, with the idea that slowing access to property financing might defuse the rising inequality resulting from skyrocketing prices. The government implemented credit controls in April 1990 stipulating that any increase in bank lending for property must be smaller than the increase in a bank's overall loan book. Given the high percentage of lending that had been collateralized using property prior to this mandate, credit effectively stopped flowing toward property. Deregulation of the bond market also ensured that this mandate had teeth as corporate nonproperty borrowing (a very traditional role for Japanese banks) was slowly shifting away from banks to the bond market, a trend that accelerated concomitantly with financial deregulation.[30] The market rapidly swung from "an illiquid market where no one wants to sell (the traditional condition of this land-worshipping society) to an equally illiquid market where no one wants to buy."[31]

Housewives, Preschool, and Pollock

The two lenses of Chapter 5 are quite powerful in evaluating the Japanese bubble economy. The epidemic model provides a view of the bubble economy's maturity and the relative proximity of a bust. The *Far Eastern Economic Review* noted in 1988 that "stocks have become a national street-level preoccupation" and near the top of the best-seller list was a Japanese comic book about the economy and the stock market.[32] By the late 1980s, more than 22 million people were investing in the stock market, up from around 13–14 million in the mid 1980s. Nomura Securities, the largest of the domestic brokerage firms, had more than 5 million customers, mainly Japanese housewives, who regularly invested with Nomura salesmen. Speculation was encouraged, and through broker "guidance," more than a third of stocks held in private accounts were held in margin accounts.[33]

Given the high proportion of the infectable population that appeared infected, an imminent slowdown of infections seemed likely. In fact, the rapid acceleration in the number of brokerage accounts opened by individual investors was a spectacular early warning indicator of the beginning of the end of the bubble economy.

Any consensus-oriented collection of individuals is highly prone—like the bees in a swarm—to the silent leadership of a seemingly informed individual. Consider the earlier preschool example, in which the establishment of the "we don't like crackers" conclusion in the classroom is not dissimilar to the movement of ants described in Chapter 5. The investment climate in Japan through the middle of the 1980s was a stable equilibrium with everyone "tied," in an opinion sense, to everyone else. Social harmony, conformity, and consensus ruled the day. For whatever reason, once the balance tipped[34] toward the pursuit of immediate individual gain, the whole swarm of formerly long-term-oriented social beings became speculators. The cohesive power of communal thinking that had stabilized Japanese society for so long was now creating a speculative frenzy. The result was a spectacular manifestation of herd behavior in speculation, despite the view that gambling was a Chinese vice from which the Japanese were immune:

> The Japanese were particularly susceptible to the lure of the stock market. . .[because] they have a tendency to exhibit herd-like behavior when pursuing a certain activity, whether at work or play. This was said to stem from the communal demands of rice farming, which had fostered a national *shudankizoku ishiki* (group consciousness). During the war, Japan was portrayed in government propaganda as "one hundred million hearts

Table 8.2   The Five-Lens Approach to the Japanese Boom and Bust

Lens	Notes
Microeconomics	Reflexive credit/collateral dynamic Higher prices induced buyers Lower prices induced sellers
Macroeconomics	Inappropriately cheap money Financial innovation (100 year mortgages)
Psychology	New era thinking (economic power) Conformity-driven social harmony Conspicuous consumption (trophy art) Economic overconfidence
Politics	Supply/demand distortions (penal property taxation) De-regulation of the banking industry Credit regulations that distorted incentives
Biology	Amateur investors (housewives) Silent Leadership (communal philosophies) Popular Media (*Japan as Number One*)

beating as one." After the October crash, the president of a securities house boasted that Japan had survived the period of volatility because it was "a consensus society—a nation that likes to move in one direction."[35]

Being a consensus society is definitely a two-edged sword, for if consensus were organized around a stable equilibrium, all would be well. However, if the accepted perspective was one of disequilibrium, short-termism, or speculative behavior, then instability would dominate and the former stability would evaporate.

The Multilens Look

As the discussion above has demonstrated, the five lenses presented in Part I were able to shed light on the bubble economy of Japan in the late 1980s and the subsequent bust during the 1990s in a manner not possible with the use of only one lens. Table 8.2 summarizes the five lens approach to thinking about the "Bubble Economy." The next chapter utilizes the fives lenses to evaluate the Asian financial crisis that emerged in the mid 1990s and the contagion effects it had on the rest of the world.

CHAPTER

9

The Asian Financial Crisis

THE MIRAGE OF A MIRACLE

*The great Asian slump is one for the record books. Never in the
course of economic events—not even in the early years of the
Depression—has so large a part of the world economy experienced so
devastating a fall from grace.*

—Paul Krugman

In many ways the seeds of economic success in Asia were sown in
the early aftermath of World War II. In an effort to rebuild societies and generate long-term economic growth, many Asian countries adopted export-oriented development policies designed to
utilize their abundant (and therefore cheap) labor to meet global
demands. Combined with increased opportunities for trade, the
economic strategies caught a massive tailwind in the early 1990s
and asset markets took notice, rising to lofty heights. The resulting bubble eventually collapsed in 1997 and 1998, with the ripple
effects being felt around the world.

Boom Times in East Asia

The early to mid-1990s were a spectacular time for many East Asian
economies (Japan, as we have just learned, was an exception).

A 1993 book titled the *East Asian Miracle: Economic Growth and Public Policy*, began with this summary:

> East Asia has a record of high and sustained economic growth. From 1965 to 1990 the twenty-three economies of East Asia grew faster than all other regions of the world. Most of this achievement is attributable to seemingly miraculous growth in just eight economies: Japan; the "four Tigers"—Hong Kong, the Republic of Korea, Singapore, and Taiwan, China; and the three newly industrializing economies of Southeast Asia—Indonesia, Malaysia, and Thailand.[1]

Against this backdrop of economic performance, it is not surprising that booms might develop across the region's asset markets. According to Robert Barbara, "the booms were initially sensible, reflecting sound investment opportunities. The dynamics were straightforward. The collapse of the former Soviet Union and China's newfound willingness to interact with capitalist nations supercharged trade and capital flows between the developed world and emerging Asian economies."[2]

Rapid growth was taking place throughout the entire region, albeit with slightly nuanced and different driving factors in each country. South Korea, which had been devastated by the war, embarked on a remarkable period of economic growth that utilized high savings rates, cheap labor, an inexpensive currency, and strong industrial policy to produce products needed by global consumers and corporations. Singapore, which was literally a swamp in the 1950s, embarked on a strategy to become a corruption free, rule-of-law oriented outpost in a land of crony capitalists and in so doing, elevated itself to first-world status. Deng Xiaoping's rise to power in China resulted in an economic revival that opened the country up to international trade and global investment, as well as an economic reform agenda more typically found in capitalist nations. For many years following this policy shift, China grew its GDP in excess of 10 percent per year. Hong Kong transformed into a regional, if not global, financial center. Manufacturing activity surged in Thailand, Indonesia, and Malaysia as globalization took hold, trade barriers were lowered, and protectionism retreated.

Many stock markets in the region rose at rapid rates. In 1993, for instance, many East Asian countries saw their stock markets double in value, with growth continuing into 1994. Figure 9.1

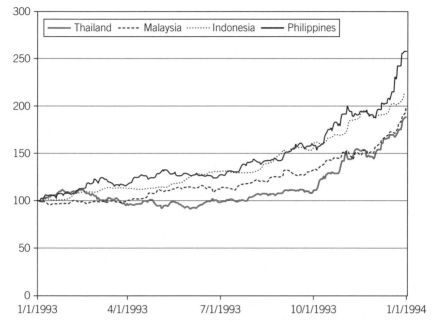

Figure 9.1   The Performance of Selected Asian Stock Markets in 1993
Source: Bloomberg Finance L.P.

graphs the performance of the Philippine, Thai, Malaysian, and Indonesian markets in 1993. Real estate prices rose throughout the region as the optimistic outlook combined with inexpensive capital to create significant demand. In sum, Asian economies and asset markets boomed.

In essence, what occurred was simple: Abundant capital combined with cheap labor to produce competitive economies. The developed world (or more precisely, the rich world) got excited about these prospects and began pouring money (primarily dollars) into the East Asian markets. As a result, many Asian currencies appreciated quite rapidly and banks and local corporations borrowed significant sums of U.S. dollars (i.e., not local currency). Kindelberger and Aliber note the importance of the interconnections that began to form between East Asian countries and the developed world:

> China, Thailand, and the other East Asian countries were on the receiving end of outsourcing by American, Japanese, and European firms that wanted cheaper sources of supply for established domestic markets. Rapid economic growth was

both the result and cause of the inflow of foreign capital, especially from Japan. Japanese investment initially took the form of construction of manufacturing plants to take advantage of lower labor costs . . . from there a large part of the production would be exported, some to the United States, some to Japan, and some to third countries. . . . The buzzword was export-led growth, which was almost always based on a low value for the countries' currency in the foreign exchange market.[3]

The system fed upon itself, and soon Americans were outsourcing jobs to Korea, and in turn the Koreas were outsourcing jobs to China and Indonesia, where labor was even cheaper. In many ways, the whole chain was based on two primary enabling factors in the production country: inexpensive labor, and cheap currencies. As part of this "game," countries sought to constantly keep their currencies undervalued. In fact, on January 1, 1994, the Chinese government effectively devalued their currency relative to the U.S. dollar by ~50 percent. Might this action have provided a tremendous boost to Chinese exporters (at the expense of other Southeast Asian exporters)? In fact, it's possible that the 1994 Chinese devaluation may have in fact been one of the primary catalysts for the Asian financial crisis.

"Ground zero" in this Asian export-oriented game was Thailand. It typified everything about the boom and also served as the catalyst for the regional bust. Let us now turn to Thailand to understand what occurred within it and how it illustrates the boom dynamics of the region.

Thailand Catches the Flu

On the surface, it seems odd that a country like Thailand could be responsible for a global economic meltdown that resulted in debt defaults in Russia, the collapse of perhaps the world's largest hedge fund, and economic and currency contractions to rival the largest in history. In *The Return of Depression Economics*, Paul Krugman explains:

The world economy is almost inconceivably huge, and in the commercial scheme of things, Thailand is pretty marginal. Despite rapid growth in the 1980s and 1990s, it is still a poor country; all those people have a combined purchasing power no greater than that of the population of Massachusetts. One might have thought that Thai economic affairs, unlike those of an economic behemoth like Japan, were of interest only to the Thais, their immediate neighbors, and those businesses with a direct financial stake in the country. But the 1997 devaluation of Thailand's currency, the baht, triggered a financial avalanche that buried much of Asia.[4]

It was the devaluation of the Thai baht that eventually snowballed into a global mess, but before the bust, there had been a great boom. From 1985 to 1996, Prime Minister Prem Tinsulanonda enacted policies that opened the doors of the economy to the outside world. During this time, Thailand was one of the world's fastest growing economies and averaged annual GDP growth of 9.4 percent. Cheap labor, fiscal conservatism, and natural resources formed a powerful cocktail that modernized the formerly agricultural-dominated economy into a manufacturing-led, export-oriented powerhouse.

Foreign capital came to Thailand in droves in the early 1990s, and with its arrival, the country's financial self-sufficiency began to rapidly erode. Although it had basically self-funded its growth from domestic savings through the early 1990s[5], Thailand grew increasingly dependent on foreign capital, most of which was being lent in U.S. dollars.[6]

Several factors contributed to the rapid inflow of capital into Thailand during the early to mid-1990s, including several external factors. To begin, the resolution of the Latin American debt crises and the fall of the Soviet Union made investing in riskier places in the world more fashionable. Second, the sharp drop of interest rates in the developed world drove investors on a global search for better yields. Third, development agencies like the International Monetary Fund and the World Bank began rapidly increasing their funding into emerging Asian countries like Thailand. And finally, there was the rapid growth of emerging markets funds (due in no small part to the name change—see "Third World Becomes Emerging Markets") that began allocating capital in a diversified manner to developing countries like Thailand, Malaysia, Indonesia, and the like.

As foreign inflows began coming into Thailand in greater and greater volumes, the stock market rose simultaneously. Might

"Third World" Becomes "Emerging Markets"

We often hear of countries such as China and Brazil referred to as emerging markets. This was not always the case. In perhaps one of the greatest marketing coups of all time, former investment banker Antoine van Agtmael managed to rename the less developed countries of the world the "emerging" markets. He did so after struggling to raise a diversified fund to invest in what were then known as third world countries. Van Agtmael recounts the experience he had after a prospective client (Francis Finlay of JP Morgan) said to him, "This is a very interesting idea . . . but you will never sell it using the name 'Third World Equity Fund'!"

> I immediately knew he had a point. We had the goods. We had the data. We had the countries. We had the companies. What we did not have, however, was an elevator pitch that liberated these developing economies from the stigma of being labeled as "Third World" basket cases, an image rife with negative associations of flimsy polyester, cheap toys, rampant corruption, Soviet style tractors, and flooded rice paddies. Over the weekend, I disappeared into one of the mental isolation spells that my wife and children so heartily dislike, but which I often find oddly productive. Racking my brain, I at last came up with a term that sounded more positive and invigorating: Emerging Markets. "Third World" suggested stagnation. "Emerging Markets" suggested progress, uplift, and dynamism.

Van Agtmael went on to found a firm (Emerging Markets Management) focused exclusively on investing in emerging markets and he continues to run the firm today.

Source: Antoine van Agtmael, *The Emerging Markets Century: How a New Breed of World-Class Companies Is Overtaking the World* (New York, NY: The Free Press, 2007).

this have been a sign that capital was being recycled into speculative investing in shares? Krugman describes the phenomenon as follows:

> As more and more loans poured in from abroad, then, the result was a massive expansion of credit, which fueled a wave of new investment. Some of this took the form of actual construction, mainly office and apartment buildings, but there was a lot of pure speculation too, mainly in real estate, but also in stocks.[7]

As the credit-fueled boom continued, non-bank finance companies sprung up everywhere. These institutions were usually controlled by a relative of a government official and were believed to have implicit government guarantees—enabling them to raise money at advantageous rates from respected banks and foreign lenders. These finance companies could then re-lend the capital to riskier projects or speculative ventures at higher rates to capture the spread. The implication of these relationships is that the government would backstop any losses, but that gains would accrue only to the finance company. Such "crony capitalism," as this system was later named, was widespread in Asia. Some have argued that this crony capitalism was in fact a very rational way of doing business as it enabled transactions in the absence of strong contract law.[8]

In the winter of 1996, against this backdrop of inefficient capital allocation via relationship lending practices, a dramatic concern emerged that began to spook foreign investors. Consumer finance companies began reporting large losses. Might this have been a manifestation of the 1994 Chinese devaluation that decreased the competitiveness of Thai exports (relative to Chinese exports)? Many of these companies had been set up by large domestic banks to circumvent regulations that prevented them from growing their consumer lending practices as rapidly as they would like. Foreign inflows began to slow, and eventually reversed.[9] Although capital inflows into the emerging Asian countries had been approximately $93 billion in 1996, by 1997 that number had turned into an outflow of approximately $12 billion.[10]

Eventually, the outflow of currency created downward pressure on the currency, something the government sought to prevent. On July 2, 1997, after expending significant reserves in an attempt to defend the currency, the Thai baht was allowed to depreciate and moved from a price of 25 baht per U.S. dollar to more than 55 baht per dollar in early 1998. Such a currency move could have a devastating effect on those with misalignment between their earning currency and their borrowing currency; to illustrate the point, consider the following hypothetical example.

Mr. T is a Thai businessman who decides to borrow $10,000,000 to expand his business. He doesn't need dollars, but because the rate to borrow them is cheaper and the bank is willing to lend to him at a good rate, he takes the $10 million loan and converts it to Thai baht. At the time, 25 baht = 1 US$, so he gets 250 million baht for his loan. He is not concerned about the loan because his business is healthy (but his earnings are all in baht). His business continues to grow, and Mr. T uses the cash flow to reinvest in the business rather than to repay the loan. Then disaster strikes. For simplicity of math, let's say that the baht is now worth 50 baht = 1 US$. Now, in order to repay the $10 million loan, Mr. T must come up with 500 million baht. The loan value doubled in local currency terms, effectively bankrupting Mr. T.

This is exactly what happened to thousands of individual entrepreneurs, banks, and big businesses in Thailand during the Asian financial crisis. Because foreign capital sources feared that they might not get paid back, they all retrenched and began recalling capital whenever possible, thereby creating an effective bank run on Thailand. Everyone wanted their money back at the same time, creating a self-fulfilling vicious cycle of selling assets at depressed values to repay loans, but also further depressing values in the process. The largest Thai finance company, Finance One, which was worth over $5.5 billion at one point, collapsed completely.[11]

To complicate the situation, in order to prevent the currency from continuing to fall, Thai authorities began to sharply raise interest rates to attract capital. Although the strategy worked to stabilize the currency (the baht was trading at ~36 baht = 1 U.S. dollar by the end of 1998), it increased the cost of doing business and slowed the economy so dramatically it entered a recession, with GDP shrinking by approximately 2.2 percent in 1998. Needless to say, confidence in the Thai economy was shattered. This loss of confidence led to less economic activity, which fulfilled fears of a slowing economy, which hurt companies, banks, and consumers, which led to lower confidence. The feedback loop was nasty.

But the question remains: How and why did the problems in Thailand create a financial tsunami that engulfed so many other, seemingly unrelated countries and organizations? Although Thailand's trading partners would be hurt because of the economic slowdown in Thailand, an important new mechanism through which Thailand's contagious disease spread were the same emerging markets funds that had enabled its boom. When bad news and financial losses came in from Thailand, fund managers needed to reduce holdings throughout the region to meet redemption requests from investors. Regardless of how countries may have differed, they were linked in the portfolios of these fund managers and hence were all vulnerable to self-validating panics.

To illustrate this concept in action, consider the following simplified scenario. A fund manager has chosen to invest in five countries and has spread his money equally between them (20 percent of the portfolio to each). Now, because of economic hardships in Country A, the stock market of Country A has fallen 50 percent. Now, instead of having 20 percent in each of five countries, our fund manager has 11.1 percent in Country A and 22.2 percent of his portfolio in each of the other countries. Assuming he wants to return to his prior country weightings, he must now sell shares of companies in Country B, Country C, Country D, and Country E—despite the fact that these countries have not had the same economic difficulties as Country A. This contagion effect is further complicated by the risk that our fund manager faces investor redemptions, in which case he might indiscriminately be selling all countries. Thus, even though the spark started in Country A, the flames might eventually engulf all five countries.

Through such capital market linkages, the panic spread from Thailand and eventually engulfed most of Asia, Russia, most other emerging markets, and the famed U.S. hedge fund Long-Term Capital Management. To appreciate the magnitude of the capital markets impact, particularly when combined with currency impacts, consider Figure 9.2, which illustrates the performance of the Jakarta Stock Exchange Composite Index from January 1, 1995 through December 31, 1999 in U.S. dollar and Indonesian rupiah terms. Note that the U.S. dollar–denominated chart reflects what most emerging markets managers experienced. Peak to trough declines during this period were 65 percent in local currency terms and 93 percent in U.S. dollar terms. Over the 5-year period displayed in the chart, the index actually rose 44 percent in Indonesian rupiah terms (granted, the currency fell a great deal) but fell more than 55 percent in U.S. dollar terms.

The Boombustology of the Asian Financial Crisis

Given the complexity of the East Asian financial crisis in terms of number of countries, governments, nongovernmental organizations, and currencies involved, it is impossible in several pages to

Figure 9.2   Indonesian Stock Market, 1995–1999
Source: Bloomberg Finance L.P.

utilize the five lenses of Part I in a comprehensive manner. Instead, this section will highlight a handful of illustrative issues.

The Reflexivity of Confidence

As the rapid transmission of bank losses into a reversal of foreign fund flows and a self-validating panic demonstrated, the events in Asia during 1997 and 1998 were highly reflexive. They were not self-correcting in the traditional sense of efficiency. The primary cause of this reflexivity was the use of borrowed money that was collateralized by assets—assets which had their values inflated by the excess purchasing power generated through borrowed money. Because these are not self-correcting dynamics, they become quite disruptive and tend toward disequilibria.

The dynamics leading to disequilibrium can be summarized as a self-reinforcing, self-validating reflexive feedback loop that connects what I label the five Cs—confidence, collateral, credit, conditions, and capital, as shown in Figure 9.3. During the boom phase of the cycle, confidence inspires credit, credit improves collateral values, which generates confidence and better economic conditions via increased activity. The improved conditions drive more confidence

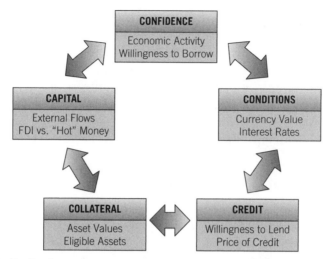

Figure 9.3   The Five Cs

and attract capital, which results in greater availability of credit. The greater availability of credit broadens the universe of acceptable collateral, which generates better conditions, and on it goes.

Unfortunately, the world discovered that these highly interconnected and reinforcing five Cs can also work in reverse. So, during the bust phase of the cycle, reduced confidence led to less credit, credit contraction hurt collateral values, which hurt confidence and conditions. Deteriorating conditions further hurt confidence, which caused capital to flee, while further reducing access to credit. The contraction in credit tightens collateral standards, which further hurts conditions, and so on.

A classic example of a positive feedback loop and the role of signal strength can be found with a microphone in an auditorium. If the signal is too strong, then the speakers will generate noise sufficiently loud enough that the microphone will pick it up, with the speakers amplifying that feedback even more, generating even greater feedback, and so on. If the signal is dampened by other noises or interference of any sort, then the signal strength does not multiply. If, however, the feedback loop combines with a strong signal, the result is that utterly offensive nails-on-a-chalkboard, toe-curling screeching noise.

If confidence is the root of our signal, then the shock to one's confidence is what tips the balance and turns our virtuous cycle into a vicious one. How intensely might Mr. T's confidence have been shaken when he woke up one day and found he was effectively bankrupt? Quite seriously, I assume. How intensely might the foreign bank's confidence have been shaken when it learns that it lent money out to borrowers that suddenly appear highly unlikely to repay, even though last month those very same loans appeared quite safe? Again, one can only assume quite severely. Thus, the highly iterative and self-reinforcing loop is very reflexive and can lead the system to extremes of instability, rather than any resemblance of a calm equilibrium.

Miracle or Myth?

In an aptly timed essay published in *Foreign Affairs* at the end of 1994, Paul Krugman warned that Asia's economic success was more likely to be a mirage than a miracle. His essay, "The Myth of Asia's Miracle," began by describing the supposed economic success story of the Soviet Union. He describes how the idea of central planning and the prioritization of collective objectives over individual pursuits was considered by some as a better alternative to Western market-dominated individualism. Of course, his writing of such thoughts in 1994 after the Soviet Union had imploded upon itself was intentional.

His example provided a powerful reminder that growth by itself is meaningless, but rather, one needs to consider the sources of economic growth and their sustainability. The Soviet Union, claimed Krugman, was able to outgrow the United States in the 1950s and 1960s not because it had a more sustainable system, but rather because it had been very efficient at mobilizing inputs. Productivity, he noted, holds the key to long-term sustainable growth.

In order to fully appreciate Krugman's argument and its applicability to the East Asian story, we need to understand the basics of growth accounting. The term was first introduced by MIT professor Robert Solow in a 1957 paper published in the *Review of Economics and Statistics*. The basic framework suggested that there are two primary sources of growth: a change in inputs and a change in the productivity of those inputs. Inputs can further be broken down into capital and labor. Isolating each of these three variables (capital, labor, and total productivity) helps to understand how each affects economic growth.

Suppose for a moment that a country has 100 people and only one revenue-generating activity—picking apples. Fifteen of the people are too old to work, and fifteen are too young, so the working population is 70 people. Suppose on any given day, only 30 of those 70 are actually working. One very obvious way to grow the output of the economy is to have some of the 40 idle workers begin working. If the average worker can pick 1,200 apples a year, then our initial output was 36,000 apples. Now after adding additional workers (suppose another three workers join the effort), our production will grow to 39,600 apples, representing 10 percent growth. In this case, because the input of labor grew by 10 percent and output grew by 10 percent, we can say 100 percent of our growth is accounted for by labor inputs.

Now suppose we are able instead to purchase some machines (cost = 1,200 apples per machine, paid for 100 percent from savings) that help us gather more apples per worker. The machine (a handheld apple-picking arm extender that eliminates the need for climbing trees) is able to help each worker pick 1,320 apples per year. Assuming that we have added no new workers, but that each worker now has the machine, annual production will rise to 39,600 apples—exactly 10 percent higher than previously. But how can we account for this new growth, since it comes at a cost of the machines? One method is to weight the cost of the machine by the return it generates and consider that our capital investment. In our case, the machine costs 1,200 apples and generates 120 apples per year of additional production. Capital thus produced a 10 percent return. In this example, because capital grew by 10 percent and output grew by 10 percent, we can say that 100 percent of our growth is accounted for by capital inputs.

Finally, let us consider a third scenario in which our 30 workers neither get additional colleagues in the fields or new equipment to help them. Instead, they are able to grow output by simply increasing their productivity. In this case, 100 percent of the growth in output can be accounted for by efficiency gains.

Because neither capital nor labor inputs can be grown indefinitely, growth from inputs is ultimately unsustainable. Krugman argued in 1994 that the supposedly miraculous growth rates of Asia were destined to fall. They were unsustainable because they were based on growth of inputs. He highlights the case of Singapore:

> Between 1966 and 1990, the Singaporean economy grew at a remarkable 8.5% per annum, three times as fast as the United States; per capita income grew at 6.6%, roughly doubling every

decade. This achievement appears to be some kind of economic miracle. But the miracle turns out to have been based on perspiration rather than inspiration: Singapore grew through a mobilization of resources that would have done Stalin proud. The employed share of the population surged from 27 to 51 percent. The educational standards of that work force were dramatically upgraded: while in 1966 more than half the workers had no formal education at all, by 1990 two-thirds had completed secondary education. Above all, the country had made an awesome investment in physical capital: investment as a share of output rose from 11% to more than 40%...

Singapore's growth has been based largely on one-time changes in behavior that cannot be repeated. Over the past generation the percentage of people employed has almost doubled; it cannot double again. A half-educated work force has been replaced by one in which the bulk of workers has high school diplomas; it is unlikely that a generation from now most Singaporeans will have PhDs. And an investment share of 40% is amazingly high by any standard; a share of 70% would be ridiculous. So one can immediately conclude that Singapore is unlikely to achieve future growth rates comparable to those of the past.[12]

Similar stories, albeit less extreme, can be found across Asia. Because money was being thrown at countries like Thailand by external investors and the five Cs were in a virtuous phase, capital was easy to come by. Combined with the overconfidence developed through the prior years of spectacular economic performance, it is conceivable that money was allocated to projects with unrealistic return expectations. In an outcome that would not have shocked Austrian economists, malinvestment seemed not only likely, but inevitable.

"Hasn't Happened" Is Not "Can't Happen"

One of the great financial industry disclaimers is that "past performance is no guarantee of future results." I've always found this statement a bit odd, even misleading. Perhaps it should be modified to "past performance is not related to future performance" or "insofar as past performance indicates a replicable skill and the future looks like the past, then we might think it possible that future results might or might not resemble past results," or something like that. In any case, just because something has happened, doesn't mean it will continue to happen. Likewise, just because something has not happened, does not mean it cannot or will not happen. In fact, underestimation of the probability of events that have not happened is a common cognitive bias. It is the natural result of employing an availability heuristic. Obviously, images and stories of an event that has not happened are less available.

Many Thai individuals, companies, banks, and government officials did not spend much time thinking about the currency mismatches that plagued their financial structures. Given the role that such mismatches played in the rapid unraveling of the economy, let us consider how the decision-making biases discussed in Chapter 3 might have affected Thai thinking.

From a psychological perspective, why were major movements in the currency not seen as possible by lenders or borrowers? Perhaps it was because the Thai currency had been very stable prior to the crisis. Perhaps it was because there was not any available data on Thai currency volatility. (Surely, however, foreign lenders would have been aware of the recent Mexican depreciation.) Perhaps they were anchored on the current ratio of ~25 baht per dollar and made insufficient adjustments for the range of likely outcomes. Might lenders and borrowers alike have thought the baht might move by ~10 percent?

There are clearly dozens upon dozens of questions that one can ask about the decision-making processes that led to the currency mismatch, but one thing remains certain—the decision to borrow in dollars while earning in baht created vulnerabilities, risks that were inappropriately considered (likely for one of the many psychological reasons discussed in Chapter 3) in the course of making that decision.

Another indicator of overconfidence (as well as excess liquidity and loose monetary conditions driven by foreign inflows) was the construction of Malaysia's Petronas Towers. The twin skyscrapers, which were completed in 1997 and almost perfectly marked the top of Asian financial markets prior to the Asian financial crisis, were the tallest buildings in the world. Chapter 11 will discuss the skyscraper indicator in greater detail.

Crony Capitalism as Cultural Coping

Although there are hosts of political issues and policies that one can consider through a political lens, this section will focus on the idea of rights and prices (the two primary elements presented in Chapter 4). Let us begin with property rights, which are, across most emerging markets, less well developed than those in the United States or the "first" world. Nevertheless, property rights did exist in many emerging Asian countries, but were significantly less well protected and infringements on them less well enforced. How might individuals and companies attempt to cope with such an environment?

One way to gain greater comfort in your claim for certain property is to have strong relationships (even blood-based relationships, i.e., family) with those with whom you might end up having a dispute. Harvard University Professor Dwight Perkins summarizes the issue at hand:

> Societies made up of self-contained villages or autonomous feudal estates do not have to worry much about the security of economic transactions. The village elders or the feudal lord can enforce whatever rules they choose. However, when trade takes place over long distances, local authority can no longer guarantee that a transaction will be carried out in accordance with a given set of rules. . . . A general authority must provide security along the road or river; each individual trader should not have to provide it on his own . . .
>
> In Europe and North America, the required security was supplied by laws backed up by a judiciary that over time became increasingly independent of the other functions of government. This development of the rule of law backed up by an independent judiciary took place over centuries, and the process was well along by the eighteenth century. . . . There was no comparable development of this kind of legal system in East and Southeast Asia. There was, however, the development of long-distance commerce both within and between economies in Asia, and that commerce had to have something that substituted for the rule of law. That substitute drew on one of the strengths of East Asian culture: close personal relationships based on family ties, as well as ties that extended beyond the family.[13]

Thus, it seems at least reasonably likely that the lack of strong institutional structures to enforce property rights led to the mass adoption of lending based on noneconomic considerations. Perhaps the simple lack of well-defined property rights should have been an alarm bell for foreign lenders.

In terms of price considerations, perhaps the greatest government-inspired distortions took place in the currency markets. Given the export-oriented nature of most of the region's economies, most governments worked to keep their currencies cheap relative to their trading partners. The result of these efforts was an increase in the country's relative dependence on exports as cheap currencies supported exporter profits. Likewise, it hurt importers and therefore discouraged the generation of domestically oriented industries. The managed foreign exchange rates also drove, as discussed previously in the example involving Mr. T, significant currency mismatches in the financial structures of domestic companies. Thus, by interfering with the price mechanism's efforts to determine the price of a currency, many Southeast Asian governments magnified their vulnerability to currency volatility.

Asian Harmony vs. Western Individualism

Our epidemic lens provides little value here. As is evident by the now common reference to the East Asian financial crisis (not boom or bubble), the story here is really one of a bust. Sure, stories exist of property prices and stock prices going through the roof, but there are few stories of taxi-drivers, housewives, and gardeners investing in the market. Rather, it was a story of global capital flows (some might argue "hot money") that filled the void and provided the fuel for the boom to take place.

The emergence lens, however, does provide insight. As we found in our study of the Japanese boom and subsequent bust, Asian philosophies tend to be less individualistic and more communal. They emphasize social harmony and group cohesion over individual pursuits. The impact of this pack mentality is that markets become highly tippable in one direction or another. Just as was discussed in the previous chapter about Japan, so too is the swarm/herd framework applicable with respect to Asia. We won't recount the same logic here, but it might make sense to review Chapter 8 in light of the East Asian scenario. It will seem eerily pertinent.

Another "herd" that emerged during the early 1990s was the group of fund managers focused on emerging markets. Inherent

Table 9.1   The Five-Lens Approach to the Asian Financial Crisis

Lens	Notes
Microeconomic	Pro-cyclical capital flows Reflexivity of confidence
Macroeconomic	Hot money inflows providing cheap capital Financial innovation (finance companies to hide leverage) Moral hazard motivated lending
Psychology	Anchoring on currency values, insufficient adjustment World's tallest skyscraper (Petronas Towers) New era thinking ("miracles" and "tigers")
Politics	Crony capitalism inspired moral hazard Political focus on undervalued currencies
Biology	Silent Leadership (communal philosophies) Herd of emerging markets funds

in their design as diversified managers was a linkage and coupling of very different economies into one bucket. Further, given they merely allocate other people's money, these fund managers became herdlike in their behavior because of client flows. Thus, in good times (think early 1990s), flows into their funds would likely be positive and the herd would stampede in—bringing capital along. However, if the herd changed direction, the stampede would occur in the opposite direction, with capital flight from the country.

In discussing the Asian crisis, Michael Lewis described this phenomenon bluntly: "The collapse of the Thai baht in July 1997 caused the people who had invested in places that reminded them a bit of Thailand (South Korea, the Philippines, Indonesia, Malaysia) to take their money and go home."

The Multilens Look

Given the East Asian financial crisis was really a set of many different crises that fell like dominoes, this chapter attempted to focus on the case of Thailand as representative of the situation. The five-lens approach to thinking about the events that unfolded yields some striking similarities to other booms and busts. Table 9.1 provides a quick summary of the chapter via the lenses discussed.

10

The U.S. Housing Boom and Bust

THE HOMEOWNER'S SOCIETY CREATES
THE PEOPLE'S PANIC

*It's the English speaking world's favorite economic game: property.
No other facet of financial life has such a hold on the popular
imagination. No other asset-allocation decision has inspired so
many dinner-party conversations. The real estate market is unique.
Every adult, no matter how economically illiterate, has a view on its
future prospects.*

—Niall Fergusson

The global credit crunch that began with a hiccup in the U.S.
subprime markets in February 2007 and snowballed into greatest economic contraction since the Great Depression is still under
way as this book is being written. Although it is often risky to write
about events as they unfold, I have nevertheless chosen to do
so—recognizing that the chapter will necessarily focus upon a discussion of the boom with a cursory mention of the bust. While the
impact of this boom and bust sequence on the rest of the world is
yet to be fully understood, the events that have transpired so far
have tremendous value in our study of bubbles before they burst.

"Safe as Houses"

In his book *The Ascent of Money: A Financial History of the World,*
Niall Fergusson explains what property ownership can mean to

individuals as well as the world of finance. For very good reasons, investing in housing seems like a safe bet:

> "Safe as Houses": the phrase tells you all you need to know about why people all over the world yearn to own their own homes. But that phrase means something more precise in the world of finance. It means that there is nothing safer than lending money to people with property. Why? Because if they default on the loan, you can repossess the house. Even if they run away, the house can't. As the Germans say, land and buildings are "immobile" property. So it is no coincidence that the single most important source of funds for a new business in the United States is a mortgage on the entrepreneur's house. Correspondingly, financial institutions have become even less inhibited about lending money to people who want to buy property.[1]

The ending of the Internet, media, and telecom boom of 2000 resulted in an unprecedented asset bubble implosion in the United States. In an effort to stimulate the economy, monetary policy became extraordinarily loose, with a host of unintended consequences. Krugman describes leadership at the Federal Reserve as follows: "Greenspan acted like a parent who sternly warns teenagers against overdoing it but doesn't actually stop the party, and stands ready to act as designated driver when the fun is over."[2] And so it was that the Greenspan Fed lowered rates in the aftermath of the Internet bubble's bursting, and proceeded to hold them at low levels for an extended period of time.

Writing in 2005, economist Robert Shiller, co-creator of the widely followed Case-Shiller housing price index whose March 2000 publication of Irrational Exuberance proved extraordinarily well timed in predicting the Internet bust—predicted a housing bust. He noted that "the market for real estate, particularly individual homes, would seem likely to display speculative booms from time to time, since the psychological salience of the prices of the places we see every day and the homes we live in must be very high, and because home prices are such a popular topic of conversation."[3] Just as he meticulously dismissed popular explanations for why the Internet boom was different and would not bust, so too did he address the numerous rationalizations explaining why the housing boom would not bust. He notes:

One such explanation is that population pressures have built up to the point that we have run out of land, and that home prices have shot up as a result. But we didn't just run out of land since the late 1990s: population growth has been steady and gradual. Another theory is that the things that go into houses—the labor, the lumber, the concrete, the steel—are in such heavy demand that they have become very expensive. But construction costs are not out of line with long-term trends. Another glib explanation is that the boom is due to the interest rate cuts implemented in many countries in an effort to deal with a weak global economy. But while low interest rates are certainly a contributing factor, central banks have cut interest rates many times in history, and such actions never produced such concerted booms.[4]

To understand the magnitude of the bubble that was created in the U.S. housing market, consider the charts (using data compiled by Shiller going back to 1890) that show the U.S. home price index (a proxy for the real, inflation-adjusted values of homes) compared to the long-run drivers of housing costs, namely the cost of building materials and the demand (i.e., population) for housing.

As visible in Figure 10.1, inflation in building materials and labor does not adequately explain the sudden and rapid rise of

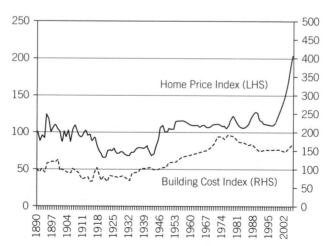

Figure 10.1   Shiller's Home Price Index vs. Building Cost Index
Source: www.econ.yale.edu/~shiller/data.htm

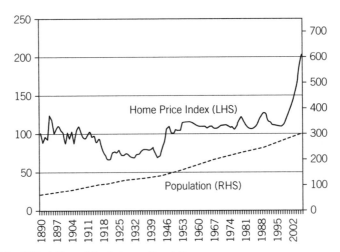

Figure 10.2   Shiller's Home Price Index vs. Population
Source: www.econ.yale.edu/~shiller/data.htm

the home price index. Might demand for housing be the culprit? Figure 10.2 plots that same home price index against the U.S. population.

As seen in Figure 10.1 and Figure 10.2, U.S. home prices very clearly had appreciated at a rate faster than that of the fundamental housing market drivers. Between 1890 and 2005, when this chart was produced, housing prices were up 85 percent in real terms, far greater than the appreciation in building costs. Likewise, prices grew more rapidly than population, and the additional cost of money (i.e., interest rates) does not amount to much of a cost pressure on housing. In 2006, these figures clearly indicate an unsustainable boom in progress.[5]

The Music Stops

In July 2007, the chief executive officer of Citigroup, Chuck Prince, granted an interview to the *Financial Times*. During the interview, he was asked about the potentially excessive housing market lending that Citigroup was conducting, particularly in light of early indications of problems in the subprime market. In a now famous response that captures the competitive risk taking that took place among virtually all participants in the housing finance markets, Prince noted, "When the music stops, in terms of liquidity, things will be complicated. But as long as the music is playing, you've

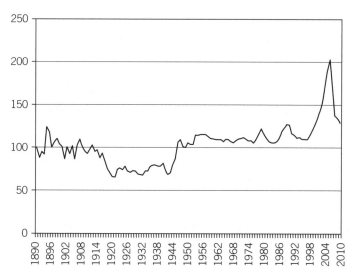

Figure 10.3   Shiller's Home Price Index, 1890–2010

Source: www.econ.yale.edu/~shiller/data.htm

got to get up and dance. We're still dancing."[6] Unfortunately for Citigroup and the rest of the housing finance complex, the music definitely stopped at some point in 2007 or 2008, and inappropriately undertaken risks were blatantly exposed—resulting in what has been to date one of the worst economic contractions and credit crunches of all time.

The magnitude of the pullback at the time of this writing (it's not clear if the decline is over) is best captured by the above-referenced home price index. Professor Robert Shiller maintains the data and updates it quarterly. Figure 10.3 includes the most recent data as of September 2010.

The "canaries in the coal mine" of the housing boom were the subprime lenders, many of which began keeling over in early 2007. A March 2007 article in *BusinessWeek* noted, "After years of easy profits, the $1.3 trillion subprime mortgage industry has taken a violent turn: at least 25 subprime lenders, which issue mortgages to borrowers with poor credit histories, have exited the business, declared bankruptcy, announced significant losses, or put themselves up for sale."[7] After significant losses due to subprime exposure were reported during the summer of 2007 by hedge funds managed by Bear Stearns, the matter snowballed into a global problem by the fall of 2007 when French bank BNP Paribas indicated that it could not accurately value assets in three of its asset-backed securities (ABS) funds because of exposure to U.S. subprime assets.

In order to fully understand how and why the housing bust accelerated and spread, it's important to understand the dynamics of the "shadow banking" system and how it differs from traditional banking operations. To do so, we need to take a step back and understand the process of securitization and how it applies to the mortgage industry.

Securitization is a process by which a pool of assets (such as mortgages or credit card loans) is divided into several pieces known as collateralized debt obligations (CDOs). For instance, if 5,000 mortgages, each of $500,000, are put into one structure, the entire pool has assets worth $2,500,000,000 (assuming all mortgages are considered good.). Let's also suppose that the pool is divided into 250 individual securities, each worth $10,000,000. Because each security has a claim against the whole pool (and not against 20 specific mortgages), the securities created in this process are seemingly less risky and more diversified. Investors such as pension funds may be able to get $10 million of exposure to mortgages without the concentration risk of having 20 direct obligations. Further, because securitization allows for the allocation of cash flows coming from the mortgages in any manner desired, each tranche (piece of the pool) need not be treated equally. Thus, senior tranches may be shielded from the first losses. This unique element allows for significant structuring flexibility and enabled the creation of seemingly very secure tranches out of arguably very insecure pools of mortgages.

The ramifications of securitization were numerous. First, it necessarily broke the symbiotic relationship between lender and borrower. Whereas banks would historically keep the mortgages on the books and service the loan directly (maintaining a relationship with the borrower), securitization enabled the separation of mortgage origination and mortgage servicing. Thus, originators no longer had a vested interest in the long-term viability of a borrower, resulting in definitively lower lending standards. At the very least, it allowed banks to issue more loans than their balance sheet might otherwise allow as they were able to securitize loans made with bank capital and thereby continue lending to more customers with recycled resources.

Secondly, securitization made dealing with problem loans particularly difficult. Because mortgages are in a pool that had their cash flows allocated according to prearranged dynamics, no one party is responsible for a particular mortgage. Whereas a delinquent borrower might previously have been able to negotiate directly with the bank holding her mortgage, securitization made such negotiations and potential loan modifications almost impossible. The result is likely to be more foreclosures and forced sales in a falling market.

The third and final element of the shadow banking system is that it is effectively part of the global capital market, and is therefore subject to the whims and vagaries typical of capital markets. For instance, a successful securitization requires there to be willing buyers of the securitized products. If capital markets become unreceptive, or downright hostile, to further securitization, as they did in 2008, then the shadow banking system is likely to shut down and generate dynamics comparable to banking failures.

At the end of the day, shadow banking is just another form of credit provisioning as it allows borrowers to obtain money from lenders. When the system broke down following the subprime market implosion, the results were felt far and wide. Banks that had previously depended on the shadow banking market to take loans off their hands were stuck with more loans than they desired, the secondary market in collateralized obligations slowed dramatically, and fearful originators stopped lending. The whole system came to a screeching halt with a dramatic contraction in the availability of credit. The resulting impact upon commerce, housing markets, and other asset classes was severe.

The Boombustology of the U.S. Housing Boom and Bust

Because the events relating to the boom–bust sequence of the U.S. housing market are still unfolding, this section does not attempt to be comprehensive, but instead highlights issues representative of insights that may be gleaned through a multidisciplinary lens.

Reflexivity Relationships Between Credit and Collateral

One of the primary factors that drove the boom in mortgage lending was that "loans are made on the basis of the value of the property, not on the ability of the borrower to repay,"[8] resulting in a powerful reflexive dynamic. Had lenders constrained their issuance of loans to those able to repay (i.e., adopting income or cash flow–based lending criteria), it's unlikely a reflexive dynamic would have been as drastic, even if it did take hold. Nevertheless, because asset-based lending was the order of the day, a virtuous cycle ensued during the boom phase and turned into a vicious cycle during the bust phase. Although related impacts from this dynamic were evident in capital flows, confidence, and economic conditions, the primary impact was found in the relationship between collateral and credit.

Cheap Money = Expensive Housing

The relationship between the cost of money (i.e., the interest rate a buyer might pay) and the value of an asset that can be bought with that money (i.e., a house) is perhaps most obvious in those assets that are typically bought with a high percentage of borrowed money. Housing provides the clearest example of this phenomenon at work. See Chapter 2 for a referesher.

Consider the following situation. A house is sold for $400,000 to a buyer who secures a mortgage for 80 percent of the purchase price ($320,000) at an interest rate of 10 percent. For ease of calculation, let's assume that the mortgage is interest only. In this case, the monthly payments would equal $320,000 × 10% / 12 months = $2,667. Now if interest rates were to fall to 5 percent, those same payments would fall by 50 percent, with the new monthly required payments equal to $320,000 × 5% / 12 months = $1,333.

Although lower interest rates have tremendous power to lower mortgage payments, the connection with house prices—which may be less obvious—is equally powerful. Suppose now that a person had a budget of $2,667 per month. How much could he afford to pay for the same house with the lower mortgage rates? Simple algebra facilitates this calculation: $2,667 × 12 months / 5% = $640,000 of loan amount. Add to this loan amount the original down payment of $80,000 and we see that the lower interest rate might increase the amount that our buyer can afford to pay to $720,000—assuming no minimum down payment percent.

Given the dynamics between interest rates and housing prices, then, it should come as no surprise that monetary policy, which brought interest rates down to 1 percent by 2002, ignited a serious property boom. By manipulating the cost of money down to highly stimulative levels to encourage economic activity, the Federal Reserve unintentionally created tremendous upside pressure on the prices of highly leveraged assets such as houses.

Further, it might make sense to revisit Hyman Minsky's financial instability hypothesis and the role of financing structures in generating instability. In particular, there appears to be a remarkable similarity between Minsky's description of Ponzi finance and the terms on which some mortgages were underwritten. Stories of mortgages with 1-year teaser rates abound. Likewise, it now appears that many loans were taken by individuals who had neither the ability to service the debt nor pay it back with income. They were "banking" (pun intended) on the value of the home rising, thereby allowing them to either sell the property at a profit or to cash out adequate money to pay the mortgage. Such financing structures are inherently unstable, as discussed in Chapter 2.

"House Values Don't Go Down"

The phrase "it takes two to tango" is highly applicable when it comes to the U.S. housing boom and bust. Ambitious homeowners-to-be were eager to "lever up" in a quest to buy the largest, most expensive home they could purchase, and eager lenders were willing to design various mortgage products to meet their needs. The seemingly symbiotic relationship was taken to extremes by both lenders willing to lend more money than a borrower could afford, and borrowers willing to borrow more than they could repay. Both parties were operating under an extraordinarily flawed assumption—namely, that house values simply do not fall.

Before we dive into the social psychology of home ownership and its virtues, we should consider some of the mortgage innovations that emerged prior to the housing boom and fueled it to lofty heights. In particular, the emergence and rapid growth of subprime loans (loans made to those with problematic credit histories), adjustable rate mortgages (mortgages that have floating interest rates that can go up over time—many of which were accompanied by very low initial teaser rates), interest-only mortgages (loans in which the borrower did not have to repay any principal), and stated-income loans (mortgages that required no documentation of income) greatly enlarged the pool of available homebuyers by increasing access to credit. Down payment assistance programs further enlarged the universe of homebuyers by providing capital for down payments.

Media reports about the housing boom and seemingly ubiquitous dinner party conversations about the rapidly rising prices of homes also contributed to the belief that house prices don't fall. The cover of *Time* magazine in 2005 highlighted the role of housing in wealth creation and how low interest rates were making the housing market more affordable to more people. Its headline tells the whole story: "Home $weet Home: Why We're Going Gaga Over Real Estate." As if that wasn't enough, *Boston* magazine's cover story (see Figure 10.4) in May 2006 (quite possibly the absolute top of the real estate market) was titled "Buy! Buy! Buy! The Smart Real Estate Moves Right Now." Unfortunately, no one appeared to be questioning whether it was even smart to be invested in real estate.

In addition to the obvious sense of overconfidence that existed among U.S. home buyers in 2005 and 2006, it seems as if even cautious home buyers suffered from cognitive biases such as anchoring and insufficient adjustment. Sure, the logic went, house prices could fall a bit, but not meaningfully enough to matter. This logic is textbook insufficient adjustment. Likewise, the fact that these adjustments were made from lofty current prices (i.e., that buyers anchored on them) made the adjustments even less useful for even cautious buyers.

Homes for Everyone!

Another critical factor in the U.S. housing boom and bust was political encouragement for every American to own a home. In a well-written article that shed light on the role of government in the housing boom and bust, Peter Wallison, the Arthur F. Burns Fellow in Financial Policy Studies at the American Enterprise Institute, noted that "the crisis has its roots in the U.S. government's efforts to increase homeownership, especially among minorities and other underserved or low-income groups, and to do so through hidden financial subsidies rather than direct government expenditures."[9]

How exactly did the government go about promoting homeownership? Wallison argues that the "Community Reinvestment Act, Fannie Mae and Freddie Mac, penalty-free refinancing of home loans, tax preferences granted to home equity borrowing, and reduced capital requirements for banks that hold mortgages and mortgage-backed securities" all contributed to a system that grew to be increasingly vulnerable as lending standards fell to accommodate these and other government efforts.

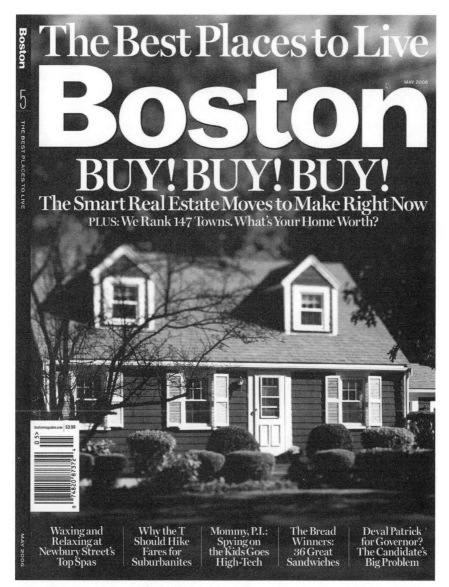

Figure 10.4   Cover of *Boston* Magazine
Source: © 2006 Metro Corp. Reproduced with permission.

The Community Reinvestment Act (CRA), originally enacted in 1977, underwent a major revision in 1995, the impact of which was immediately felt in homeownership rates. CRA was adopted to prevent discrimination in access to capital and encouraged banks to focus on community needs. After the 1995 revisions were enacted, homeownership jumped from the stable 64 percent level it had been for several decades to over 69 percent by 2005.

Freddie and Fannie were two government entities designed to purchase loans from banks in an effort to encourage additional mortgage lending. In this sense, these entities were the original securitizers of mortgages and effectively created the secondary market in mortgages. As pressure mounted during the Clinton administration to increase the availability of housing finance, Freddie and Fannie responded. Wallison notes,

> By 1997, Fannie was offering a 97 percent loan to value mortgage, and by 2001, it was offering mortgages with no down payment at all. By 2007, Fannie and Freddie were required to show that 55 percent of their mortgage purchases were LMI (low to moderate income) loans and, within this goal, that 28 percent of all purchases were from underserved areas (usually inner cities) and 25 percent were purchases of loans to low-income and very-low-income borrowers.[10]

Clearly, these were the least creditworthy borrowers in the system, perhaps explaining why profit-oriented banks had not previously paid attention to them as potential borrowers. It was only after the securitized market took off, and government mandates were clear, did those banks begin paying attention to this group of potential customers.

The final area of political influence on the housing market that deserves discussion is that of tax policies. Specifically, the mortgage interest deduction has effectively served as a subsidy to homeowners, with the largest subsidies going to the homeowners with the largest mortgages (presumably associated with the largest incomes). To see the subsidy in action, let's compare the difference between a person who has a $2000 per month rent payment and one who has a $2200 a month mortgage payment, of which $2000 is interest and is therefore deductible. Because the renter is not able to deduct his rent payments, his after-tax cost of housing remains $2000 per month. The homeowner with mortgage, however, is able to deduct (subject to certain limitations) the interest from his taxable income. Assuming the homeowner is in a 30 percent tax bracket, his after-tax cost of housing will be $2000 \times (1 - 30\%) + $200 = 1600. This basically equates to a governmental handout of $600 per month to our homeowner. Further, given that $200 of this $1600 payment is for repayment of principal, the rent equivalent is $1400 per month, $600 per month less expensive than our renter.

In an eloquent *New York Times Magazine* article titled "Who Needs the Mortgage Interest Deduction?" Roger Lowenstein describes the logic of the mortgage interest deduction as follows:

> Some fellow in the Treasury Department had long ago decided it would be a good thing for families like ours not to suffer through our lives as tenants. In fact, he (whoever he was) decided it would be good for our neighbors and for society in general if we could be owners and not just dwellers. In early America, only those who owned property were eligible to vote, and the notion that tenants were only provisional citizens, or at least had a lesser stake in things, has somehow endured. According to studies, people who own their homes take better care of them; they fix the roof more often and plant more lilacs. They join more clubs and community groups; they vote more often; they move around less often; and their kids do better in school. The government is subsidizing my house so I will do more gardening. Or something like that.[11]

Further, because interest on home equity loans and lines of credit are also deductible, homeowners are encouraged to take out second and sometimes third mortgages against a property to fund (over)consumption. As noted by Wallison,

> Interest on consumer loans of all kinds—for cars, credit cards, or other purposes—is not deductible for federal tax purposes, but interest on home equity loans is deductible no matter what the purpose of the loan or the use of the funds. As a result, homeowners are encouraged to take out home equity loans to pay off their credit card or auto loans, or to make purchases that would ordinarily be made with credit cards, auto loans, or ordinary consumer loans.[12]

By encouraging the use of home equity financing for consumption purposes, the government promotes lower equity values in homes—thereby inadvertently enhancing the likelihood of defaults and foreclosures during a real estate downturn.

Epidemics and Emergence

The fact that the subprime market served as the last untapped universe of potential homebuyers to access the housing market indicates that their increasing participation in the housing market was an indicator of the boom's maturity. In the spectrum of mortgage quality, prime loans are considered the safest and are offered to the most creditworthy borrowers. Following prime, there is a category known as Alt-A loans, which are offered to borrowers without full documentation, with lower collateral values, and with lower credit scores. Subprime is the riskiest of the mortgages and was offered to borrowers who had historically been deemed uncreditworthy.[13] Figure 10.5 highlights the growth in subprime and Alt-A lending that took place during the final stages of the housing boom.

In addition to the absolute growth in the number of subprime and Alt-A loans issued (as evidenced in Figure 10.5), the absolute dollar amount of the risky loans (defined as subprime and Alt-A) grew exponentially, as seen in Figure 10.6. Figure 10.6 also demonstrates how these risky loans became an increasingly large share of all mortgage originations, having risen from under 10 percent in 2002 to almost 34 percent by 2006. Within this category, it is interesting

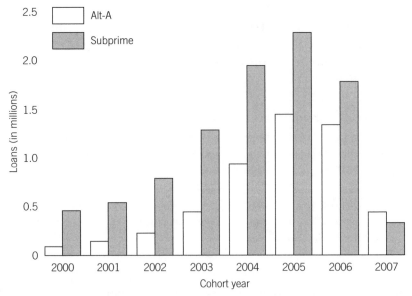

Figure 10.5   Rapid Growth in Number of Subprime and Alt-A Loans

Source: General Accounting Office report accessed via www.gao.gov/new.items/d09848r.pdf

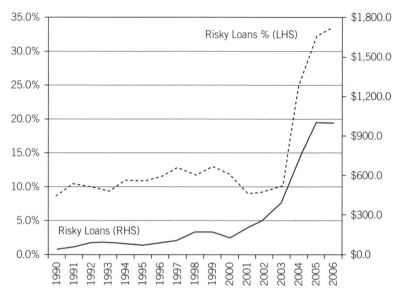

Figure 10.6   Exponential Growth in Risky Loans
Source: The 2010 Mortgage Market Statistical Annual, Volume 1 (Bethesda, MD: Inside Mortgage Finance Publications, 2010).

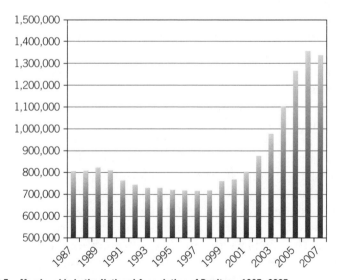

Figure 10.7   Membership in the National Association of Realtors, 1987–2007
Source: D. McCormick, *Field Guide to NAR Membership Statistics, 1908–Present.* Accessed electronically via www.realtor.org/library/library/fg003.

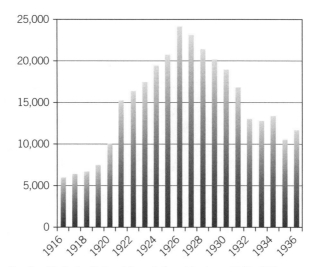

Figure 10.8   Membership in the National Association of Realtors, 1916–1936

Source: D. McCormick, *Field Guide to NAR Membership Statistics, 1908–Present.* Accessed electronically via www.realtor.org/library/library/fg003.

to note that the riskiest of loans, subprime, grew during the same period from approximately 5 percent of the total mortgage market in 2002 to over 20 percent of the mortgage market by 2006.[14]

From the data, it definitely appears that most of the eligible buyers (i.e., prime, creditworthy borrowers) had already been infected, thereby leaving the "disease" only to infect the historically uncreditworthy. Obviously, the available universe of infectable potential homebuyers was rapidly shrinking. By enabling the most amateur of investors to enter the housing markets, the boom in subprime lending was a useful indicator of the housing bubble's maturity and imminent burst. The fact that TV shows like "Flip This House" were in competition with other TV shows like "Flip That House" further validates the maturity of the boom. If ordinary, television–watching non-speculators enter the housing investment business, who is left to infect?

The popularity of real estate not only grew as an investment activity, it also grew (unsustainably) as a professional activity. Figure 10.7 displays the number of members in the National Association of Realtors (NAR). Given the licensing requirements of the profession, NAR membership is a reasonable proxy for the number of real estate salespersons in the United States.

Lest we get lulled into thinking that NAR membership only rises, consider Figure 10.8, which illustrates NAR membership

Table 10.1   The-Five Lens Approach to the U.S. Housing Boom and Bust

Lens	Notes
Microeconomic	Reflexive credit/collateral dynamic Higher prices induced buyers Lower prices induced sellers
Macroeconomic	Financial innovation (subprime, Alt-A, etc.) Securitization enabled "shadow banking" Ponzi finance via teaser rates, etc.
Psychology	New era thinking (housing demand) Anchoring on prices, insufficient adjustments
Politics	Tax policies encouraging homeownership for all Moral hazard (government role in mortgage finance: Fannie, Freddie) Supply/demand distortions (Community Reinvestment Act, mortgage interest deduction)
Biology	Amateur Participants (Subprime, NAR members) Silent Leadership (Donald Trump) Popular Media (Flip This House, Flip That House)

before, during, and after the Florida land boom. As is clear from the chart, membership clearly does fall. Given our anchoring and insufficient adjustment biases, how many observers believe that NAR membership could decline by an additional 500,000?

The emergence perspective on the U.S. housing bubble does not seem to offer many vivid lessons, with the possible exception of Donald Trump's revival as a cult figure among young ambitious business professionals. In addition to his bestselling books about thinking like a real-estate billionaire and his popular TV show "The Apprentice," Trump had a more subtle effect on the seemingly uninformed swarm. His personal wealth creation in real estate had been enormous and included the launch of a Vegas casino resort and some of the most prominent real estate developments in major cities. Surely if The Don was investing it was safe for Joe Six-Pack to invest.

The Multilens Look

The U.S. housing boom and bust is a classic case of a credit-fueled reflexive bubble formed by the interaction of the five Cs described above. However, an equally supportive role was played by government policies in supporting the five Cs through both the creation of a securitization market and the encouraging of homeownership and home finance. Table 10.1 summarizes the five lens view of the U.S. housing boom and bust.

PART III

Looking Ahead

Part One presented various disciplinary lenses through which to evaluate financial extremes, and Part Two illustrated the use of those lenses on five historical cases. Part Three brings together the lenses of Part One and the case study evidence of Part Two into a framework for identifying bubbles before they burst. The real power and usefulness of the multilens approach lies in its application to unresolved mysteries, and so the last chapter evaluates the likelihood the boom in China is a bubble about to burst.

11

Spotting Bubbles before They Burst

A METHOD FOR IDENTIFYING
UNSUSTAINABLE BOOMS

When a person with money meets a person with experience, the person with experience winds up with the money and the person with the money ends up with the experience.

—Harvey MacKay

Although studying booms and busts provides significant fodder for academic discussions and intellectual debates, it is perhaps most useful if it helps one to make money, avoid losses, or, ideally, both. In order to be useful, then, our study of booms and busts must provide tools for proactively understanding if one is investing in an unsustainable boom with the corresponding risks of an imminent bust. As mentioned in the preface, this book does not provide a map of the market. It also does not attempt to provide any insight into market timing. Rather, it provides a probabilistic framework for understanding the likelihood of being in a bubble. The underlying belief of this approach is that, although asset markets may be well behaved and efficient most of the time, they do on occasion stray to extremes. These extremes matter a great deal, and this chapter provides a seismograph to identify the tremors that precede a quake.

Many an academic has made a career out of explaining events from a historical perspective. Few practitioners have had the luxury of living in a world of 20/20 vision comparable to that provided by hindsight. As such, this chapter provides a tool—in the form of a checklist—that individuals and institutions might use to spot bubbles before they burst. Findings of the previous chapters have been coalesced into a framework to recognize unsustainable booms.

The booms and busts discussed in Part II demonstrate many similar characteristics. Most exhibited reflexive dynamics, excessive and unsustainable leverage, overconfidence and biased decision making, policies distorting price-discovery processes, and herdlike behavior. This chapter summarizes each of these characteristics and concludes with a checklist of the common indicators associated with being in the midst of bubble.

Reflexivity and Self-Fulfilling Dynamics

The first lens presented in Chapter 1 focused on the forces of supply and demand and questioned whether they generate an equilibrium. This physics-inspired approach to microeconomics suggests that supply and demand meet to create a stable price. A rise in prices generates supply, which in turn offsets the price rise. Likewise, similar logic suggests that a fall in prices generates demand, which provides upward pressure on prices. Chapter 1 concluded that although supply and demand dynamics usually generate a stable equilibrium, they occasionally do not. There are instances in which higher prices stimulate additional demand, not additional supply—a situation that often characterizes a boom. Likewise, busts might be characterized by situations in which lower prices stimulate additional supply, not demand. The theory of reflexivity provides an alternative to the equilibrium-oriented efficient market hypothesis.

The five Cs framework captures the essence of the reflexive dynamics that dominate most boom and bust sequences. By definition, booms and busts are events that deviate significantly from equilibrium, and it is often highly likely that reflexive dynamics are responsible for these deviations. Because the five Cs framework has broad applicability to the study of booms and busts, we instead focus in this section on more specific reflexivity signposts that involve an interplay with credit and leverage—namely, the prevalence of asset-based lending and the simultaneous growth of credit volumes and asset prices.

During the course of the five case studies presented, the most prominent examples of reflexive dynamics at work involved the self-reinforcing, pro-cyclical dynamic between credit and collateral.

This often occurred in times of extreme optimism when lenders modified their lending criteria from income-oriented toward asset-focused approaches. When the primary criteria for extending credit switches from income-based affordability to collateral value, watch out. This is a spectacular early warning sign of a powerful reflexive dynamic being unleashed.

Because increased collateral values inspire more credit, reflexive dynamics can often be identified by the concomitant growth of credit and collateral values. If credit is rising rapidly along with asset prices, there is a high probability that reflexive dynamics are under way. These dynamics were prominent in the Florida, Japan, and U.S. housing cases studied in previous chapters. As these dynamics unfolded, they were accompanied by a similar boom in confidence at banks as they felt they were increasingly secure in their loans, not realizing that when the music slowed (if not stopped), then they would suddenly find that they were less intelligent than they themselves once thought.

A change in lending standards and a simultaneous growth in lending and asset prices are both indicators of what might also be termed easy or loose money. Let's review selected events that transpired in the cases to evaluate the prevalence of reflexive dynamics and their interactions with loose money.

Tulipomania

The tulip mania discussed in Chapter 6 exhibited many of the characteristics typical of a reflexive dynamic. Higher prices generated more demand, and, following the bursting of the bubble, lower prices generated more supply. Aside from these price-based indicators of reflexive dynamics, there appears to have been the possibility of foreign inflows (i.e., hot money) into the Netherlands as it became the financial center of the world. Foreign capital inflows seeking higher returns often cause the very returns they are seeking, thereby creating a very unstable situation.

The Great Depression

The Florida land boom that preceded the Great Depression provides a spectacular example of the two reflexivity indicators in action. As is typical in most property-related booms, credit provided the fuel for the asset boom with banks. Liquidity was rampant and credit ubiquitous. Remember the total U.S. money supply during the 1920s?

One can also note that credit was expanding at the same time as asset prices were rising and although evidence on the methodology of bank approvals is hard to come by, it seems conceivable that banks were finding comfort that as asset prices rose, the collateral pledged against their loans made the loans (seem) less risky. It was only once the music stopped that banks realized their comfort was unwarranted.

The Japanese Boom and Bust

Given that land was the centerpiece of the Japanese boom and bust sequence, it should come as no surprise that reflexive credit and collateral dynamics were present. The mere existence of mortgage products with a 100-year term (see the following section on financial innovation) indicate that leverage was being extended on terms other than ability to repay as banks could not have reasonably expected individuals to live long enough to repay their loans. Many of these loans simply must have been extended by banks operating under the assumption that asset values would protect them against this inability to repay the loan from income. Further, Japanese credit grew rapidly during the 1980s, simultaneous with the boom in asset prices. It seems highly unlikely that this was coincidental.

The Asian Financial Crisis

The Asian Financial Crisis was in many ways a story of hot money inflows and outflows. The reflexive dynamic created by such money flows was not dissimilar to those generated in other unsustainable booms. Money came into East Asia seeking higher returns, but the very arrival of such money at least partially created those returns. As long as the flows continued, the story remained in tact. Once the money flows stopped, and reversed, the virtuous cycle rapidly turned vicious. This is exactly the dynamic that took place in Thailand and the rest of Southeast Asia during the Asian Financial Crisis.

The U.S. Housing Boom and Bust

The housing boom that took place in the early to mid-2000s in the United States was a period that definitively exhibited telltale signs of reflexive dynamics. To begin, the multitude of mortgage innovations that took place were specifically designed to extend leverage and mortgage power to those who had been previously unable to access such credit. Such innovations included subprime, Alt-A,

Table 11.1   Signs Revealing Reflexive Dynamics toward Disequilibrium

Indicator	Examples
Change in Criteria Used to Evaluate and Extend Credit from Income-Oriented Toward Collateral-Focused	100-year mortgages issued during the Japanese property boom
Concomitant Growth in Credit and Collateral Value	Simultaneous boom in mortgage values and housing prices during the U.S. housing boom
"Hot Money" Inflows Seeking (and creating) Outsized Returns	Foreign capital flowing into the Netherlands, Foreign capital flowing into Thailand

and NINJA (No-Income, No-Job or Assets) loans. Securitization (see the following financial innovation section) was the enabling force behind banks willing to look beyond historical warning signs (i.e., bad credit in the case of subprime and Alt-A mortgages, or unemployment in the case of NINJA loans) of potential losses. By not having to (directly) worry about the ramifications of extending inappropriate credit, banks felt empowered to change the historical basis upon which mortgages were extended. Additional confidence was gained by rapidly rising collateral values. Further, it should come as no surprise that the amount of outstanding credit rose alongside asset values.

Red Flags of Reflexivity

Two of the primary criteria for identifying the onset of destabilizing reflexive dynamics in asset markets thus seem to be the modification of the standards by which credit has historically been granted (i.e., affordability) toward collateral-based lending and the simultaneous growth in credit and asset values. A third indicator is the presence and growth of "hot money" inflows seeking outsized returns, which usually enable the very returns sought. Table 11.1 summarizes these indicators.

Leverage, Financial Innovation, and Cheap Money

Chapter 2 introduced several non-traditional macroeconomic approaches to thinking about booms and busts. Specifically, the dynamics of debt and the ability of a borrower to repay form the heart of Hyman Minsky's financial instability hypothesis. The nasty impact of deflation on debt (increasing the real burden of debt) was then considered before evaluating the Austrian school of economics and their "cheap money as the root of all evil" explanation for boom and bust cycles.

A common adage about banking and leverage captures the spirit of the boom and bust dynamic quite eloquently: "If you owe the bank $100 and can't pay, then you have a problem. If you owe the bank $100 million and can't pay, then the bank has a problem." Financial innovation, which often creates effective leverage, is an enabling culprit in the credit game and when combined with cheap money, creates a dynamic that is particularly fragile and prone to instability. Credit is inherently destabilizing, and misunderstood credit can be lethal. In a recent article titled "Financial Innovation and Financial Fragility," Nicola Gennaioli and two colleagues noted the following sequence of events through which financial innovation can become destabilizing:

> Many recent episodes of financial innovation share a common narrative. It begins with a strong demand from investors for a particular, often safe, pattern of cash flows. Some traditional securities available in the market offer this pattern, but investors demand more (so prices are high). In response to demand, financial intermediaries create new securities offering the sought after pattern of cash flows, usually by carving them out of existing projects or other securities that are more risky. By virtue of diversification, tranching, insurance, and other forms of financial engineering, the new securities are believed by the investors, and often by the intermediaries themselves, to be good substitutes for the traditional ones, and are consequently issued and bought in great volumes.
>
> At some point, news reveals that new securities are vulnerable to some unattended risks, and in particular are not good substitutes for the traditional securities. Both investors and intermediaries are surprised by the news, and investors sell these "false substitutes," moving back to the traditional securities with the cash flows they seek. As investors fly for safety, financial institutions are stuck holding the supply of the new securities (or worse yet, having to dump them as well in a fire sale because they are leveraged). The prices of traditional securities rise while those of the new ones fall sharply.[1]

Although the quote above is clearly referencing the AAA-rated debt derivatives which were a false substitute for U.S. Treasuries, we should not lose track of the fact that financial innovation has the ability to create instability. Indeed, whether it was the development of futures contracts in 1630s Holland or the sliced and diced mortgage-backed securities of the 2000s makes no difference: *financial innovation often embeds or conceals leverage.*

Tulipomania

The structure of the tulip market in the 1630s was one based on futures. Because the actual tradable bulb market only existed for several months, most trading that took place in tulip bulbs took place in derivative markets that effectively enabled (via down payments that enabled control of larger values) leverage. Richard Bookstaber, while reviewing the perils of financial innovation, notes that the Tulipomania "reached full bloom only with the innovation of forward contracts and the leverage these contracts afforded, which allowed traders to buy and sell commodities they did not own, had no intention of owning, and indeed did not even have the money to purchase outright."[2] Further, ubiquitous money and liquidity (see Table 6.1) provided monetary fuel for tulip prices.

The Great Depression

Here again, the use of effective leverage was prevalent. It was the "pay only 10 percent to get economic exposure to 100 percent of an asset" mind-set. By simply putting down a deposit that was 90 percent less than the actual price, speculators in Florida were able to achieve 10× leverage on the price movement of the properties they had supposedly committed to purchasing. Not dissimilar to the Bookstaber quote above, it was later revealed that many of these properties were held by individuals who had no intention of owning them and likely lacked adequate resources to own them outright. The result, like the events that had transpired almost 290 years prior, was identical. The house of cards, which was built on a precarious foundation of extreme leverage, eventually imploded.

In a series of articles published in the *Saturday Evening Post,* Garet Garrett described the bubble of the 1920s as follows: "An ephemeral, whirling, upside-down pyramid, doomed in its own velocity. Yet it devours credit in an uncontrollable manner, more and more to the very end; credit feeds its velocity."[3] From brokerage margin provided to eager speculators to credit fueling the purchases of automobiles, radios, and other new devices, much of the boom of the 1920s took place with borrowed funds. Ultimately, as noted in "Whirlwinds of Speculation," a 1931 article published in *The Atlantic* magazine, the credit fueled its own demise by producing a supply response in the "units of speculation" (i.e., stocks, bonds, and developments in Florida) creating the inevitable crash.

Finally, the lowering of interest rates in 1925 to assist the British in fighting the outflow of gold from their country was unintended fuel on top of the already existing speculative fire. This spurred credit growth, and by the early 1930s, U.S. existing credit to GDP reached an all-time high of 299 percent.[4]

The Japanese Boom and Bust

Macroeconomic policy during the Japanese boom was marked by tremendous growth in credit. In fact, it has only been in the years following the bust that the magnitude of the credit overhang has been made patently evident. By encouraging the use of credit to facilitate asset-gain wealth effects, the monetary authorities of Japan were hoping to alleviate the pain that would likely be felt by exporters due to currency appreciation. The result was a cheap money credit explosion that resulted in the final vertical ascent of Japanese asset markets.

The lethal combination of debt and deflation has since plagued the island nation and resulted in what has been labeled by Richard Koo as a balance sheet recession. Traditional economic incentives like profit maximization were effectively brushed aside in a quest for balance sheet repair. This act of deleveraging generated a reflexive dynamic of its own, in which debt deflation firmly took hold.

The Asian Financial Crisis

Perhaps the most dramatic innovation that enabled the inflow of portfolio investments into Southeast Asia was the emergence of emerging markets funds. As highlighted in Chapter 9, the fact that increasing pools of global capital were organized into common funds focused on emerging economies enabled the rapid transmission of economic hardships in one country into capital flight from another. As fund managers began taking significant losses in Thailand, they found themselves overly exposed to other countries and hence began selling them as well. Further, redemptions by the fund's investors led to a general selling pressure across all emerging markets as fund managers indiscriminately sold stocks in an effort to meet requests for the return of capital.

Although the topic of cultural homogeneity and crony capitalism will be touched on below, it is worth noting here that the development of financial intermediaries such as the Thai finance companies spurred the disbursement of credit. The crony capitalism that led to inefficient and risky lending made for the ultimate in moral hazard. Banks and others freely lent inappropriate amounts of capital to connected individuals with the belief that relationships in the government would ultimately protect them. Thus, capital flowed more freely than it otherwise might have.

The U.S. Housing Boom and Bust

If one had to focus on only one cause of the U.S. housing boom and bust, it would likely be the ease of leverage and credit that enabled a slew of individuals—unable to afford the homes they purchased—to enter the market and thereby bid up the prices of real estate. There were many contributing factors to this plot, but central to it are the innovations in securitization and collateralization that created the mortgage-backed securities, collateralized debt obligations, and a host of other credit-derived securities that were served up to yield-hungry global investors seeking the comfort of highly rated and supposedly safe securities.

Another enabling factor in the housing boom was the inappropriately low interest rates that were in effect to combat the ramifications of the Internet bubble bursting. By keeping rates extraordinarily low for an extended period of time, the U.S. Federal Reserve unintentionally fueled the next bubble, a far larger and wide-reaching credit-fueled housing boom with significantly greater ramifications.

Finally, the predominant role played by government-sponsored enterprises such as Fannie Mae and Freddie Mac in the housing markets created a sense of comfort on the part of those buying housing securities guaranteed by these organizations. After all, the U.S. government would not allow a default on mortgage-backed securities, would it?

Signs of Unsustainable Credit Conditions

The signposts for unsustainable credit conditions fall under three primary indicators: financial innovations that enhance or enable leverage, inappropriately (and often unintended) cheap money, and the issuance of credit to non-creditworthy borrowers due to

Skyscrapers as a Bubble Indicator

One of the first skyscrapers was designed and built in 1887 by Bradford Lee Gilbert. It was designed to solve a problem of space: He had an unusually shaped 6.5 meter plot on Broadway in Manhattan. His solution: Maximize space for occupancy by building vertically. The press ridiculed the idea, fearing that the 160-foot structure might fall over should a strong wind arrive. Friends, lawyers, and engineers suggested repeatedly that Gilbert abandon the idea, warning that if the building did fall over, the legal bills would ruin him. To overcome the skepticism, Gilbert took the top two stories of the building for his personal offices.[*]

From that project forward, the skyscraper has come to symbolize so much more than creativity. It has become a symbol of success, or one's literal ascent toward the heavens. It became "the great architectural contribution of modern capitalistic society and is even one of the yardsticks for twentieth-century superheroes."[†]

Nevertheless, because skyscrapers are rarely built by their anticipated tenants with cash, they are inherently speculative ventures. In many ways, the tallest skyscrapers under construction are an indicator of where money is easiest, speculative juices are flowing most briskly, and confidence is high. Noting this relationship in a fascinating piece of research, Dresdner Kleinwort property analyst Andrew Lawrence developed what he calls "the Skyscraper Index" as an indicator of forthcoming economic contractions.[‡] Consider the following buildings, all of which were the world's tallest at the time of their completion, and their associated economic contractions:

World's Tallest Skyscrapers and Related Busts

Building	Location (Completed)	Spire Height	Financial Crisis
Singer	New York (1908)	187 meters	Panic of 1907
Metropolitan Life	New York (1909)	247 meters	Panic of 1907
40 Wall Street	New York (1929)	283 meters	Great Depression
Chrysler	New York (1929)	319 meters	Great Depression
Empire State	New York (1931)	443 meters	Great Depression
World Trade Center	New York (1973)	526 meters	70's Stagflation
Sears Tower	Chicago (1974)	527 meters	70's Stagflation
Petronas Towers	Kuala Lumpur (1997)	452 meters	Asian Financial Crisis
Taipei 101	Taipei (2004)[a]	509 meters	Tech Bubble
Burj Dubai	Dubai (2008/2009)[b]	828 meters	Global Credit Crunch

Source: Mark Thornton, "Skyscrapers and Business Cycles," *The Quarterly Journal of Austrian Economics* (Vol 8, No 1, Spring 2005); www.skyscraperpage.com; Phil Anderson, "A Recession Indicator That's Hard to Miss," *Moneyweek* (February 11, 2008).

[a] Taipei 101 was financed and construction begun in 1999, quite near the peak of the technology boom.

[b] It is interesting to note that the uncompleted Burj Dubai tower was classified as the world's tallest structure on July 21, 2007, perhaps the peak of the U.S. market before the ensuing financial meltdown.

Thus, we might consider the construction of skyscrapers to be symptomatic of bubble conditions, namely easy money and overconfidence. Thorton summarizes the common pattern quite eloquently: "First, a period of easy money leads to rapid expansion of the economy and a boom in the stock market... credit fuels a substantial increase in capital expenditures . . . This is when the world's tallest buildings are begun."[§]

[*] Phil Anderson, "A Recession Indicator That's Hard to Miss," *Moneyweek* (February 11, 2008).
[†] Mark Thornton, "Skyscrapers and Business Cycles," *The Quarterly Journal of Austrian Economics* (Vol 8, No 1, Spring 2005), 51–74.
[‡] Andrew Lawrence, "The Skyscraper Index: Faulty Towers!" *Property Report, Dresdner Kleinwort Benson Research* (January 15, 1999).
[§] Mark Thornton, "Skyscrapers and Business Cycles," *The Quarterly Journal of Austrian Economics* (Vol 8, No 1, Spring 2005).

Table 11.2   Signs Revealing Leverage Excesses

Indicator	Examples
Financial Innovation(s) that enhance or enable leverage	Forward contracts for tulips, 10% down binders during the Florida land boom, 100-year mortgages in Japan, pooled funds for diversified emerging markets investing, securitization and the boom in credit derivatives
Cheap/Excessive Money	1925 lowering of interest rates to facilitate British gold retention, Japanese engineered asset boom to mitigate currency-driven export slowdown, lowering rates to combat bursting of the Internet bubble
Moral Hazard–Motivated Lending	Crony capitalism, Fannie/Freddie

implicit government guarantees (moral hazard–inspired lending). See Table 11.2 for a summary.

Overconfidence

Chapter 3 evaluated several decision-making biases that consistently impact rational behavior. Several rules of thumb were considered, and other forms of individual-level behavior that appear contrary to economic theory were evaluated. Overconfidence surfaced as perhaps the most relevant of the decision-making issues that emerge as a product of anchoring, insufficient adjustment, and reliance on the availability and representativeness heuristics.

Among the manifestations of overconfidence, perhaps the most revealing is the belief in the onset of a new era where the belief "this time is different" pervades popular sentiment. This new era belief often gains traction because there is believability to the story that things are genuinely different. Classic manifestations of this new-era inspired confidence often include conspicuous consumption and the purchase of trophy assets and art.

Tulipomania

The 1600s in Amsterdam felt like it was indeed the beginning of a new era. As noted in Chapter 6, the political economic context supported such a view and the virtual domination of world trade by the Dutch basically confirmed this new-era belief for even the most ardent of doubters. Holland had just won a hard fought war, was reaping fantastic economic gains from the redeployment of resources from military pursuits to commercial endeavors, and was now reaping the economic rewards of a dominating position in world trade. This perspective, combined with the conspicuous display of rare bulbs and the broad participation of amateur investors, provided ample evidence of a broad, Holland-wide (over)confidence in the existence of a new era. Indeed, to many participants and observers, the time seemed to have come for a Dutch domination of the world in matters of economic and non-economic consideration. Why wouldn't the world's wealthy flock to Amsterdam to procure bulbs of the most beautiful flower?

The Great Depression

The Western world had just won World War I and new technologies were promising a new era in American convenience and modern living. Just as the war had accelerated the mobilization of rural resources into industrial efforts, the ending of the war resulted in the redeployment of resources from military to economic pursuits. Automobiles and radios, both newly accessible by the presence of previously unavailable consumer credit, promised a different life in the years and decades ahead. Roads were connecting previously faraway places and a burgeoning aerospace industry enabling human flight was being formed. Lindbergh's solo crossing of the Atlantic Ocean made this new-era belief all the more real.

In a spectacular manifestation of the confidence (and hubris) of the times, speculative and competitive juices were flowing rapidly in the development of New York City's skyscrapers. Shortly after 40 Wall Street was completed and deemed the world's tallest tower, the Chrysler building chose to erect a spire tall enough to claim the title. Not to be outdone, the Empire State Building opened shortly thereafter, transferring the "world's tallest tower" title for a third time in less than three years.

The Japanese Boom and Bust

The postwar economic miracle exhibited by the transformation of a completely devastated Japan into a world-leading economic superpower provided the new era belief so representative of over-confidence. The comparisons of real estate values in Japan and the United States, several of which were detailed in Chapter 8, high-light one manifestation of this confidence.

Trophy asset purchases such as those described in Chapter 8 also typify the extreme overconfidence that accompanied the Japanese economic success story. Paying hundreds of millions of dollars more than asking price for a trophy building in Manhattan simply to get into the *Guinness Book of World Records* is the quintessential embodi-ment of overconfidence and hubris. Equally reflective of the times was the Japanese role in driving the art market to new heights.

The 1979 publishing of Harvard professor Ezra Vogel's book *Japan as Number One* provided an argument that a new era of pros-perity was coming. Although the book seemed correct in the 1980s, it has since come to represent folly. Interestingly, Jon Woronoff published a compelling *Japan as (Anything But)Number One* in 1991, very close to the top of the Japanese bubble. But as is so often the case in situations of overconfidence, contrary evidence to the pre-vailing "wisdom" was not well received at the time.

The Asian Financial Crisis

For a decade-long period leading up to the mid-1990s, Thailand was one of the fastest growing economies in the world. Similar dynamics took place across many of the Southeast Asian emerging economies. Despite the fact that much of this increase in economic output came from a growth in inputs, virtually no commentators

(Paul Krugman being a notable exception) were willing to question the region's economic sustainability. Popular books on the subject included the World Bank's *The East Asian Miracle* and Ezra Vogel's *Four Little Dragons*. With such global infatuation with the export-led development model and the success of Southeast Asia, overconfidence was effectively preordained.

Another manifestation of overconfidence was the rampant and widespread currency mismatches that left Thai (and other) borrowers extremely vulnerable to currency movements. By earning in local currency but borrowing in U.S. dollars (or other currencies), currency depreciations created a debt–deflation-like dynamic in which the effective (i.e., local currency–valued) amount of debt ballooned. The dynamics that inspired so many borrowers to undertake such a risk are at least partially clarified through a behavioral decision-making lens. As noted in Chapter 9, perhaps the likelihood of currency moves was underestimated due to a lack of recently available data regarding adverse currency moves (i.e., availability bias). Or perhaps the analogy of another country borrowing in a different currency proved more vivid (i.e., representative bias). Regardless, it does seem that borrower beliefs underweighted the probability of adverse outcomes.

As a final indicator of overconfidence (and easy money), Malaysia took the crown for the world's tallest skyscraper with the completion of the twin Petronas Towers in Kuala Lumpur in 1997.

The U.S. Housing Boom and Bust

Aided in great part by low-cost financing and increasingly flexible mortgage terms, many homebuyers and investor participants in the U.S. housing boom and bust were operating under the false belief that "real estate prices don't fall." Despite the elevated levels of objective measures of value (measures such as median price to median income, percent of income for debt service, etc.), many borrowers (and lenders for that matter) failed to note the rising risks.

Consider the art market of 2006, considered by many to be the year during which the U.S. housing market peaked. The three highest prices ever paid for paintings took place during 2006 art auctions. In June of 2006, cosmetics magnate Ronald Lauder paid a record-breaking $135 million for a Gustav Klimt painting. Only months later, a new record was set when U.S. hedge fund mogul Steven A. Cohen of SAC Capital paid roughly $137.5 million for a de Kooning painting titled "Woman" in November 2006.[5]

Table 11.3   Overconfidence Indicators

Indicators	Examples
Conspicuous Consumption	Trophy purchases, record art prices, world's tallest skyscrapers
New-Era Thinking	War victories (Spain, WWI); economic champion status (Japan, East Asian miracle), technological developments (radio, car, airplane)

It's Different This Time

Table 11.3 provides a summary of ways in which overconfidence can signal the presence of an unsustainable boom.

Policy-Driven Distortions

Chapter 4 introduced a political lens. Two big-picture issues dominated the discussion: property rights and the price mechanism. After establishing the need for protected property rights, the chapter considered the ways government actions meddle with the price mechanism—namely, mandated prices and tax distortions affecting buy/sell decisions. Price ceilings and floors were also addressed.

Most tax or price-affecting policies are meant to incentivize a certain politically desirable behavior. Unfortunately, most policies are accompanied by unintended consequences, many of which distort the price mechanism and therefore negatively affect the stability of asset markets. Three primary signposts highlight an increased likelihood of an unsustainable boom. The first, moral hazard, effectively creates a dynamic in which lenders are willing to underweight the risk of failure because they believe (rightly or wrongly) that governments do not have the political will to allow the failure of certain key stakeholders. The second involves active government manipulation of supply and demand dynamics via price controls, tax policies, and/or direct government actions. The third indicator, shifting regulations, is usually a sign of flux in the rules of play vis-à-vis business that allows for the emergence of a new paradigm and industry structure by destabilizing established industrial patterns.

Let us now turn to each of the cases to briefly consider the policy distortions that manifested themselves as the unsustainable boom was under way.

Tulipomania

Recall from Chapter 6 that the political dynamic of having prominent public officials suffering substantial personal financial losses led to a modification of the "rules" and the proposed conversion of futures contracts (in which the buyer had purchased the asset for future delivery) into call options (in which the buyer had the right but not the obligation to purchase the asset in the future). By modifying property rights as transactions were taking place, government inspired investor reevaluations of the risk–reward trade-offs.

It was this action that whipped speculation into a powerful fury and led to the last upward surge in tulip prices. Thus, proposed political legislation and the subsequent political theater in which planters and buyers negotiated prices were among the key causal factors driving the extreme volatility in tulip prices.

The Great Depression

The flow of money into Florida during the land boom may in fact have been the unintended consequence of Prohibition. Banks were flush with money from the brisk commerce in liquor that was present in Florida due to its somewhat porous borders with countries that did not prohibit alcohol. In many ways, one can therefore think of American money flying into Florida as a form of interstate "hot money" that, due to the fact that many of the banks had state (rather than national) charters, resulted in excessive lending within Florida. Might some of this capital have helped fuel the Florida land boom?

Although several policy distortions, such as the adherence to the gold standard, confounded policy actions during the early stages of the Great Depression, few policy distortions were responsible for the onset of the bubble. Many policy shifts took place in the aftermath of the bust that laid the groundwork for future busts (consider the fact that the homeownership society was a political goal set out during the 1930s in America, or that FDIC insurance on bank deposits—a prototypical example of policy-induced moral hazard—was a policy that emerged from the Great Depression).

The Japanese Boom and Bust

Chapter 8 described in detail the punitive taxation on short-term real estate sales in Japan. By artificially suppressing supply from hitting the market and decreasing the effectiveness of the price mechanism due to depressed liquidity, policy makers had inadvertently provided pricing support while intending to minimize speculative short-term trading. It was precisely by seeking to minimize speculation that they created price dynamics that attracted speculators and led to dangerously high levels of debt and real estate values. Additional complications arose from the inheritance tax and the demand it created for highly-leveraged transactions, as discussed in Chapter 8. Given that Japanese tax policies effectively decreased supply and increased demand, might the government have inadvertently fueled the real estate boom?

Further, the rapid deregulation of the financial sector led to significant competition in risk-taking by banks. Credit boomed in no small part because of these shifting regulations. Further, credit controls specifically implemented to cool the housing market contributed to the ultimate bursting of the property bubble.

The U.S. Housing Boom and Bust

Among the many policy distortions that ended up fueling the fire of the U.S. housing boom and bust were the mortgage interest deduction and an overarching political belief that homeownership was a right to which every American was entitled. The involvement of government-sponsored enterprises such as Fannie Mae and Freddie Mac further bolstered the belief that the government was prepared to underwrite mortgages to facilitate the conversion of this objective into reality. The Community Reinvestment Act (CRA) went on to further encourage lending to the least creditworthy of borrowers.

A virtuous (which later turned vicious) cycle soon ensued, with Freddie and Fannie issuing bonds to global investors seeking effective U.S. government guarantees with greater reward than U.S. Treasuries. The proceeds of these offerings were then used to purchase mortgage-backed securities. This facilitated banks lending more money, knowing a ready and willing market existed for unloading the mortgages to pseudo-government entities. This enabled banks to worry less about the quality of the mortgages because they were not going to bear the risk of default or nonpayment. Thus, the whole house of cards was built on a belief that the government would not tolerate a failure of Freddie or Fannie.

Further fueling the housing boom were advantageous tax policies available to those who utilized mortgages to finance the purchase of their property. Because interest is deductible against earned income, the net result of mortgage interest deductibility is a subsidy to homeowners in the form of reduced taxes. Thus, in the case of an individual in a 35 percent tax bracket (and assuming no other special circumstances), the government agreed to pay 35 percent of the individual's interest payments.

Unintended Consequences of Policy Developments

Table 11.4 summarizes the findings of this subsection. Although policy is usually a politically motivated outcome of legislative processes, it is unfortunately often accompanied by unintended consequences—many of which are likely to enhance the probability of booms and busts.

Table 11.4   Policy Distortion Indicators

Indicators	Examples
Supply/Demand Manipulation	150% property transaction tax, inheritance tax, mortgage interest deduction, Community Reinvestment Act
Regulatory Shift	Conversion of futures contracts into call options, Prohibition-related "hot money" inflows into Florida, de-regulation of Japanese banking sector

Epidemics and Emergence

The biological framework presented in Chapter 5 focused on two primary lenses—epidemics and emergence. The power of the epidemic lens is in its ability to shed light on the relative maturity of a boom (i.e., to provide some guidepost as to how imminently the sustainability of the boom will be questioned). The participation of amateur investors provides that guidepost, as it is analogous to the final stages of an epidemic (who else is left to be infected?).

The emergence of group order (and consensus) from seemingly chaotic individual efforts and beliefs was the second biological perspective introduced in Chapter 5. The behaviors of locusts, bees, and ants illustrated how swarm logic via silent leadership can lead to consensus and herdlike behavior. Although it probably goes without saying, such herd mentality increases the likelihood of rapid changes in sentiment (and therefore the prices in asset markets).

Tulipomania

As discussed in Chapter 6, a telltale indicator of the boom's unsustainable progression was found in the mass participation of "nobles, citizens, farmers, mechanics, seamen, footmen, maid-servants, even chimney sweeps and old clotheswomen"[6] in the tulip markets. Further, the involvement of prominent—and therefore seemingly knowledgeable—individuals in the market for tulips provided the impetus for beelike silent leadership of the speculating swarm.

The Great Depression

According to Allen, participation in the stock market in 1929 was characterized not only by professional and traditional investors, but also by "grocers, motormen, plumbers, seamstresses, and speakeasy waiters."[7] Allen goes on to note how the "Big Bull Market had become a national mania. . ... The speculative fever was infecting the whole country. Stories of fortunes being made overnight were on everybody's lips." If the entire population of potential investors was already active in the market, who else might be attracted to it so as to help propel it higher?

The silent leadership of seemingly informed individuals in leading the uninformed is perhaps best demonstrated by Yale professor Irving Fisher who is unfortunately[8] most remembered for noting that "stocks have reached what looks like a permanently high plateau" just weeks before the 1929 stock market crash. Further, the involvement of JP Morgan and others on the Thursday before the market crash helped bring a swarm of speculators "back to the honey" that afternoon.

The Japanese Boom and Bust

Once again, we find the relative maturity of the Japanese boom revealed quite blatantly in 1988 with a notation by the *Far Eastern Economic Review* that "stocks have become a national street-level preoccupation." The broad participation of Japanese housewives in the market also indicated that the universe of individuals yet to be infected had dramatically shrunk.

Further, the consensus-oriented nature of Japanese society led to a particular susceptibility to herd behavior. Combined with popular media such as the economy-focused comic book bestseller or the publication of *Japan as Number One*, the collectivist Japanese instincts were channeled into a herd focused exclusively on upside. Just as the dramatic shift from a long-term oriented savings-focused society into a collective of speculators demonstrated emergent group behavior, so too did the rapid dejection that ensued following the bust.

The Asian Financial Crisis

Although the epidemic model did not provide immediate or obvious stories to highlight the maturity of the boom, the opening of many capital markets to "hot money" or portfolio inflows might be seen as one extreme form of infection. If global risk appetites had clearly extended to the least developed economies of the world, how much greater might risk appetite grow?

As for herd behavior emanating from consensus beliefs, here too the Asian philosophical mind-set is a factor as it has been deemed to be more collectivist and consensus oriented than the individualistic Western models. If everyone else was borrowing in U.S. dollars, why shouldn't I? Further, collective confidence was surely bolstered by the publication of books such as the World Bank's *The East Asian Miracle.*

The most important form of herd behavior, however, might have originated from outside the region with the proliferation of emerging markets funds. By diversifying exposure to many countries in a common pool, managers would indiscriminately sell if one country suffered economic woes. Further, because emerging markets managers were compared against a common benchmark (such as the MSCI Emerging Markets Index), many behaved quite similarly in effectively replicating the index and mimicking each other. Emerging markets funds thus became an efficient mechanism through which the economic woes of one country were transmitted to others.

The U.S. Housing Boom and Bust

An epidemic interpretation of the U.S. housing boom logically begins with a focus on the quality of mortgages (i.e. prime vs. subprime). In the quest to "infect" more and more potential homeowners with mortgages, several financial innovations enabled the participation of a greater population of infectable individuals. Using this lens, subprime and other mortgages to individuals with poor credit history represent the epidemic equivalent of a very mature stage. The rapid rise of risky mortgages as a percentage of total mortgage lending, as shown in Chapter 10, provided powerful evidence that the pool of potential participants was being exhausted. After those with good and bad credit histories have mortgages, to whom else might a mortgage be sold? Further evidence of the boom's maturity was found in the boom in real estate salespeople.

From a consensus-oriented perspective, the political goals of broad homeownership were manifested into a common belief that everyone had a right to buy a home. Further, history suggested that home prices did not fall nationally and as such, money was to be made. Low interest rates provided a spectacular tailwind to this belief, and soon shows like "Flip This House" and "Flip That House" were popular on television. Magazine covers highlighted the ease with which real estate fortunes were being made, and the formerly bankrupt property mogul Donald Trump reemerged, this time writing bestselling books such as *How to Get Rich*.

Maturity and Consensus

Table 11.5 lists several indicators related to the biological lens. The table attempts to provide specific examples illustrating the evidence.

Table 11.5   Indicators of Emergence and Epidemics

Indicators	Examples
Amateur Investors	Chimney sweeps, old clotheswomen, grocers, motormen, plumbers, Japanese housewives, subprime borrowers
Silent Leadership	Pompeius de Angelis, JP Morgan, Irving Fisher
Popular Media	*Japan as Number One, The East Asian Miracle*, "Flip This House," "Flip That House"

Conclusions

There seems to be a great deal of overlap when it comes to the various signposts that telegraph an unsustainable boom. Table 11.6 summarizes the various indicators and their frequency. The shaded lines are deemed particularly important as those indicators were present in each of the studied cases.

Several preliminary conclusions emerge from this framework. First, although reflexive dynamics relating to confidence seem ever present, a reflexive dynamic between collateral values and access to credit seems particularly problematic. Thus, asset-based lending without regard to affordability is reminiscent of Minsky's Ponzi financing. Second, excessive money is a big warning sign as capital seeks a home. Combined with leverage-enhancing financial innovations and moral hazard, easy money creates a toxic combination of lofty asset prices and an unsustainable foundation.

Third, overconfidence in the form of "this time is different" and new era thinking seems consistently present and somehow provides a believability to the otherwise clear extremes. Conspicuous consumption in the form of trophy asset purchases and the world's tallest skyscraper seemed consistent as well. Fourth, policy distortion manifests itself in numerous ways, but most problematically in the belief that a meaningful fall in asset values or the failure of certain institutions is politically unacceptable. While such perspectives usually surface in excessive lending and risk-taking (i.e., easy money), regulatory shifts and the unintended consequences of tax policies also seem to exacerbate the likelihood of unsustainable

Table 11.6 Boombustology Road Map

	Tulipomania	Great Depression	Japanese Boom and Bust	Asian Financial Crisis	U.S. Housing Boom and Bust	#
Reflexive Dynamics						
Credit Criteria		X	X		X	3
Collateral/Credit	X	X	X	X	X	5
Hot Money	X			X		2
Leverage/Deflation						
Financial Innovation	X	X	X	X	X	5
Cheap / Excessive Money	X	X	X	X	X	5
Moral Hazard	X	X	X	X	X	5
Overconfidence						
Conspicuous Consumption	X	X	X	X	X	5
New-Era Thinking	X	X	X	X	X	5
Policy Distortion						
Supply/Demand Manipulation	X		X	X	X	4
Regulatory Shift	X	X	X		X	4
Consensus/Herd						
Amateur Investors	X	X	X	X	X	5
Silent Leadership	X	X	X	X	X	5
Popular Media			X	X	X	3

booms. Finally, the participation of amateur or marginal participants in an asset boom seems quite revelatory in determining the relative maturity of the boom and approaching bust. Silent leadership (either informed or uninformed) was consistently present with respect to forming consensus thinking and herd behavior, and popular media usually revealed this collective thinking.

The frequency data in Table 11.6 also provides additional insight into the relative importance of the indicators. Within the five lenses, leverage appears to be the most important, and should be weighted heavily in any analysis of forthcoming busts, for as noted by one of the most successful bubble hunters of all time, James Chanos, "Most of the time that there are bubbles that burst, they can be laid at the feet of excess credit creation."[9]

12

Boombustology in Action

IS CHINA NEXT?

There are two kinds of forecasters: Those who don't know and those who don't know they don't know.

—John Kenneth Galbraith

This chapter evaluates what appears to be a likely bubble in China. The term *likely* implies that a *Boombustology*-style, multiple lens analysis has led me to conclude that the odds of a bust in China are high. As I described in the Introduction, mysteries are inherently difficult to comprehend and understand, but probabilistic assessments of various outcomes can prove to be quite useful. This chapter uses the lenses discussed in Part I and the framework developed in Chapter 11 to gauge the probability of a Chinese bust.

Although China appears to be in the midst of an unsustainable boom, the timing of a bust is extraordinarily difficult to predict. One need only think of Gordon Chang's engaging and well-written, but early, book titled *The Coming Collapse of China* that was published in 2001. Since then, Chinese asset markets have boomed, yet many of Chang's arguments remain valid. Was Chang early or wrong? A common saying captures the treacherous nature of prediction: "Economists have predicted nine of the last five recessions." The fact that we live in such an uncertain world, however, does not imply that one cannot evaluate the probabilities of particular events transpiring. It merely means we cannot make predictions with virtual certainty.

Further, significant evidence is building that individuals are particularly poor at predicting or forecasting matters in their areas of expertise.[1] As an East Asian Studies major who once spoke Chinese well and worked at the U.S. Embassy in Beijing, it is with great trepidation, then, that I proceed with this chapter. Further hesitation comes from my acknowledgment that I too am human and suffer from the overconfidence that plagues all of us.

China is a booming economy that has been one of the world's fastest growing economies for years. Industrialization, urbanization, modernization, and entrepreneurship all appear to be on steroids in the world's most populous nation, resulting in what has become a relative consensus among global investors that China will continue growing at 8 percent for the foreseeable future, providing much needed support to the global economy.

By almost any metric, economic progress in China over the past several decades has been phenomenal. GDP per capita, literacy rates, health care, infant mortality, life expectancy, and national wealth have all improved remarkably. However, as the famous disclaimer reads on most mutual fund advertisements, "past performance is no guarantee of future performance," and indeed, this appears to be the case with respect to China's progress.

Many of the indicators highlighted in Chapter 11 are raising red flags. Reflexive dynamics seem underway, particularly between real estate prices and the credit supporting them. Money appears to be inappropriately cheap, with resulting overinvestment and capital misallocation. Returns on invested capital are falling. Confidence appears very lofty, with trophy-seeking behavior popping up in the art and wine markets. Construction of several of the world's largest skyscrapers is underway in China today. Let us not forget that China is also a communist state, with significant distortions to the price mechanism. Government-mandated lending and moral hazard appear rampant. Finally, many of the biologically-inspired indicators, such as amateur investor participation, silent leadership, and popular media attention, support the view of a Chinese bubble. Let us now evaluate these developments in greater detail via the lenses presented in Part I.

Tendencies toward Equilibrium

What dynamics have been driving the current Chinese boom and are they sustainable? Although it is impossible to provide a certain answer to this question, the discussion that follows suggests that cheap money has driven a massive credit-fueled investment boom that will eventually reverse. These dynamics do not appear likely to produce a stable equilibrium.

Perhaps the best indicator of a debt-fueled asset boom driven by reflexive tendencies is the simultaneous rise of debt levels with asset prices. Consider the following two charts taken from recent NBER research published in July 2010 about the property markets in China. Figure 12.1 shows outstanding loan balances in China, highlighting the massive growth in mortgage debt that has taken place over the past 10 years—with a particularly pronounced growth in mortgage lending over the 2007–2010 period. Likewise, Figure 12.2

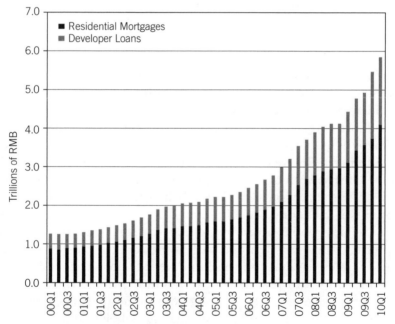

Figure 12.1   Outstanding Loans in China, 2000–2010

Source: Jing Wu, Joseph Gyourko, & Yongheng Deng, "Evaluating Conditions in Major Chinese Housing Markets," *NBER Working Paper Series,* Working Paper #16189 (Cambridge, MA: National Bureau of Economic Research, July 2010).

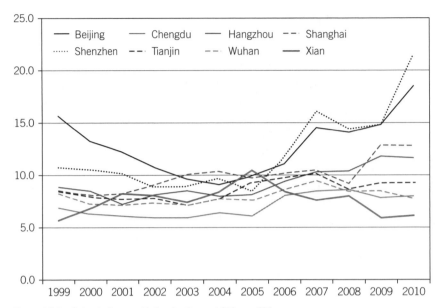

Figure 12.2   Price to Income Ratios for Several Chinese Cities

Source: Jing Wu, Joseph Gyourko, & Yongheng Deng, "Evaluating Conditions in Major Chinese Housing Markets," *NBER Working Paper Series,* Working Paper #16189 (Cambridge, MA: National Bureau of Economic Research, July 2010).

demonstrates what has occurred to property prices on a price to income basis. If a concomitant rise in both leverage and asset prices is evidence of a reflexive dynamic under way, then the data presented in these two figures suggests that China is in the midst of a reflexive debt-fueled housing boom.

Another reflexive dynamic that seems to be under way includes the belief that both the Chinese currency and land prices can only move in one direction—up. These beliefs have proven to be highly supportive, validating, and fulfilling of each other. Because both Chinese and global investors believe that the currency can only appreciate, there is a desire to park money in Chinese-denominated assets. Chinese capital controls limit the free flow of capital, leaving local investors with few viable investment destinations. As a result, many Chinese recycle their profits into domestic investments. See "Limited Options for Investing: Alternating Bubbles?"

Instead of parking excess capital in U.S. Treasuries, the Chinese have been finding yuan investments in which to leave their money.[2] However, the Chinese stock market bust in 2007–2008 was scarring to most Chinese speculators and drove them to the property market. The belief that property prices are unlikely to fall has its origins in China's rural economic roots. Not too long ago, China was a primarily agricultural country and land was the single most important asset. Land obsession is still a deep reality in today's Chinese culture.[3]

Signs of bubbly conditions in Chinese property seem ubiquitous. On one February day, a Shanghai investor purchased 54 apartments. Separately, a villa sold for more than US$30 million in late 2009. Even more spectacularly, the *New York Times* noted that developers in Tianjin "have created a $3 billion 'floating city,' a series of islands built on a natural reservoir, featuring villas, shopping malls, a water amusement park and what they say will be the world's largest indoor ski resort."[4] Andy Xiang, a Shanghai-based real estate investor, noted "the speed you buy a house here is faster than you buy vegetables."[5] In one case, more than 800 people lined up around a sports stadium—some waiting in a downpour for six hours or more—with the hope of purchasing one of the 220 units in a new Shanghai development.[6]

Further, if equilibrium-seeking dynamics were under way, it would be highly unlikely to see excess capacity and rising prices. In the land of mean-reverting, supply and demand–driven price equilibrium, it would be impossible to have empty apartments and rising apartment values. Yet that is precisely what we see in China. In addition to property prices rising rapidly (in some cases by 8–10 percent per month), there are reports of as many as 65 million urban electricity meters that are registering zero consumption over a recent six-month period of time.[7] Although Chinese authorities have tried to downplay such reports, anecdotal evidence of empty apartments has become commonplace. On the commercial property front, reports vary from the official vacancy statistic of around 22 percent to one local distressed investor's vacancy estimate of 50 percent.

Despite such high vacancy rates, hedge fund manager Jim Chanos believes that there was roughly 2.6 billion square meters (which equates to approximately 30 billion square feet) of nonresidential (i.e., office) real estate under construction in January 2010. In a speech he gave that same month at Oxford University, he noted, "There is a 5 foot by 5 foot office cubicle being built for every man, woman, and child in China." Needless to say, the equilibrium-seeking tendency of Chinese property markets seems to be temporarily suspended. When it does finally kick in and begin working, the mean reversion tendency and force will be violent and create a bust that has the potential to drag banks and the economy with it. Further, given the importance of Chinese construction in driving many commodity markets, there is a reasonable chance that such a bust will also drag with it many commodity producers and processors.

Leverage, Cheap Money, and Potential Deflation

The Mundell-Fleming model developed in the 1960s states that it is impossible for a country to simultaneously maintain a fixed exchange rate, independent monetary policy, and allow for free capital movement.[8] China has attempted to maintain a fixed exchange rate with the U.S. Dollar and also retain its monetary independence.

Limited Options for Investing: Alternating Bubbles?

Chinese laws, based on traditional beliefs that inflows into the country are good and outflows are bad, severely limit the overseas investment options available to wealthy Chinese citizens. As a result, two primary venues dominate Chinese thinking when the wealthy plan to invest: the domestic stock market and the domestic property market.

Given the relatively recent (it peaked in late 2007) and meaningful correction in the Chinese stock market, investors began to question the safety of the stock market. It is not surprising, then, that investor interest in property grew dramatically between 2007 and 2010.

Christina Larson of the New America Foundation noted that "stock markets in China are unstable and immature, and there are few tax incentives for philanthropy. As a result, the wealthiest in China are faced with a problem unimaginable a generation ago: what to do with their money."* For many, the answer is real estate, an asset that at least appears to be a store of value.

As the Chinese authorities work diligently to cool the property market, might they unwittingly be creating an unsustainable stock market boom? Although such a possibility is not to be ruled out, early details of the official 12th Five-Year Plan include a focus on creating options for Chinese citizens wishing to invest overseas. In early 2011, Wenzhou became the first Chinese city to allow individual residents to make direct overseas investments. According to Yuan Zhigang, dean of the Fudan University school of economics, "by allowing individuals to directly buy assets overseas, the government is creating a new channel to disperse excessive liquidity in the country, underlining the strong inflationary pressure the government faces this year."# Might the relaxing of capital controls spur the simultaneous deflation of both the Chinese property and stock markets?

* Christina Larson, "Bubble, Bubble, China's in Trouble: The Mad Scramble for Chinese Real Estate," *Foreign Policy* (May 2010).
# "Wenzhou tests individual DOI to cool inflation." *China Daily*, January 11, 2011, page 14.

Capital accounts are not freely convertible. Despite the allure of this approach, there is limited evidence supporting its success. As described by Sebastian Edwards, the Chief Economist for Latin America at the World Bank from 1993 to 1996, "the blunt fact is that capital controls are not only ineffective . . . but also breed corruption and inflate the costs of managing investment."[9]. In fact, the IMF's 2010 *Global Financial Stability Report* noted that capital "controls tend to lose effectiveness as market participants find ways to circumvent them . . . many studies find no effect of controls on the volume of inflows . . ."

By linking their currency to the U.S. dollar, the Chinese have effectively outsourced their monetary policy to the United States. The country can choose to manage either its currency (through interest rates and/or capital flows) or its interest rates, but not both. Attempting to manage both would create opportunities for arbitrage, which would rapidly eliminate the opportunity. So, although the pegged currency may have historically made sense, it no longer appears to do so. Historically, when the Chinese economy was very dependent on trade with the United States, the United States and Chinese economies were basically synchronized. If the U.S. economy was doing well, then so too did the Chinese economy, as U.S. imports of Chinese goods likely rose. If the U.S. economy was in the doldrums, then Chinese exports were likely down.

This synchronicity of the Chinese and U.S. economies meant that a common monetary policy worked and was logical. If the United States began to overheat as economic conditions created inflationary pressures, similar conditions would likely exist in China. The Federal Reserve would then probably raise interest rates, providing an appropriate monetary response to both countries. Likewise, if the U.S. economy was struggling, the Federal Reserve might lower interest rates in a bid to increase economic activity— providing appropriate medicine for two similarly sick patients. The system made sense. It worked. However, over time, China and the United States have become increasingly less interconnected as China has increased its trade with the rest of Asia and the world.

As the United States suffers through the worst economic slowdown it has endured since the Great Depression, the U.S. Federal Reserve has been issuing massive doses of economic adrenaline in the form of very stimulative monetary policies. Through the veins of a fixed exchange-rate system and a Chinese yuan that is pegged to the U.S. dollar, this adrenaline is being transmitted to the Chinese economy. The only problem is that the Chinese patient was not as dangerously ill as the United States economy was when the medicine was administered. The outcome is extraordinarily easy money in China (and for that matter, in all countries that either peg or manage their currency to the U.S. dollar). Thus, while the United States fights deflation and struggles to maintain low real interest rates, Chinese real rates are remarkably negative.

To understand why negative real interest rates are a recipe for an asset boom, one need only think of the fact that negative real rates mean that investors get paid to borrow from a bank and park the money in any asset that grows in nominal terms (i.e., an asset that has its price move with inflation). Accomplished hedge fund manager Jim Chanos recently highlighted the unsustainability of Chinese credit-fueled asset markets in an interview on financial news channel CNBC: "Bubbles are identified by credit excesses, not valuation excesses, and there's no bigger credit excess than in China."[10]

The sheer volume of lending in China is staggering. According to the BCA Research, "in the past two years, China's new credit creation has amounted to US$2.7 trillion—an amount equal to 4.4 percent of global GDP, or as much as the size of the U.S. credit expansion in the mid-2000s."[11] Hedge fund manager Hugh Hendry has noted that a majority of this lending has taken place since the beginning of 2009, highlighting that the $1.9 trillion of lending that took place between January 2009 and May 2010 (the first 16 months of the Chinese stimulus program) was bigger than the economies of South Korea, Taiwan, and Hong Kong—combined.[12]

Although Beijing has tried to slow the rate of credit growth during the second half of 2010 (with analysts applauding their recent success), recent research from Fitch indicates meaningful growth in a Chinese shadow banking industry has more than offset this supposed slowdown in credit growth. The report notes that recent inflationary pressures seem to have taken market participants by surprise, likely due to "the widespread misconception that the acceleration in lending in 2009 was a short-lived anomaly and that monetary conditions began to normalize in 2010."[13] The report goes on to concede that headline credit (i.e., bank lending) data points to a slowdown, but highlights that "actual credit flows in China remain as high as in 2009: lending has not moderated, it has merely found other channels."[14]

This scenario of massive credit flowing and easy money is precisely the foundation of an Austrian school prototypical unsustainable boom. Excess investment and overconsumption will result in too much capacity and an eventual bust. If money is inappropriately priced, it is likely to be inappropriately allocated. Peking University professor of finance Michael Pettis notes that "low interest rates (along with their cousin, socialized credit risk) are the main causes of capital misallocation and excess capacity in China."[15]

One manifestation of cheap money is the existence of inefficient enterprises. Consider recent analysis conducted by Hong Kong Institute for Monetary Research on the economic strength of China's state-owned-enterprises (SOEs). The authors note that their findings "show that if SOEs were to pay a market interest rate, their existing profits would be entirely wiped out."[16] For reference, it is thought that non-bank SOEs control more than 33 percent of China's assets[17] and have a disproportionately high impact on both labor and capital markets. The impact of "market interest rates" would have a devastating impact upon the Chinese economy.

The other obvious manifestation of excessively low interest rates is misallocation of capital. When thinking about overinvestment and the potential for a bust, the steel industry exemplifies overcapacity. According to Worldsteel, the trade group representing the global steel industry, Chinese steel production has grown from 23 million tons in 1977 to a run rate of approximately 650 million tons during the first half of 2010. This growth has taken the Chinese steel industry's share of global steel production from around 3 percent in 1977 to almost 50 percent by 2010.[18] Figure 12.3 summarizes the growth in reported Chinese production as well as Chinese steel's share of global production.

If we take a moment to break down the sources of demand for Chinese steel, one finds a potentially reflexive relationship with the property market described above. In fact, according to Bank of America/Merrill Lynch, 53 percent of all Chinese steel demand was for construction purposes.[19] Although such data is hard to come by, anecdotal evidence suggests that up to 20 percent of Chinese steel production is being used to construct more steel mills! Truly a reflexive dynamic if ever there was one.

Further, although the data regarding Chinese steel capacity is inconsistent across different sources, most believe that utilization has been running between 65 and 75 percent. For instance, the *Wall Street Journal* reported in 2009 that there existed 200 million tons of excess capacity[20], while UBS analysis conducted in early 2010 suggested there was about 175 million tons of excess capacity.[21] To put these numbers in context, 175 million tons of annual steel

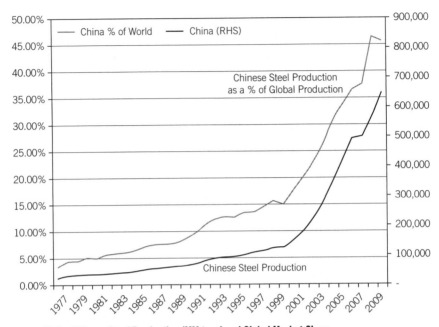

Figure 12.3   Chinese Steel Production (MM tons) and Global Market Share

Source: Steel Statistical Yearbooks, published by the International Iron and Steel Institute and Worldsteel Assocation; Yearbooks from 1980 through 2009 accessible via www.worldsteel.org.

production is more than the production of South Korea and Japan—combined! Steel does not appear to be an outlier; similar grandiose statistics can be found for the size of the Chinese cement (greater than the rest of the world, combined) and aluminum industries.[22]

Another example of unsustainable building can be found with the inner Mongolian district of Kangbashi, the urban center of Ordos City. Due to massive coal deposits in the area, Ordos is today the second wealthiest city (on a per capita basis) in China. Despite having a functioning (albeit somewhat less modern than ideal) downtown area, the government decided to utilize stimulus spending to build an entire new downtown area. The district, which is effectively completed, remains basically empty and uninhabited.

Thought by many to be a modern ghost town, *Time* magazine recently noted that Kangbashi is "filled with office towers, administrative centers, government buildings, museums, theaters, and sports fields—not to mention acre on acre of subdivisions overflowing with middle-class duplexes and bungalows. The only problem: the district was originally designed to house, support, and entertain 1 million people, yet hardly anyone lives there."[23] Firsthand accounts from recent visitors to the city are eerie: "Only a handful of cars drive down Kangbashi's multilane highways, a few government offices are open during the day and an occasional pedestrian, appearing like a hallucination, can be seen trudging down a sidewalk, like a lone survivor of some horror-movie apocalypse."[24]

Overinvestment in China has also been supported by financial innovations such as "local investment companies" and "local government funding vehicles" that have enabled municipalities to skirt around regulations designed to prevent them from accessing credit. According to recent research, outstanding debt in these vehicles (which appear off the balance sheets of Chinese banks) may be as high as $1.7 trillion, or almost 35 percent of China's GDP.[25] Most of this money, according to Northwestern professor Victor Shih, has likely channeled itself into local development projects, some of which seem unlikely to be economically viable. "A soccer stadium in the middle of nowhere is not going to generate much cash flow . . . and without massive central government subsidies, I think many of these projects will not generate enough cash even to pay interest on their loans."[26] Sounds like Minsky's Ponzi financing.

A final example of the overinvestment boom can be found with the South China Mall, labeled by Abu Dhabi's *The National* newspaper as the "Mall of Misfortune." Built in Southern China in what were agricultural lands as recently as 2003, the South China Mall is the largest mall in the world with the ability to accommodate ~1,500 businesses. The 7 million square foot complex was described by PBS as being "Disneyland, Las Vegas, and Mall of America rolled into one. There are carnival rides, mini-parks, canals and lakes amid classic Western-style buildings."[27] Although completed in 2005–2006, a PBS documentary noted in late 2009 that the mall had 10 or 12 operating tenants.[28] Originally planned to have 70,000 visitors a day, the mall has not come anywhere near achieving this objective. Paul Allen of Bloomberg visited the mall in early 2011 and described the scene as having "shuttered shops, never occupied by a single tenant, dusty escalators that lead to floor upon floor of emptiness . . ."[29] Despite these obvious problems, Kun Liu, president of the mall, noted that a further expansion is in the works, with more than 200,000 square meters (~2 million square feet) to be developed.[30]

When pondering how such a real estate failure might have taken place, Dick Groves, a retail consultant in Hong Kong, noted that, "When it's easy to get financing without having to convince

China's Growth: How Sustainable?

As eloquently described by Paul Krugman in his 1994 *Foreign Affairs* article titled "The Myth of Asia's Miracle," mobilization of resources cannot continue indefinitely. Growth derived from growth of inputs (capital and/or labor) is ultimately unsustainable as it eventually yields to diminishing returns. Economic growth slows, and the extrapolation of past input-driven growth trends are rapidly deemed inaccurate. Might China's past growth have been based on such input-driven growth?

Let us begin by evaluating what has been happening vis-à-vis capital in China. The best measure of capital-derived growth is a country's investment rates. The following chart demonstrates that China's fixed asset investment (as a percentage of GDP) over the past 15 years has surged. Clearly, growth in capital has been an important contributor to Chinese growth. Unfortunately, such investment only provides one-time gains to GDP growth leading to an ever-increasing appetite to invest. MIT professor Yasheng Huang describes this reality as "Beijing's addiction to investment-driven growth."* How likely is it that such investment-driven growth can continue without the creation of growth-limiting (or bust-inducing) overcapacity?

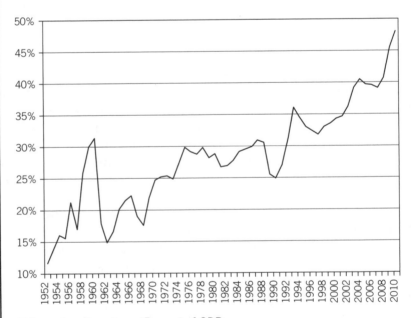

Chinese Investment as a Percent of GDP
Source: CEIC

When it comes to labor, the outlook is not much better. According to Bijal Shah, the urban labor force grew at an annualized 7.5 percent annual rate between 2000 and 2010.[†] A major driver of this growth in labor was migration-driven urbanization. How likely is it that this migration process will continue at the same rate? *The Economist* analyzed the demographics of Qilin, a rural town about 38 miles northwest of Chongqing. By 2007, urban opportunities had drawn many from Qilin; "those left behind are mostly school-age children and the middle-aged and elderly, who would have little chance of finding jobs in urban areas."[‡] Shah's research highlights that the number of 15–24-year-olds—those most likely to migrate—is falling from 230 million to 180 million between 2010 and 2015. Given the high percentage of this population that has already moved to cities, demographic realities and continued high migration rates are very likely to be incompatible.

Evidence also exists that China may be more urbanized than commonly believed. Although China is approximately 50 percent urbanized, this statistic is based upon a Chinese definition of an "urban center" as an area with population density of at least 1,500 people per square kilometer. According to such standards, Houston, TX (the fourth largest city in America with a population of more than 2.2 million) would not qualify as a city! Using Chinese definitions, the United States has a very compelling urbanization opportunity. More likely, however, is the reality that China is more urbanized than thought.

Such data on the outlook for continued growth of capital and labor led recent research presented in the *Journal of Chinese Economic and Business Studies* to bluntly conclude that "growth in China has largely been driven by factor inputs."[§] Such growth is ultimately unsustainable. As analysts work diligently to estimate future Chinese economic growth, might they be overestimating such growth because the origins of historical growth were heavily influenced by growth of inputs? Might the Chinese growth story be less sustainable than widely believed?

[*] Yasheng Huang, "Chinomics: The Fallacy of the Beijing Consensus," *The Wall Street Journal* (June 19, 2010).

[†] Bijal Shah, "Why China's Growth Rate May Halve," *Cycles Strategy*, MainFirst Bank AG research report (October 8, 2010).

[‡] "China's Chicago: A Giant City in the Southwest Is a Microcosm of China's Struggle to Move Millions from Rural to Urban Areas," *The Economist* (July 26, 2007).

[§] Yanrui Wu, "The Role of Productivity in China's Growth: New Estimates," *Journal of Chinese Economic and Business Studies* (Vol 6, No 2, May 2008).

someone of the project's feasibility, and without having to show preleasing commitment, you can start to get into trouble."[31] PBS captured the essence of the South China Mall story by describing it as "a cautionary tale of capitalist hubris."[32] Just in case you might think the South China Mall is a one-off example, consider the fact that more than 500 new malls have been built in China in the last five years, according to the Mall China Information Center.

Recent academic work has connected the overinvestment that is generated by cheap money—examples of which were just shared in this section—with overconfidence. In a recent study of Chinese companies, researchers found that overconfident managers overinvested, particularly when there was easy money.[33] Let us now turn to other indicators of overconfidence, namely conspicuous consumption.

Conspicuous Consumption and Overconfidence

The *New York Times* noted in April 2010 that Chinese influence on the art market was rising rapidly, analogizing China's soaring financial power and impact on the art markets to "a hurricane carrying off all that lies in its path."[34] Although the article focused primarily on the Chinese influence on Chinese art, the implications for the global art market were soon felt in New York. *China Daily* noted on May 24, 2010, that "the art world is at fever pitch after an anonymous telephone bidder, now believed to be Chinese, paid a world record $106.4 million for a work by Pablo Picasso at a Christie's sale in New York earlier this month."[35]

In case you think this purchase might be a random, one-time event, consider recent comments by Ken Yeh, chairman of Christie's Asia, noting that "China's billionaire art buyers are creating something of an electric atmosphere in the art world."[36] Yeh highlighted that the surge in Chinese interest has been noted by up to 20 buyers who have suddenly embarked on a mission to buy Western art. Traditional buyers have noted this newfound buying pressure, finding it frustrating when seeking to purchase art. Morgan Long, head of art services at The Fine Art Fund, noted that funds "have come across frantic bidding from people from the Chinese mainland. We haven't been able to buy anything we wanted at the prices we were looking for."[37]

A November 2010 auction held in London captured the electricity of the Chinese art appetite quite well. An 18th century vase, dating from the period of emperor Qianlong, which had been found in a dusty old attic, was purchased at auction for $70 million by a buyer from mainland China.[38]

A similar appetite seems to be forming with respect to Chinese desires for wine.[39] During an October 2010 wine auction, three bottles of Chateau Lafite's 1869 were sold for the record-setting price of US$230,000 per bottle (more than 30 times pre-auction estimates) to an undisclosed Asian buyer. Immediately following the sale, however, Sotheby's head of international wine Serena Sutcliffe highlighted that "there's a lot of speculation why the Chinese like Lafite so much," revealing the buyer's nationality as Chinese.[40]

Might speculative juices in China be constrained to the art and wine markets? Evidence from a host of other markets suggests not. Consider the fact that the best performing commodity in China in 2009 was garlic. As noted by *The Guardian*, "it is tastier than property, more pungent than gold, and rising in value faster than either. An astonishing market surge has seen Chinese speculators pile into garlic deals, causing prices to rocket between 10- and 30-fold in the last 18 months."[41] Rare teas have been equally exciting to Chinese speculators. Dahongpao tea, grown only in a small mountainous region of Fujian province, is a noteworthy case. Prices for Dahongpao tea have risen more than tenfold between 2009 and 2010 and recent prices have approached £1,000 per kilogram.[42] Or consider the fact that "mutton fat" jade, so named for its marbled white appearance, now sells for more than $3,000 per ounce, more than double the price of gold. This represents a ten-fold increase from a decade ago, for "rocks" that had 20 years ago been used to fill sandbags to control flood waters![43] Finally, in early 2011, a Chinese buyer paid $200,000 for a racing pigeon (a world record) at a Belgium auction. The bird, named "Blue Prince," was one of 218 birds that fetched $1.8 million at the auction.[44]

Perhaps the Chinese fascination with art, wine, jade, garlic, tea, and pigeons is a coincidental phenomenon with no relation to national overconfidence and/or conspicuous consumption. Although definitely possible, consider Chinese buying intentions recently in professional sports. In early August 2010, it was reported that the $200bn+ China Investment Corporation, the government's overseas investment vehicle, was behind a bid to buy Liverpool Football Club.[45] Further, in 2009, the Chinese were reported to have purchased a minority stake in the Cavaliers Operating Company, the corporate entity that owns the Cleveland Cavaliers and operates the Quicken Loans Arena.[46]

Trophy asset purchases have been done more discreetly with use of intermediaries such as private equity firms, state-owned enterprises, and other indirect methods under the umbrella of state capitalism. Perhaps as a reaction to the public relations nightmare of China National Offshore Oil Company's (CNOOC) attempted purchase of Unocal, the Chinese have opted to interface with trophy assets on a more discreet basis. Consider the fact that Chinese entities currently own Volvo (purchased from Ford) and a large stake in Blackstone, the successful U.S. investment firm.

Although overinvestment (see preceding section) is a telltale sign of managerial overconfidence, Chinese confidence can be reflexively validated into overconfidence through popular media noting "it's different this time" or by announcing the arrival of a new era. It is precisely with this logic that Martin Jacques's well-written, thoroughly researched, and thought-provoking book *When China Rules the World* is so concerning. By providing a believable story as to why it's different this time and how we are about to embark on a "changing of global leadership," the book has a very "toppy" feel to it and is eerily reminiscent of *Japan as Number One*.

A final indicator of (over)confidence and easy money coming together in a potentially unsustainable manner can be found by looking at our skyscraper indicator. Although surpassing the Burj Dubai is an unlikely event in the near future, a simple look at the world's tallest buildings currently under construction provides insight into where speculative juices are flowing, credit is easy, and confidence is high. According to Skyscraperpage.com, 5 of the 10 largest buildings under construction as of this writing are in China.[47] By 2015, Chinese skyscrapers will occupy spots #2, 3, 5, 9, and 10 of the top 10 tallest buildings in the world.[48]

Rights, Moral Hazard, and Political Distortion

Charles Goodhart, former advisor to the Bank of England and Emeritus Professor at the London School of Economics, has noted that economic indicators lose their informational content if used as a target of economic policy. Known as "Goodhart's law," this perspective captures one of the primary problems in China today. Whereas GDP had historically been a useful indicator (i.e., it was an outcome of economic activity), it has now become a policy target subject to manipulation in the quest to achieve the "number." Economic activity no longer drives GDP; rather, GDP drives economic activity.

What might the impact of "GDP targeting" be upon economic activity? Consider the fact that government-mandated lending has driven local governments to demolish usable roads and dynamite functioning bridges in a quest to develop projects through which to deploy investment dollars and generate GDP.[49] These actions, while illogical to most observers, actually make a great deal of sense from the perspective of incentives at the local level—not only does the creation of new infrastructure generate economic activity (i.e., GDP), but so too does the act of destruction! Given that local officials are often evaluated on GDP growth in their geography, such infrastructure destruction and re-creation might also accelerate one's climb up the communist party's ladder.

The tension between local objectives of rapid growth and the national desire for sustainability of growth has recently resulted in Beijing pronouncements asking the provinces to "slow down." In early January 2011, Zhang Ping, director of the National Development and Reform Commission, asked China's provinces to lower growth targets and to consider environmental impacts. Stratfor analysts noted that "the top technicians in control of the country's financial system face the dilemma of making forceful demands to slow the economy at the risk of driving it into the ground—or continuing with small adjustments and thereby revealing their weak will and emboldening the provincial warlords."[50] Further, the analysts note that "the provinces show no self-restraint because they are profiting from the easy credit and endless economic boom . . ."[51]

In his provocative book *The Next 100 Years: A Forecast for the 21st Century*, George Friedman of Stratfor notes China may be a paper tiger by the year 2020. One of his central arguments rests on the contradiction of the political reality (communist, centrally managed) with the economic perception (market oriented), and the enormous misallocation of capital that may be taking place:

> China appears to be a capitalist society with private property, banks, and all the other accoutrements of capitalism. But it is not truly capitalist in the sense that the markets do not determine capital allocation. Who you know counts for much more than whether you have a good business plan. Between Asian systems of family and social ties and the communist systems of political

relationships, loans have been given out for a host of reasons, none of them having much to do with the merits of the business. As a result, not surprisingly, a remarkably large number of these loans have gone bad—"nonperforming" in the jargon of banking. The amount is estimated at somewhere between $600 billion and $900 billion, or between a quarter and a third of China's GDP, a staggering amount.[52]

How might this have occurred? As our study of previous booms and busts found, moral hazard and a belief in government backing often leads to significant confidence on the part of depositors, with a correspondingly robust confidence manifested within banks through brisk and voluminous lending. When thinking about the presence of moral hazard in China and its banking system, one need only stop to think about the all-powerful role of the government in terms of owning, running, and regulating most of the large financial institutions in the country. In addition, the communist, top-down approach to managing most matters implies not only that traditional moral hazard (i.e., depositors willing to give their money to any bank, confident that the government will protect them in the event of a bank failure) exists, but one might go so far as to suggest the Chinese system creates moral hazard on steroids.

In addition to de facto deposit insurance that banks need not pay a premium for, the China Banking Regulatory Commission also imposes several constraints (such as a capital adequacy ratio, a debt–assets ratio, and limitations on nonperforming loans) on Chinese banks intended to ensure their safety, liquidity, and so forth. Further, regulators visit, audit, and monitor banks to ensure banks are in compliance with these requirements.

Northwestern University professor Victor Shih notes the implicit deposit guarantee and "intrusive regulations make the system less secure, not more."[53] Shih notes, "Profits from risky behavior can be so high that banks are willing to share some of the spoils with corrupt regulators who can help them circumvent bothersome rules." He then follows up his argument with recent examples involving corruption related to lending practices; in one case, bankers bribed police to arrest auditors investigating a bank's books, and in another case, the vice president of a large commercial bank was convicted of receiving bribes to grant loans against lending policies and regulations.

Noting that such behavior is tougher to pull off in states with a free media, independent judiciary, and rule of law, Shih concludes that "small crises are not allowed to emerge to inform the public of accumulating systemic risks," thereby allowing the covert building of large problems.

In addition to such politically motivated bank lending and the moral hazard that accompanies it, even the casual observer of Chinese property markets cannot help but be overwhelmed by the magnitude of policy intervention that affects supply and demand dynamics. Just over the past 10 years, for instance, property-related policy objectives in China have shifted from stimulating demand (1998–1999) to stabilizing supply (2002–2004) to suppressing demand (2005–2007) to simulating demand (2008) to suppressing demand (2009–2010).[54] For instance, in 1998, housing reform allowed for the transfer of property-use rights to non-government entities and individuals, and to stimulate demand, in 1999 mortgages with a 30-year term were introduced and down payment requirements lowered from 30 to 20 percent. By 2005, however, the required down payment was raised back to 30 percent and lending rates rose six times in 2007 alone. However, by the time the global economy began slowing in 2008, the Chinese authorities felt the need to lower the down payment requirement to 20 percent again, as well as to reduce property transaction-related taxes.

Lots of policies have been implemented since 2010 in an effort to control the property market, including policy restrictions on developers, limitations on banks' lending to the sector, and so forth. Even within the realm of down payment mandates, households purchasing property of greater than 90 sq. meters (~1000 square feet) must put down at least 30 percent, and those purchasing a second home need to put down at least 50 percent. Further, in an effective acknowledgment of extraordinary speculative interest, Chinese authorities stated that mortgages would not be allowed for the purchase of third homes in certain geographies.[55] Third homes! The People's Bank of China also raised the deposit reserve ratio multiple times to cool lending activities, and nonlocal (i.e., foreign) participation in the property market was prohibited.[56] In an additional effort to cool property markets, Beijing telegraphed that it plans to introduce property taxes in 2011 to curb speculative buying.[57]

In aggregate, the government's multiple means of attempting to restrict speculation in the property market has led Deutsche Bank's chief China economist Jun Ma to note that these actions were driven by "strong public discontent with housing affordability" and in aggregate, the cooling measures are "the most draconian in history."[58]

Consensus, Silent Leadership, and Epidemics

Like most Asian cultures and most Asian nations, China comprises a quite homogenous group of people. Although variations exist, most citizens are Han Chinese and think of themselves as similar. Asian cultural values are still said to be quite consensus-oriented and tend to shun individualistic behavior or accomplishment. As noted in the case studies presented in Chapters 8 and 9, a social harmony–seeking, consensus-oriented society is one that is particularly prone to swarm and herd behavior.

China's stock market, effectively closed to foreign investors by regulatory mandates, has more investors than any other market in the world. There are more than 124 million brokerage accounts.[59] Former Morgan Stanley chief economist Andy Xie, now a fund manager in Shanghai, has noted how prevalent the stock market has become as a topic of conversation among ordinary Chinese citizens. In one conversation with a bartender, Xie found that his bartender was convinced that the Communist party would make sure that the Shanghai market would rise to over 8,000 points (it was 2,600 at the time) in the next five years. The logic was as revealing as the conviction expressed: "Look, the Hong Kong market is at 20,000 . . . Shanghai at 8,000 would be very reasonable." It is worth noting, however, that because of the relatively recent (2007–2008) stock market bust in China, investors still recall the possibility of prices falling. When it comes to real estate and property prices, however, the Chinese seem not to be seriously entertaining the idea that prices can meaningfully fall.

An August 2010 cover story of *Bloomberg Markets* magazine profiled Zhang Xin, the billionaire real estate developer who founded Soho China, one of the country's most successful real estate companies. The essence of her message: "I don't see any bubbles. . . . The next few months will be a fantastic time to buy."[60] If knowledgeable investors such as she are bullish on Chinese real estate, surely the uninformed will consider deferring to her judgment. In this way, large groups of investors can be led as a swarm into buying assets at perhaps exactly the wrong time. In addition to specialized media such as Bloomberg providing high-profile, consensus-generating stories, the publishing of popular media such as the Martin Jacques book can have a substantial effect on directing consensus beliefs. Perhaps the countrywide real estate obsession is driven by the fact that few Chinese real estate investors have experienced a bust. Might this collective (lack of) experience generate a herdlike behavior among the inexperienced?

It should come as no surprise, then, that with such silent leadership, speculative juices in the property market are flowing in full force. For instance, Xie notes the preponderance of housemaids running out and buying property. As noted above, Beijing took notice of the massive property price escalation across major cities and has dramatically increased regulations against those purchasing second (as well as third!) homes. Throughout the country, individuals seem to have developed an earnest belief that property is a safe bet. If housemaids are now real estate speculators, an epidemic lens might suggest that the disease is very close to having maximum infection. Might the real estate speculative frenzy be approaching its final hours?

Perhaps more concerning, however, than the "property is a sure thing" belief on the part of individual investors is the "property is a sure thing" belief on the part of large, state-owned businesses in mundane industrial sectors. The *New York Times* reported in August 2010 that approximately 82 percent of all land auctions in Beijing have been won by big state-owned companies outbidding private real estate developers.[61] Further, research from the National Bureau of Economic Research published in July 2010 suggests that Beijing may be among the frothiest of China's real estate markets. Between 2003 and the first quarter of 2010, Beijing real estate prices rose between 350 and 900 percent.[62]

Defense equipment manufacturers, salt miners, railway groups, oil companies, chemical processers, shipbuilders, and telecom companies are all active in the property development business—industrial activity that seems eerily similar to that of Japanese corporations in the late 1980s. Anhui Salt Industry Corporation is currently developing Platinum Bay, a complex of luxury high-rise apartment condominiums. China Ordinance Group, a defense contractor, recently paid $260 million for land upon which it plans to build a residential and retail development. Sino Ocean, a large state-owned shipbuilder, recently paid $1.3 billion in December 2009 and March 2010 for land in Beijing upon which to build residential communities.

Su Chuanbo, marketing manager for Anhui Salt's Platinum Bay development, suggested in the *New York Times* that the central government had been encouraging state-owned enterprises to become more profitable. Given that real estate development was "incredibly lucrative," he implied it was quite logical for them to be entering such an attractive business.[63]

The government has recently taken notice of this phenomenon, with the State Assets Supervision and Administration Commission ordering 78 companies to dispose of or spin off their real estate divisions. Despite these efforts, experts believe that more than 90 of the 125 state-owned companies entirely under Beijing's control still have actively operating real estate efforts.[64] Considering these facts via an epidemic lens is quite concerning: industrial companies are entering the real estate development business, developers are rapidly producing significant supply, and housemaids have already bought properties. Who might be left to purchase more real estate?.

Finally, in a reflection of the national obsession with real estate, a TV series called "Snail House" airing on many major stations became "the hottest primetime soap opera in China."[65] The primary theme of the show: real estate and the burdens of rapidly rising prices on a young family.[66] In a story titled "The Soap Opera of China's Housing Boom," *The Financial Times* provided a quick summary:

> The most talked-about television programme in China at the moment is a soap opera called *Snail House*, which offers the viewer sex, corruption, and political intrigue. Really, however, it is about house prices. One character becomes the mistress of a party official to help her buy a flat, while another young couple struggles unsuccessfully to raise the deposit for an apartment in a city that looks suspiciously like Shanghai. . .[67]

Given the immense popularity of the show and the potential it had to create social unrest, Chinese authorities took it off the air at the end of 2009[68]—thereby providing strong confirmatory evidence

for the thesis that the housing frenzy had infected a large percentage of the population.

The Unsustainable Chinese Story

As indicated at the outset of this chapter, making predictions about the *timing* of a boom turning into a bust is inherently risky business. It is impossible be certain exactly when a boom will bust. However, as noted by fund manager and bubbleologist Jeremy Grantham, "In dealing with the soft sciences of economics and finance, certainty is too high a hurdle."[69] With this spirit in mind, this chapter applied the *Boombustology* framework to one of the most important investment questions of today: Is the Chinese boom sustainable? Given data available at the time of this writing, the odds point to "No!" Table 12.1 summarizes the findings of this chapter.

According to historian Edward Chancellor, "China's real estate market, and indeed its economy and financial system, have been shaped by a belief that past rates of economic growth will continue into the future. This assumption justifies more investment, which spurs the growth, leading to more investment . . . China has become a field of dreams; a build-and-they-will-come economy."[70]

When China decelerates, the ramifications on both China and the global economy are likely to be quite dramatic. Noting the difficulty of converting an investment-oriented economy to one driven by consumption, Michael Pettis stated "the world needs to prepare itself for a decade during which, if all goes well, China grows at a still respectable but much lower rate of 5–7 percent."[71] *Bloomberg* columnist William Pesek notes that "for a nation at China's level

Table 12.1   Troubling Indicators Point to a Forthcoming China Bust

	China	Notes
Reflexive Dynamics		
Credit Criteria	X	Stimulus-induced/mandated lending
Collateral/Credit	X	Concomitant rise in property prices and credit
Hot Money		Universal expectations of rising currency, offset by capital controls
Leverage/Deflation		
Financial Innovation	X	Local government funding vehicles to allow municipalities to borrow for development
Cheap / Excessive Money	X	Negative real interest rates
Moral Hazard	X	State-owned banks, mandated lending
Overconfidence		
Conspicuous Consumption	X	Art, wine, jade, garlic, pigeons, world's tallest skyscrapers under construction
New-Era Belief	X	Economic champion status, *When China Takes Over the World*
Policy Distortion		
Supply / Demand Manipulation	X	Supply of bank loans mandated by the state and controlled by regulatory fiat
Regulatory Shift	X	Down payment requirements, mandates that developers pay 50% of land prices up front
Consensus / Herd		
Amateur Investors	X	Bartender chitchat, maids buying real estate, state-owned enterprise activity in real estate
Silent Leadership	X	*Bloomberg Markets* story about Soho China developer
Popular Media	X	"Snail House" as prime-time TV hit

of development, 5 percent growth is crisis territory. The chances of social unrest would explode . . . putting the onus on the government to take drastic measures to boost growth."[72]

Given these facts, it should come as no surprise that Vitaliy Katsenelson has compared the Chinese economy to the runaway bus in the movie *Speed*.[73] Just as the movie's bus needs to maintain a certain speed to prevent the explosion of an on-board bomb, so too must China continue growing at high single digit rates to prevent social unrest,[74] an explosion in bad loans, and potentially destructive debt-deflation driven by overcapacity.

With respect to the impact on the external world, consider the interconnections that China has developed with the rest of Asia through increased regional trade, or the impact that Chinese development has had on commodities markets. A material slowdown in China would have massive implications for the economies of Australia, Indonesia, Russia, Brazil, Canada, Norway, South Africa, and other nations that generate a large percentage of their economic activity and growth from feeding the Chinese growth machine.

Further, in a balance sheet–constrained world in which developed countries struggle to generate meaningful economic growth, a Chinese bust is the equivalent of the sole locomotive pulling the global economic train breaking down, or worse yet, derailing. The magnitude of the impact alone necessitates careful and continued vigilance, even if timing the bust exactly is not possible. At the very least, one should understand that the *Boombustology* seismograph is generating significant activity. Simply knowing a quake is forthcoming will hopefully help you navigate its arrival.

Hedgehogs, Foxes, and the Dangers of Making Predictions

The fox knows many things, but the hedgehog knows one big thing.
Archilochos

Within the fragments of ancient Greek poetry found among archaeological remnants was the short but insightful line by the poet Archilochos, quoted above.[1] In the 2,700 or so years since those words were written, the distinction between foxes and hedgehogs has been used countless times, perhaps made most recently famous by Isaiah Berlin's entertaining essay titled "The Hedgehog and the Fox," which was written in 1953.

Berlin expands on the ancient Greek poet's insight to develop the difference between the ideological hedgehog and generalist fox:

There exists a great chasm between those, on one side, [the hedgehogs] who relate everything to a single central vision, one system, less or more coherent or articulate, in terms of which they understand, think and feel—a single, universal, organizing principle in terms of which alone all that they are and say has significance—and, on the other side, those [the

foxes] who pursue many ends, often unrelated and even contradictory, connected, if at all, only in some de facto way, for
some psychological or physiological cause, related by no moral
or aesthetic principle.[2]

The basic underlying logic of *Boombustology* has been that, when
it comes to spotting financial bubbles before they burst, it is better
to be a fox. Foxes are more suited to attack mysteries. Hedgehogs,
with their depth of understanding, are more effective in solving
puzzles.

Ultimately, one adopts a framework for thinking about uncertain
future events in the hope that one might be able to gain insight into
the probabilities of various scenarios. Is there any way to tell if foxes
are genuinely better than hedgehogs in making predictions? Actually,
recent research conducted by Philip Tetlock does just that. Tetlock
conducted a 20+ year study of 284 professional forecasters and asked
them to predict the probability of various occurrences both within
and outside of their areas of expertise. By 2003, Tetlock had accumulated data on more than 80,000 forecasts.

The results indicate that experts are less accurate predictors
than nonexperts vis-à-vis predictions in their area of expertise.[3] Two
members of the faculty at The Wharton School note that this finding "assaults common sense with evidence."[4] Tetlock himself uses
the language of hedgehogs and foxes to summarize his results:

> If we want realistic odds on what will happen next, coupled
> with a willingness to admit mistakes, we are better off turning
> to experts who embody the intellectual traits of Isaiah Berlin's
> prototypical fox—those who "know many little things," draw
> from an eclectic array of traditions, and accept ambiguity and
> contradiction as inevitable features of life—than we are turning
> to Berlin's hedgehogs—those who "know one big thing," toil
> devotedly within one tradition, and reach for formulaic solu-
> tions to ill-defined problems.[5]

Tetlock's conclusion that those with the ability to incorporate
new information, to update their beliefs, and to adapt to a changing reality by employing multiple perspectives are better predictors
provides strong support for the *Boombustology* approach.

The frameworks presented in this book are explicitly designed to avoid the "one big thing" approach and to generate a "many little things" approach. Idealogical reliance on any single lens might prove, as suggested by Tetlock, detrimental to one's ability to navigate uncertain, vague, or poorly-defined situations. The multidisciplinary approach presented in this book mitigates the likelihood of falling into the "hedgehog trap."

The five-lens methodology of identifying bubbles before they burst is built on the philosophical foundations of liberal education. Richard Levin, president of Yale University, noted that "it is not subject-specific knowledge but the ability to assimilate new information and solve problems that is the most important characteristic of a well-educated person."[6] He goes on to explain the rationale for this belief: "The logic behind this approach is that exposing students to multiple disciplines gives them alternative perspectives on the world, which prepares them for new and unexpected problems."[7] Given that few financial bubbles are "expected" or are certain, a liberal arts approach is ideally suited to thinking about such ambiguous developments.

As you utilize the frameworks presented in this book, remember that the only thing that appears certain is uncertainty. Remember that the dynamic, interconnected world in which we live is likely to present situations that transcend the tools provided by single disciplinary lenses. Remember that there are inherent differences between puzzles and mysteries. Last, but not least, remember that despite the allure of "it's different this time" explanations, it's usually *not* different.

Notes

Introduction The Study of Financial Extremes

1. Some U.S. senators suggested that the fact that the CIA had missed the implosion of the Soviet Union had cost U.S. taxpayers hundreds of millions of dollars in unnecessary military expenditures that could have been used for other purposes. This was reason enough, they claimed, to fold the CIA into the State Department.
2. Gregory F. Treverton, "Risks and Riddles." *Smithsonian Magazine* (June 2007).
3. Joseph Nye, "Peering into the Future," *Foreign Affairs* (July/August 1994).
4. Ibid.
5. Ibid.
6. Malcolm Gladwell, "Open Secrets: Enron, Intelligence, and the Perils of Too Much Information," *The New Yorker* (January 2007).

Chapter 1 Microeconomic Perspectives

1. Adam Smith, *The Wealth of Nations*, Book IV, Chapter II, Paragraph IX, Accessed via http://www.econlib.org/library/smith/smWN.html
2. Paul Samuelson, *Economics: An Introductory Analysis* (New York: McGraw Hill, 1967).
3. Justin Fox, *The Myth of the Rational Market* (New York: HarperCollins, 2009), xiii.
4. The dissertation was eventually published; see Davis and Etheridge, *Louis Bachelier's Theory of $peculation: The Origins of Modern Finance* (Princeton: Princeton University Press, 2006).
5. Eugene Fama, "Efficient Capital Markets: A Review of Theory and Empirical Work" (paper presented at the 28th annual meeting of the American Finance Association in New York City, December 28–30, 1969). The paper was later published in the *Journal of Finance* 25, no. 2 (May 1970).
6. Eugene Fama, "Efficient Capital Markets: A Review of Theory and Empirical Work," *Journal of Finance* 25, no. 2 (May 1970).
7. Ibid.
8. Justin Fox, *The Myth of the Rational Market* (New York: HarperCollins, 2009), xiv.
9. The Sveriges Riksbank Prize in Economic Sciences in Memory of Alfred Nobel; accessed via http://nobelprize.org/nobel_prizes/economics/laureates/1997/
10. Roger Lowenstein, *When Genius Failed: The Rise and Fall of Long-Term Capital Management* (New York: Random House, 2000); Robert Rubin et al., "Hedge

Funds, Leverage, and the Lessons of Long-Term Capital Management: Report of The President's Working Group on Financial Markets," published on April 28, 1999; accessed via www.ustreas.gov/press/releases/reports/hedgefund.pdf.

11. Peter Coy and Suzanne Woolley, "Failed Wizards of Wall Street," *BusinessWeek* (September 21, 1998).

12. Michael Lewis, "How the Eggheads Cracked," *New York Times Magazine* (January 24, 1999).

13. Ibid.

14. Raj Patel, *The Value of Nothing: How to Reshape Market Society and Redefine Democracy* (New York: Picador, 2009) 4.

15. As quoted by Representative Henry Waxman during Alan Greenspan's testimony to the Government Oversight Committee, October 23, 2008.

16. Alan Greenspan, testimony to the Government Oversight Committee, October 23, 2008.

17. Ibid.

18. Karl Popper, *The Open Society and Its Enemies* (Princeton: Princeton University Press, 1971).

19. George Soros, Speech given to the MIT Department of Economics World Economy Laboratory Conference in Washington, DC, April 26, 1994.

20. Ibid.

21. George Soros, *The Soros Lectures at the Central European University* (New York: Public Affairs, 2010).

22. George Soros, speech given to the MIT Department of Economics World Economy Laboratory Conference in Washington, DC, April 26, 1994.

23. George Soros, testimony before the U.S. House Banking Committee, April 13, 1994.

24. George Soros, testimony before the U.S. House of Representatives Committee on Oversight and Government Reform, November 13, 2008.

25. George Soros, *The Crisis of Global Capitalism: Open Society Endangered* (New York: Public Affairs, 1998).

26. Andrew Cave, "'I got it wrong' on collapse of global capitalism, says Soros." *The Telegraph* (February 23, 2001).

27. George Soros, testimony before the U.S. House of Representatives Committee on Oversight and Government Reform, November 13, 2008.

28. In the language of professional economists, such instability is endogenously generated and does not require any exogenous shock to be created.

Chapter 2 Macroeconomic Perspectives

1. Paul A. McCulley, "The Shadow Banking System and Hyman Minsky's Economic Journey," *PIMCO's Global Central Bank Focus* (May 2009).

2. George Cooper, *The Origin of Financial Crises: Central Banks, Credit Bubbles, and the Efficient Market Fallacy* (New York: Vintage Books, 2008).

3. Please note that by naming my aggressive borrowers the "Carefree Carrolls," I am in no way attempting to diminish the role of aggressive lenders that convince unsuspecting borrowers into assuming more debt than might be

prudent. In fact, one could easily replace the "Carefree Carrolls" with the "Duped Daltons" in this chapter.

4. Stephen Mihm, "Why Capitalism Fails," *The Boston Globe* (September 13, 2009).
5. In fact, in a collection of his essays was titled *Can IT Happen Again?* *Boston Globe* writer Stephen Mihm eloquently noted that "it" was, "like Harry Potter's nemesis Voldemort, the thing that could not be named: The Great Depression."
6. George Magnus, "Minsky for Beginners (Transcript)," *UBS Emerging Economic Focus* (October 12, 2009), 2.
7. Hyman Minsky, *Can IT Happen Again? Essays on Instability and Finance* (Armonk, NY: ME Sharpe, 1982).
8. Ibid.
9. Hyman Minsky, "The Financial Instability Hypothesis" (working paper, Jerome Levy Economics Institute of Bard College, May 1992. No 74).
10. Ibid.
11. Paul A. McCulley, "The Shadow Banking System and Hyman Minsky's Economic Journey," *PIMCO's Global Central Bank Focus* (May 2009).
12. Fisher, a member of the Yale College class of 1888, was awarded the first ever PhD in economics from Yale University in 1891.
13. Irving Fisher, "The Debt-Deflation Theory of Great Depressions," *Econometrica* (1933).
14. Ibid.
15. Ibid.
16. Ibid.
17. Richard Koo, *The Holy Grail of Macroeconomics: Lessons from Japan's Great Recession* (Singapore: John Wiley & Sons, 2009).
18. So named because of the predominantly Austrian economists (Ludwig von Mises, Friedrich Hayek, and others) who pioneered much of the early work.
19. Llewellyn Rockwell, "Why Austrian Economics Matters More Than Ever." Talk delivered to the Mises Institute Supporters Summit, November 1, 2008, Auburn, AL.
20. Roger W. Garrison, *Time and Money: The Macroeconomics of Capital Structure* (New York, NY: Routledge, 2001).
21. Friedrich von Hayek, "The Pretence of Knowledge." Nobel Prize Lecture, delivered upon accepting the Sveriges Riksbank Prize in Economic Sciences in Memory of Alfred Nobel on December 11, 1974; accessed via http://nobelprize .org/nobel_prizes/economics/laureates/1974/hayek-lecture.html.
22. Llewellyn Rockwell, "Why Austrian Economics Matters More Than Ever." Talk delivered to the Mises Institute Supporters Summit, November 1, 2008, Auburn, AL.
23. The clearest visualizations of Austrian belief are provided by Auburn University professor Roger Garrison in *Time and Money: The Macroeconomics of Capital Structure* (New York, NY: Routledge, 2001). Many of the figures in the section about the Austrian business cycle theory are based on Garrison's frameworks.
24. The one notable exception took place when Paul Volker raised rates quite dramatically to contain inflation. While it is possible to imagine a democratic

capitalist society keeps rates at their appropriate level or higher, in practice this has proven quite difficult to do for any extended period of time as it has the potential to result in a significant political backlash against elected officials.

25. Roger W. Garrison, *Time and Money: The Macroeconomics of Capital Structure* (New York, NY: Routledge, 2001).

26. Richard Koo, *The Holy Grail of Macroeconomics: Lessons from Japan's Great Recession* (Singapore: John Wiley & Sons, 2009).

27. Murray M. Rothbard, *The Case against the Fed* (Auburn, AL: Ludwig von Mises Institute, 2007).

28. Ron Paul, *End the Fed* (New York, NY: Grand Central Publishing, 2009).

29. Ibid.

Chapter 3 The Psychology Lens

1. John Scott, "Rational Choice Theory" in Browning, Halcli & Webster, *Understanding Contemporary Society: Theories of the Present.* (London, UK: Sage Publications, 2000).

2. Steven Green, "Rational Choice Theory: An Overview" (working paper, Baylor University, May 2002).

3. Friedrich A. von Hayek, "The Pretence of Knowledge." Nobel Prize Lecture, December 11, 1974; accessed via http://nobelprize.org/nobel_prizes/economics/laureates/1974/hayek-lecture.html.

4. Dan Ariely, "The End of Rational Economics," *Harvard Business Review* (July-August 2009): 78–84.

5. Daniel Kahneman, "A Psychological Perspective on Economics," *The American Economic Review* 93, no. 2 (May 2003):162.

6. J. Edward Russo and Paul Shoemaker, *Winning Decisions: Getting it Right the First Time* (New York, NY: Currency Books, 2002) 79–80.

7. *Metaknowledge* is knowledge about one's knowledge. In some senses, it's a test of how calibrated an individual may be in knowing what they know and knowing what they don't know.

8. J. Edward Russo and Paul Shoemaker, *Winning Decisions: Getting it Right the First Time* (New York, NY: Currency Books, 2002) 80.

9. Amos Tversky and Daniel Kahneman, "Judgment Under Uncertainty: Heuristics & Biases," *Science* (1974).

10. Ibid.

11. Example modified from an example provided in Tversky and Kahneman, "Judgment Under Uncertainty: Heuristics & Biases," *Science* (1974).

12. By *bias* I mean a predictable and consistent misestimation of either probabilities or values.

13. Amos Tversky and Daniel Kahneman, "Judgment Under Uncertainty: Heuristics & Biases," *Science* (1974).

14. Ibid.

15. Max Bazerman and Don Moore, *Judgment in Managerial Decision Making* (Hoboken, NJ: John Wiley & Sons, 2008).

16. Amos Tversky and Daniel Kahneman, "Judgment Under Uncertainty: Heuristics & Biases," *Science* (1974).

17. Daniel Kahneman and Amos Tversky, "On the Psychology of Prediction," *Psychological Review* 80, no. 4 (July 1973).

18. Max Bazerman and Don Moore, *Judgment in Managerial Decision Making* (Hoboken, NJ: John Wiley & Sons, 2008).

19. Amos Tversky and Daniel Kahneman, "Judgment Under Uncertainty: Heuristics & Biases," *Science* (1974).

20. Ibid.

21. Max Bazerman and Don Moore, *Judgment in Managerial Decision Making* (Hoboken, NJ: John Wiley & Sons, 2008).

22. Ibid.

23. As cited in Bazerman and Moore, *Judgment in Managerial Decision Making* (Hoboken, NJ: John Wiley & Sons, 2008).

24. Amos Tversky and Daniel Kahneman, "Availability: A Heuristic for Judging Frequency and Probability," *Cognitive Psychology* 5, no. 2 (1973): 207–232.

25. Ibid.

26. Amos Tversky and Daniel Kahneman, "Judgment Under Uncertainty: Heuristics & Biases," *Science* (1974).

27. Amos Tversky and Daniel Kahneman, "The Framing of Decisions and the Psychology of Choice," *Science* 211, no. 4481 (Jan 1981): 453–458.

28. Daniel Kahneman and Amos Tversky, "Prospect Theory: An Analysis of Decision Under Risk," *Econometrica* 47, no. 2 (March 1979) 263–291.

29. Dan Ariely, "The End of Rational Economics," *Harvard Business Review* 87, no. 7/8 (July-August 2009): 78–84. As an additional illustration of how free goods create confusing behavior, consider the fact that I witnessed one of my colleagues (a well-paid hedge fund investor) literally dropping everything, walking several blocks, and pretending to be a random person walking by a promotion booth that was handing out free sample boxes of pasta. (Note: The pasta was available for under $2 at any grocery store.)

30. Daniel Kahneman, J. L. Knetsch, and Richard H. Thaler, "Fairness as a Constraint on Profit Seeking: Entitlements and the Market," *American Economic Review* 76, no. 4 (1986).

31. Richard H. Thaler, *The Winner's Curse: Paradoxes and Anomalies of Economic Life* (Princeton, NJ: Princeton University Press, 1992), Chapter 3: "The Ultimatum Game."

32. Gary Belsky, and Thomas Gilovich, *Why Smart People Make Big Money Mistakes and How to Correct Them: Lessons from the New Science of Behavioral Economics* (New York, NY: Fireside, 1999), 31–32.

33. Richard H. Thaler, *Quasi-Rational Economics* (New York, NY: Russell Sage Foundation, 1994), Part 1: "Mental Accounting and Consumer Choice."

34. Daniel Kahneman, J. L. Knetsch, and Richard H. Thaler, "Anomalies: The Endowment Effect, Loss Aversion, and Status Quo Bias," *The Journal of Economic Perspectives* 5, no.1 (Winter 1991): 193–206.

35. Peter Ubel, *Free Market Madness: Why Human Nature is at Odds with Economics— And Why it Matters* (Boston, MA: Harvard Business School Press, 2009).

36. Daniel Kahneman, J. L. Knetsch, and Richard H. Thaler, "Experimental Tests of the Endowment Effect and the Coase Theorem," *Journal of Political Economy* 98, no. 6 (Dec 1990): 1325–1348.

37. So named by Baron, Beattie, and Hershey, "Heuristics and Biases in Diagnostic Reasoning: Congruence, Information, and Certainty," *Organizational Behavior and Human Decision Processes*, 98,88–110.

Chapter 4 Political Foundations

1. The author acknowledges that it is possible to argue that socialist systems in which the state owns all assets are subject to terminal busts as occurred in the former Soviet Union. Such terminal busts that destroy entire political economic organizational systems are beyond the scope of discussion in this book.
2. Armen Alchian, "Property Rights," *The Concise Encyclopedia of Economics*, 2008, Library of Economics and Liberty. Accessed May 16, 2010 via www.econlib .com/library/Enc/PropertyRIghts.html
3. Karl Marx, "The Communist Manifesto," as published in Robert C. Tucker, *The Marx Engels Reader,* 2nd ed. (New York, NY: WW Norton & Company, 1978).
4. Karl Marx, "Critique of the Gotha Program," as published in Robert C. Tucker, *The Marx Engels Reader,* 2nd ed. (New York, NY: WW Norton & Company, 1978), 531. Needless to say, such an approach has deleterious effects upon individual incentives to succeed.
5. Press release dated May 22, 2009 from Tenaris management.
6. A sale that had been properly pre-cleared through the Committee on Foreign Investments in the United States.
7. Adam Smith, *An Inquiry into the Nature and Causes of The Wealth of Nations.* Accessed electronically via www.econlib.org/library/Smith/smWN.html
8. Adam Smith, *An Inquiry into the Nature and Causes of The Wealth of Nations, Book I, Chapter IV.* Accessed electronically via www.econlib.org/library/Smith/smWN.html.
9. Joseph Stiglitz, *Economics* (New York, NY: WW Norton & Company, 1993).
10. Donald Boudreaux, "Information and Prices," *The Concise Encyclopedia of Economics.* 2008. Library of Economics and Liberty; accessed May 17, 2010 via www.econlib.com/library/Enc/InformationandPrices.html.
11. Joseph Stiglitz, *Economics* (New York, NY: WW Norton & Company, 1993).

Chapter 5 Biological Frameworks

1. Robert Shiller, *Irrational Exuberance* (New York, NY: Broadway Books, 2000).
2. Ibid.
3. Ibid. Emphasis in original.
4. Brian Partridge, "Internal Dynamics and the Interrelations of Fish in Schools," *Journal of Physiology* 144 (1981): 313–325.
5. Len Fisher, *The Perfect Swarm: The Science of Complexity in Everyday Life* (New York, NY: Basic Books, 2009).
6. Social insects are those species that, when considered as a group, possess the following three characteristics: (1) flexibility to changing circumstances, (2) robustness to individual failure, and (3) self-organization free from central control or local supervision.

7. Len Fisher, *The Perfect Swarm: The Science of Complexity in Everyday Life* (New York, NY: Basic Books, 2009).

8. Stephen Simpson and Gregory Sword, "Locusts," *Current Biology* 18 (2008): 364–366.

9. J. Buhl et al., "From Disorder to Order in Marching Locusts," *Science* 312 (2006): 1402–1406.

10. For more information, see Simpson and Sword, "Locusts," *Current Biology* 18 (2008): 364–366.

11. Sepidah Bezazi et al., "Collective Motion and Cannibalism in Locust Migratory Bands," *Current Biology* 18 (2008): 735–739.

12. Len Fisher, *The Perfect Swarm: The Science of Complexity in Everyday Life* (New York, NY: Basic Books, 2009).

13. Michael Anstey et al., "Serotonin Mediates Behavioral Gregarization Underlying Swarm Formation in Desert Locusts," *Science* 323 (2009): 627–630.

14. Stephen Simpson and Gregory Sword, "Locusts," *Current Biology* 18 (2008): 364–366.

15. A waggle dance is one in which scout bees shake their abdomen and waggle their bodies in a figure eight pattern. The direction of the dance points toward a future hive destination or a source of food. The speed of the waggles provides an indication of distance to the destination.

16. Although this was first studied by Karl von Frisch, who was awarded a Nobel Prize in Medicine for this work, more recent evidence comes from the work of John Riley et al., "The Flight Paths of Honeybees Recruited by the Waggle Dance," *Nature* 435 (2005): 205–207.

17. Len Fisher, *The Perfect Swarm: The Science of Complexity in Everyday Life* (New York, NY: Basic Books, 2009).

18. M. Beekman et al., "How Does an Informed Minority of Scouts Guide a Honeybee Swarm as It Flies to Its New Home?" *Animal Behavior* 71 (2006): 161–171.

19. D. Couzin et al., "Effective Leadership and Decision Making in Animal Groups on the Move," *Nature* 455 (2005): 513–516.

20. Len Fisher, *The Perfect Swarm: The Science of Complexity in Everyday Life* (New York, NY: Basic Books, 2009).

21. S. Goss et al., "Self-Organized Shortcuts in the Argentine Ant," *Naturwissenschaften* 76 (1989): 579–581.

22. I say "at least twice" because of the way dissipation and evaporation happens over time. If the evaporation removes 50 percent of the pheromone by the time the ant makes a round trip, then the shorter trail will have three times the pheromone as the longer path.

23. Eric Bonabeau and Christopher Meyer, "Swarm Intelligence: A Whole New Way to Think About Business," *Harvard Business Review* (May 2001): 107–114.

24. Steven Johnson, *Emergence: The Connected Lives of Ants, Brains, Cities, and Software* (New York, NY: Scribner, 2001).

25. For a good overview of the research presented in the issue, please see Larissa Conradt and Christian Lists's "Group Decisions in Humans and Animals: A Survey," *Philosophical Transactions of the Royal Society – Biological Sciences* 364 (2009): 719–742.

26. John R. G. Dyer, Andres Johansson, Dirk Helbing, Iain Couzin, and Jens Krause, "Leadership, Consensus Decision Making and Collective Behavior in Humans," *Philosophical Transactions of the Royal Society – Biological Sciences* 364 (2009): 781–789.

27. Dyer et al., "Consensus Decision Making in Human Crowds," *Animal Behavior* 75 (2008): 461–470.

28. Stanley Milgram is most famous for research on individual adherence to authority. His famous experiments involved the fictional administration of pain and tested the participants' abilities to defy orders from an authority when their concerns against doing so arose. The experiments demonstrated a surprising willingness in individuals to follow orders, even when they had tremendous reservations about doing so.

29. Stanley Milgram et al., "Note on the Drawing Power of Crowds of Different Sizes," *Journal of Personal and Social Psychology* 13 (1969): 79–82.

30. Len Fisher, *The Perfect Swarm: The Science of Complexity in Everyday Life* (New York, NY: Basic Books, 2009).

31. The example is a modified version of a similar story presented in Robert Shiller, *Irrational Exuberance* (New York, NY: Broadway Books, 2000).

Chapter 6 Tulipomania

1. Donald Rapp, *Bubbles, Booms and Busts: The Rise and Fall of Financial Assets* (New York, NY: Copernicus Books, 2009).

2. John K. Galbraith, *A Short History of Financial Euphoria* (New York, NY: Penguin Books, 1990).

3. Donald Rapp, *Bubbles, Booms and Busts: The Rise and Fall of Financial Assets* (New York, NY: Copernicus Books, 2009).

4. Michael Dash, *Tulipomania: The Story of the World's Most Coveted Flower* (New York, NY: Crown Publishers, 2000), 59–60.

5. Peter Garber, *Famous First Bubbles: The Fundamentals of Early Manias* (Cambridge, MA: MIT Press, 2000).

6. Michael Dash, *Tulipomania: The Story of the World's Most Coveted Flower* (New York, NY: Crown Publishers, 2000).

7. Peter Garber, *Famous First Bubbles: The Fundamentals of Early Manias* (Cambridge, MA: MIT Press, 2000).

8. Peter Garber, "Tulipmania," *Journal of Political Economy*, 97, no. 3 (1989): 59.

9. Donald Rapp, *Bubbles, Booms and Busts: The Rise and Fall of Financial Assets* (New York, NY: Copernicus Books, 2009).

10. Charles Mackay, *Extraordinary Popular Delusions and the Madness of Crowds* (New York, NY: John Wiley & Sons, 1996).

11. "The Tulip Mania," *Harper's New Monthly Magazine* LII, no. CCCXL (April 1876); accessed via http://en.wikisource.org/wiki/The_Tulip_Mania.

12. Mark Frankel, "When the Tulip Bubble Burst" (Book Review of *Tulipomania: The Story of the World's Most Coveted Flower*), *BusinessWeek* (April 24, 2000).

13. Peter Garber, *Famous First Bubbles: The Fundamentals of Early Manias* (Cambridge, MA: MIT Press, 2000).

14. Mark Frankel, "When the Tulip Bubble Burst" (Book Review of *Tulipomania: The Story of the World's Most Coveted Flower*), *BusinessWeek* (April 24, 2000).

15. Peter Garber, *Famous First Bubbles: The Fundamentals of Early Manias* (Cambridge, MA: MIT Press, 2000).

16. Charles Mackay, *Extraordinary Popular Delusions and the Madness of Crowds* (New York, NY: John Wiley & Sons, 1996).

17. Earl A. Thompson, "The Tulipmania: Fact or Artifact?" *Public Choice* 130, no. 2 (2007).

18. Charles Mackay, *Extraordinary Popular Delusions and the Madness of Crowds* (New York, NY: John Wiley & Sons, 1996).

19. Peter Garber, "Tulipmania," *Journal of Political Economy*, 97, no. 3 (1989): 536.

20. Doug French, "The Dutch Monetary Environment During Tulipmania," *The Quarterly Journal of Austrian Economics* 9, no. 1: 3–14.

21. Ibid.

22. Charles Mackay, *Extraordinary Popular Delusions and the Madness of Crowds* (New York, NY: John Wiley & Sons, 1996).

23. Earl A. Thompson, "The Tulipmania: Fact or Artifact?" *Public Choice* 130, no. 2 (2007).

24. Charles Mackay, *Extraordinary Popular Delusions and the Madness of Crowds* (New York, NY: John Wiley & Sons, 1996).

25. Ibid.

26. Ibid.

Chapter 7 The Great Depression

1. This chapter is merely intended to be illustrative of the five lenses presented, not a comprehensive review of the Great Depression. Other treatments of the era are more thorough, and the curious reader is pointed toward them.

2. Frederick Lewis Allen, *Only Yesterday: An Informal History of the 1920s* (New York, NY: Harper & Row, 1931).

3. Ibid.

4. Ibid.

5. Donald Rapp, *Bubbles, Booms and Busts: The Rise and Fall of Financial Assets* (New York, NY: Copernicus Books, 2009).

6. Frederick Lewis Allen, *Only Yesterday: An Informal History of the 1920s* (New York, NY: Harper & Row, 1931).

7. Ibid.

8. Some scholars, including Irving Fisher of Yale University, cited the work of Professor Paul Nystrom of Columbia University to justify the belief that America had entered a new level of productivity because of Prohibition, which began in 1920. By some estimates, eliminating alcohol might save $7bn+ of lost productivity.

9. Donald Rapp, *Bubbles, Booms and Busts: The Rise and Fall of Financial Assets* (New York, NY: Copernicus Books, 2009).

10. John Kenneth Galbraith, *The Great Crash 1929* (Boston, MA: Houghton Mifflin, 1954).

11. Ibid.
12. Ibid.
13. Edward Chancellor, *Devil Take the Hindmost: A History of Financial Speculation* (New York, NY: Plume, 1999).
14. Ibid.
15. For more detailed analysis, see Milton Friedman and Anna Jacobson Schwartz, *The Great Contraction: 1929–1933* (Cambridge, MA: National Bureau of Economic Research, 1963).
16. For more detailed analysis, see Ben S. Bernanke and Kevin Carey, "Nominal Wage Stickiness and Aggregate Supply in the Great Depression," in Ben S. Bernanke, *Essays on the Great Depression* (Princeton, NJ: Princeton University Press, 2000).
17. For more detailed analysis, see Ben S. Bernanke and Harold James, "The Gold Standard, Deflation and Financial Crisis in the Great Depression: An International Comparison," in Ben S. Bernanke, *Essays on the Great Depression* (Princeton, NJ: Princeton University Press, 2000); and Barry Eichengreen, *Golden Fetters: The Gold Standard and the Great Depression* (New York, NY: Oxford University Press, 1992).
18. For more detailed analysis, see Edward Chancellor, *Devil Take the Hindmost: A History of Financial Speculation* (New York, NY: Plume, 1999).
19. For more detailed analysis, see Richard C. Koo, *The Holy Grail of Macroeconomics: Lessons from Japan's Great Recession* (Hoboken, NJ: John Wiley & Sons, 2009).
20. Robert Samuelson, "The Great Depression," *The Concise Encyclopedia of Economics*, 1st ed.; accessed via www.econlib.org/library/Enc1/GreatDepression .html.
21. Frederick Lewis Allen, *Only Yesterday: An Informal History of the 1920s* (New York, NY: Harper & Row, 1931).
22. Ibid.
23. Edward Chancellor, *Devil Take the Hindmost: A History of Financial Speculation* (New York, NY: Plume, 1999).
24. Robert Shiller, *Irrational Exuberance*, 2nd ed. (New York, NY: Broadway Books, 2005).
25. Frederick Lewis Allen, *Only Yesterday: An Informal History of the 1920s* (New York, NY: Harper & Row, 1931).
26. Edward Chancellor, *Devil Take the Hindmost: A History of Financial Speculation* (New York, NY: Plume, 1999).
27. Ibid.
28. Frederick Lewis Allen, *Only Yesterday: An Informal History of the 1920s* (New York, NY: Harper & Row, 1931).
29. John Kenneth Galbraith, *A Short History of Financial Euphoria* (New York, NY: Penguin Books, 1990).
30. Edward Chancellor, *Devil Take the Hindmost: A History of Financial Speculation* (New York, NY: Plume, 1999).
31. Frederick Lewis Allen, *Only Yesterday: An Informal History of the 1920s* (New York, NY: Harper & Row, 1931).

32. Edward Chancellor, *Devil Take the Hindmost: A History of Financial Speculation* (New York, NY: Plume, 1999).

33. Frederick Lewis Allen, *Only Yesterday: An Informal History of the 1920s* (New York, NY: Harper & Row, 1931).

Chapter 8 The Japanese Boom and Bust

1. Edward Chancellor, *Devil Take the Hindmost: A History of Financial Speculation* (New York, NY: Plume, 1999).

2. The author concedes that this fact may be changing as this book is written.

3. Japan had remained a feudal society with no individual rights until the mid-1800s. The entire economy was closed off to the outside world and virtually everything was hierarchically controlled.

4. Paul Krugman, *The Return of Depression Economics and the Crisis of 2008* (New York, NY: WW Norton, 2009).

5. Perhaps the best account of the spectacular excess that characterized Japan in the 1980s is found in a book written by a financial journalist at *The Economist* named Christopher Wood. His book, *The Bubble Economy: Japan's Extraordinary Speculative Boom of the '80s and the Dramatic Bust of the '90s* was written in 1993 and accurately predicted much of what transpired during the time since it was written.

6. Christopher Wood, *The Bubble Economy: Japan's Extraordinary Speculative Boom of the '80s and the Dramatic Bust of the '90s* (Jakarta, Indonesia: Solstice Publishing, 1993).

7. Ibid.

8. Charles P. Kindelberger and Robert Aliber, *Mania, Panics, and Crashes: A History of Financial Crises* (Hoboken, NJ: John Wiley & Sons, 2005).

9. Christopher Wood, *The Bubble Economy: Japan's Extraordinary Speculative Boom of the '80s and the Dramatic Bust of the '90s* (Jakarta, Indonesia: Solstice Publishing, 1993).

10. Edward Chancellor, *Devil Take the Hindmost: A History of Financial Speculation* (New York, NY: Plume, 1999).

11. Francis Clines, "Van Gogh Auction Sets Record: $39.9 Million," *The New York Times* (March 31, 1987).

12. Rita Reif, "Japanese Developer Buys Picasso at Record Price," *The New York Times* (December 1, 1989).

13. David Usborne, "Missing Van Gogh Feared Cremated with its Owner," *The Independent* (July 27, 1999).

14. Vartanig Vartan, "Big Stock Sale By Japanese," *The New York Times* (November 9, 1987).

15. Edward Chancellor, *Devil Take the Hindmost: A History of Financial Speculation* (New York, NY: Plume, 1999).

16. Later episodes (including the Internet boom) rivaled it, but at the time, the Japanese boom might have been the greatest one on record.

17. Takatoshi Ito, "Retrospective on the Bubble Period and its Relationship to Developments in the 1990s" in Gary Saxonhouse and Robert Stern, *Japan's*

Lost Decade: Origins, Consequences, and Prospects for Recovery (Malden, MA: Blackwell Publishing, 2004).

18. Charles P. Kindelberger and Robert Aliber, *Mania, Panics, and Crashes: A History of Financial Crises* (Hoboken, NJ: John Wiley & Sons, 2005).

19. Christopher Wood, *The Bubble Economy: Japan's Extraordinary Speculative Boom of the '80s and the Dramatic Bust of the '90s* (Jakarta, Indonesia: Solstice Publishing, 1993).

20. Ibid.

21. Charles P. Kindelberger and Robert Aliber, *Mania, Panics, and Crashes: A History of Financial Crises* (Hoboken, NJ: John Wiley & Sons, 2005).

22. Cited by Tomohiko Taniguchi, "Japan's Banks and the Bubble Economy of the Late 1980s." Princeton University, Center for International Studies, Working Paper no. 4, Program on U.S. Japan Relations, 1993.

23. Charles Mackay, *Extraordinary Popular Delusions and the Madness of Crowds* (New York, NY: John Wiley & Sons, 1996).

24. Christopher Wood, *The Bubble Economy: Japan's Extraordinary Speculative Boom of the '80s and the Dramatic Bust of the '90s* (Jakarta, Indonesia: Solstice Publishing, 1993).

25. Ibid.

26. Ibid.

27. Ito, Takatoshi. "Retrospective on the Bubble Period and its Relationship to Developments in the 1990s." in Saxonhouse, Gary and Stern, Robert. *Japan's Lost Decade: Origins, Consequences, and Prospects for Recovery*. Malden, MA: Blackwell Publishing, 2004.

28. Charles P. Kindelberger and Robert Aliber, *Mania, Panics, and Crashes: A History of Financial Crises* (Hoboken, NJ: John Wiley & Sons, 2005).

29. Paul Krugman, *The Return of Depression Economics and the Crisis of 2008* (New York, NY: WW Norton, 2009).

30. Fukao, Mitsuhiro. "Japan's Lost Decade and its Financial System." in Saxonhouse, Gary and Stern, Robert. *Japan's Lost Decade: Origins, Consequences, and Prospects for Recovery*. Malden, MA: Blackwell Publishing, 2004.

31. Christopher Wood, *The Bubble Economy: Japan's Extraordinary Speculative Boom of the '80s and the Dramatic Bust of the '90s* (Jakarta, Indonesia: Solstice Publishing, 1993).

32. Edward Chancellor, *Devil Take the Hindmost: A History of Financial Speculation* (New York, NY: Plume, 1999).

33. Ibid.

34. Gladwell, Malcolm. *The Tipping Point: How Little Things Can Make a Big Difference*. New York, NY: Little Brown & Company, 2000.

35. Edward Chancellor, *Devil Take the Hindmost: A History of Financial Speculation* (New York, NY: Plume, 1999).

Chapter 9 The Asian Financial Crisis

1. World Bank, *The East Asian Miracle: Economic Growth and Public Policy* (New York, NY: Oxford University Press, 1993).

2. Robert Barbara, *The Cost of Capitalism: Understanding Market Mayhem and Stabilizing our Economic Future* (New York, NY: McGraw Hill, 2009).

3. Charles P. Kindelberger and Robert Aliber, *Mania, Panics, and Crashes: A History of Financial Crises* (Hoboken, NJ: John Wiley & Sons, 2005).

4. Paul Krugman, *The Return of Depression Economics and the Crisis of 2008* (New York, NY: WW Norton, 2009).

5. Ibid.

6. Timothy Geithner, "Reflections on the Asian Financial Crisis." Speech at the Trends in Asian Financial Services Conference, Federal Reserve Bank of San Francisco, June 20, 2007.

7. Paul Krugman, *The Return of Depression Economics and the Crisis of 2008* (New York, NY: WW Norton, 2009).

8. Dwight Perkins, "Law, Family Ties, and the East Asian Way of Business," in Lawrence Harrison and Samuel Huntington, eds,, *Culture Matters: How Values Shape Human Progress* (New York, NY: Basic Books, 2000).

9. Charles P. Kindelberger and Robert Aliber, *Mania, Panics, and Crashes: A History of Financial Crises* (Hoboken, NJ: John Wiley & Sons, 2005).

10. Janet Yellen, "The Asian Financial Crisis Ten Years Later: Assessing the Past and Looking to the Future." Speech to the Asia Society of Southern California, February 6, 2007.

11. David Liebhold, "Thailand's Scapegoat?" *Time* 154, no. 25 (December 27, 1999).

12. Paul Krugman, "The Myth of Asia's Miracle," *Foreign Affairs* (November/December 1994).

13. Dwight Perkins, "Law, Family Ties, and the East Asian Way of Business," in Lawrence Harrison and Samuel Huntington, eds,, *Culture Matters: How Values Shape Human Progress* (New York, NY: Basic Books, 2000).

Chapter 10 The U.S. Housing Boom and Bust

1. Niall Fergusson, *The Ascent of Money: A Financial History of the World* (New York, NY: Penguin Press, 2008).

2. Paul Krugman, *The Return of Depression Economics and the Crisis of 2008* (New York, NY: WW Norton, 2009).

3. Robert Shiller, *Irrational Exuberance*, 2nd ed. (New York, NY: Broadway, 2005).

4. Ibid.

5. Just so the reader does not think I am revising my version of history, I thought I might share a bit of my personal housing story with you. Upon seeing Robert Shiller's data on the housing market in early 2005, I immediately went about selling my apartment in Boston's Beacon Hill Neighborhood. My wife and I then proceeded to rent an apartment for the next four years and only recently purchased a condo in Brookline, MA.

6. Chuck Prince, Interview with the *Financial Times*, July 5, 2007.

7. Mara Der Hovanesian and Matthew Goldstein, "The Mortgage Mess Spreads," *BusinessWeek* (March 5, 2007).

8. Christopher Dodd, Opening statement on "Mortgage Market Turmoil: Causes and Consequences," U.S. Senate Committee on Banking, Housing, and Urban Affairs. March 22, 2007.

9. Peter Wallison, "Cause and Effect: Government Policies and the Financial Crisis," *Financial Services Outlook* (November 2008). Washington, DC: American Enterprise Institute.

10. Ibid.

11. Roger Lowenstein, "Who Needs the Mortgage Interest Deduction?" *New York Times Magazine* (March 5, 2006).

12. Peter Wallison, "Cause and Effect: Government Policies and the Financial Crisis," *Financial Services Outlook* (November 2008). Washington, DC: American Enterprise Institute.

13. Frank J. Fabozzi, *The Handbook of Mortgage Backed Securities* (New York, NY: McGraw Hill, 2001).

14. Mara Lee, "Subprime Mortgages: A Primer." National Public Radio story that was summarized on the NPR website. Lee cites *Inside Mortgage Finance* for her subprime data. Accessed via www.npr.org/templates/story/story.php?storyID=9085408.

Chapter 11 A Method for Spotting Unsustainable Booms

1. Nicola Gennaioli, Andrei Shleifer, and Robert W. Vishny, "Neglected Risks, Financial Innovation, and Financial Fragility." *NBER Working Paper Series*, Working Paper #16068 (Cambridge, MA: National Bureau of Economic Research, June 2010).

2. Richard Bookstaber, *A Demon of Our Own Design: Markets, Hedge Funds, and The Perils of Financial Innovation* (Hoboken, NJ: John Wiley & Sons, 2007).

3. Garet Garrett, "Anatomy of the Bubble," *A Bubble that Broke the World* (Boston, MA: Little Brown & Company, 1932).

4. Christopher Wood, "Global and Asia Investment Strategy." Presentation to the 17th Annual CLSA Investors Forum, Hong Kong, September 2010.

5. Carol Vogel, "Landmark De Kooning Crowns Collection," *The New York Times* (November 18, 2006).

6. Charles Mackay, *Extraordinary Popular Delusions and the Madness of Crowds* (New York, NY: John Wiley & Sons, 1996).

7. Frederick Lewis Allen, *Only Yesterday: An Informal History of the 1920s* (New York, NY: Harper & Row, 1931).

8. Unfortunate because he contributed a great deal to our understanding of booms and busts, most notably via his debt-deflation theories.

9. James Chanos, Speech at the University of Oxford. Accessed via http://youtu.be/99HNFCn5RP8.

Chapter 12 Boombustology in Action

1. J. Scott Armstrong, "The Seer Sucker Theory: The Value of Experts in Forecasting," *Technology Review* (June/July 1980): 16–24; Philip Tetlock, *Expert Political Judgement* (Princeton, NJ: Princeton University Press, 2005).

2. Andy Xie, "I'll Tell You When Chinese Bubble Is About to Burst," *Bloomberg* (April 25, 2010).

3. Ibid.

4. David Barboza, "Market Defies Fear of Real Estate Bubble in China," *The New York Times* (March 4, 2010).

5. Ibid.

6. Luo Jun, "Sizzling Shanghai Homes Defy Tax, Bubble Concerns." *Bloomberg News*, December 17, 2009.

7. Andy Xie, "Fear Empties Flats in China's Property Bubble," *Caixin online* (August 3, 2010), accessed via http://english.caing.com/2010-08-03/100166589.html.

8. Robert A. Mundell, "Capital Mobility and Stabilization Policy under Fixed and Flexible Exchange Rates." *Canadian Journal of Economic and Political Science*, Vol 29, No. 4, 1963; Marcus J. Fleming. "Domestic Financial Policies Under Fixed and Floating Exchange Rates." *IMF Staff Papers No 9*, 1962.

9. Sebastian Edwards, "A Capital Idea? Reconsidering a Quick Fix." *Foreign Affairs*, May/June 1999.

10. David Barboza, "Contrarian Investor Sees Economic Crash in China," *The New York Times* (January 7, 2010).

11. Arthur Budaghyan, "Don't Fight the PBOC." *BCA Emerging Markets Research*, November 16, 2010.

12. Kevin Hamlin, "Hugh Hendry Shorts China, Betting on 1920s Style Crash" *Bloomberg Businessweek*, November 26, 2010.

13. Charlene Chu, Chunling Wen, and Hiddy He. "Chinese Banks: No Pause in Credit Growth, Still on Pace with 1999." *FitchRatings*, December 2, 2010; Charlene Chu, Chunling Wen, and Hiddy He. "Chinese Banks: Informal Securitization Increasingly Distorting Credit Data." *FitchRatings.* July 14, 2009.

14. Ibid.

15. Michael Pettis, "QE2 and the Titanic" accessed via http://mpettis.com.

16. Giovanni Ferri and Li-Gang Liu. "Honor Thy Creditors Before Thy Shareholders: Are the Profits of Chinese State Owned Enterprises Real" Hong Kong Institute for Monetary Research, working paper dated April 2009.

17. Gao Xu, "State Owned Enterprises in China" East Asia & Pacific on the rise, Accessed via http://blogs.worldbank.org/eastasiapacific/state-owned-enterprises-in-China-how-profitable-are-they.

18. Steel Statistical Yearbook, 2009. Brussels, Belgium: Worldsteel Committee on Economic Studies, 2010; accessed via www.worldsteel.org; "Crude Steel Production by Month" links on www.worldsteel.org.

19. Merrill Lynch Equity Research, *Metals and Mining Industry Primer*, April 22, 2010. Authored by Kuni Chen, Jason Fairclough, Felipe Hirai, Nik Oliver, Oscar Cabrera, Christopher Brown, and Sean Heymann.

20. Chuin-Wek Yap and Andrew Batson, "China Steps Up Its Drive to Shrink its Role as Top Global Steelmaker," *The Wall Street Journal* (December 4, 2009).

21. UBS investment research. Metal Guru Vol 55. UBS Securities Japan Ltd. Authored by Atsushi Yamaguchi, Yong-Suk Son, Hubert Tang, Navin Gupta, Katsuya Takeuchi, and Hisami Enomoto. March 23, 2010.

22. Pivot Capital Management report: "China's Investment Boom: the Great Leap into the Unknown." 2009.

23. Bill Powell, "Inside China's Runaway Building Boom," *Time* (April 5, 2010); accessed online via www.time.com/magazine/article/0,9171,1975336,00.html.

24. Ibid.
25. Dexter Roberts, "Where China Hides Its Debt: Cities Can't Borrow Much, Specially Designed Companies Can," *Bloomberg Businessweek* (July 29, 2010).
26. Ibid.
27. As noted in the PBS video posted at www.pbs.org/pov/utopia/.
28. Ibid.
29. "Dongguan's Ghost Mall Haunts China's Property Boom," accessed via www .bloomberg.com/video/65822094.
30. Ibid.
31. Michael Donohue, "Mall of Misfortune," *The National* (June 12, 2008); accessed via www.thenational.ae/article/20080612/REVIEW/206990272/1042
32. www.pbs.org/pov/utopia/
33. Wang Xia, Zhang Min, and Yu Fusheng, "Managerial Overconfidence and Over-investment: Empirical Evidence from China," *Frontiers of Business Research in China*, 2009, vol. 3, no. 3, 453–469.
34. Souren Melikan, "Chinese Bidders Conquer Market," *The New York Times* (April 2, 2010).
35. Andrew Moody, "Chinese Take the Art Market by Storm," *China Daily* (May 24, 2010).
36. Ibid.
37. Ibid.
38. John F. Burns, "This Old Thing? It's Worth Only, Oh, Close to $70 Million." *The New York Times,* November 12, 2010.
39. Rob Gifford, "Wild for Wine, China Pumps Up Demand, Prices." December 12, 2010. Accessed via www.npr.org/2010/12/12/131973813.
40. Scott Reyburn, "Lafite Sets Auction Wine Record at $230,000 a Bottle." *Bloomberg Businessweek*, October 29, 2010.
41. Tania Branigan, "Garlic bubble leaves bad taste in Chinese mouths." *The Guardian*, July 30, 2010; accessed via http://www.guardian.co.uk/world/2010/jul/30/garlic-chinese-commodity-bubble.
42. Peter Foster, "Tea bubble brews in China." *The Telegraph*, October 1, 2010.
43. Andrew Jacobs, "Jade from China's West Surpasses Gold in Value." *The New York Times,* September 20, 2010.
44. Robert Frank, "Pay $200,000 for a Pigeon?" *The Wall Street Journal,* January 15, 2011.
45. "Reds to Buy the Reds? Chinese Government Backs Bid to Take Over Liverpool FC," *The Daily Mail* (August 5, 2010); accessed via www.dailymail.co.uk/news/article-1300558/Communist-China-funds-bid-buy-Liverpool-Football-Club.html.
46. "Chinese Investors to Buy Into Cavs," ESPN.com; accessed via http://sports.espn.go.com/nba/playoffs/2009/news/story?id=4202661.
47. "World Skyscraper Construction, 2010." Accessed via http://skyscraperpage.com/diagrams/searchID=202.
48. "World's Tallest Buildings, 2015." Accessed via http://skyscraperpage.com/diagrams/searchID=201.
49. Tim Wang, "Whither China's Construction Boom?" *Forbes*, May 21, 2009.
50. "Beijing Tells the Provinces to Slow Down." *Geopolitical Diary,* Stratfor.com email, January 7, 2011.

51. Ibid.

52. George Friedman, *The Next 100 Years: A Forecast for the 21st Century* (New York, NY: Anchor Books, 2010).

53. Victor Shih, "Moral Hazard and China's Banks: Beijing Could Face Its Own Banking Crisis Unless More Market Discipline Is Introduced," *The Wall Street Journal Asia* (June 29, 2010).

54. Jinsong Du et al., China Property Policy Outlook 1: "Property Tax: Would it Crash the Market?" Credit Suisse Hong Kong Ltd. June 14, 2010.

55. Robert Fong, "2010: 2008 All Over Again?" Presentation at DB Access Asia Conference, May 2010, Singapore.

56. Chris Brooke, "Asia Real Estate Market: Boom or Bubble?" CB Richard Ellis Presentation at the DB Access Asia Conference, May 2010.

57. Stephanie Wong and Bonnie Cao, "Shanghai Prepares Property Tax to Curb 'Speculative' Buyers Raising Prices" *Bloomberg News,* January 17, 2011.

58. Jun Ma, "China: Soft or Hard Landing?" Deutsche Bank AG report. May 2010.

59. Andy Xie, "China's Stock Market Has Become a Poor Man's Casino," *Bloomberg News* (May 23, 2010).

60. William Mellor, "Beijing Billionaire Who Grew Up with Mao Sees No Housing Bubble," *Bloomberg Markets* (August 2010).

61. David Barboza, "State-Owned Bidders Fuel China's Land Boom," *The New York Times* (August 1, 2010).

62. Ilan Noy, "China's Real Estate Bubble." *UHERO*, November 22, 2010.

63. David Barboza, "State-Owned Bidders Fuel China's Land Boom," *The New York Times* (August 1, 2010).

64. Ibid.

65. Scott Tong, "Chinese Soap Opera Highlights Housing Issue," broadcast on National Public Radio, January 19, 2010. Accessed via http://marketplace.publicradio.org/www_publicradio/tools/media_player/popup.php?name=marketplace/pm/2010/01/19/marketplace_cast2_20100119_64.

66. Su Feng, "Hit TV Series Strikes Chord with China's 'House Slaves'," *The Wall Street Journal* (November 26, 2009); accessed via http://blogs.wsj.com/chinarealtime/2009/11/26/hit-tv-series-strikes-chord-with-chinas-house-slaves/.

67. Geoff Dyer,"The Soap Opera of China's Housing Boom," *Financial Times,* January 6, 2010.

68. Ibid.

69. Jeremy Grantham, "Feet of Clay: Alan Greenspan's Contribution to the Great American Equity Bubble." *GMO Special Topic Report,* October 2002; accessed via www.gmo.com.

70. Edward Chancellor. "China's Red Flags." *GMO White Paper,* March 2010; accessed via www.gmo.com.

71. Michael Pettis. "Get Ready for Lower Chinese Growth." *Financial Times,* July 29, 2009.

72. William Pesek. "China's 'Treadmill to Hell' Is Worth Mind Game." *Bloomberg,* December 5, 2010.

73. Vitaliy Katsenelson. "China—The Mother of All Grey Swans" presentation to Casey's Gold and Resource Summit, October 3, 2010.

74. Part of this social unrest might originate from the unmet expectations of China's rapidly growing pool of unemployed college graduates. According to the *New York Times*, Chinese universities graduated more than 6 million students in 2009, up from around 800,000 in 1998. Many graduates have struggled to find appropriate jobs. See Andrew Jacobs. "China's Army of Graduates Struggles for Jobs." *The New York Times*, December 11, 2010.

Conclusion Hedgehogs, Foxes, and the Dangers of Making Predictions

1. Fragment 201, trans. Douglas E. Gerber. *Greek Iambic Poetry: From the Seventh to Fifth Centuries BC* (Cambridge, MA: Harvard University Press, 1999).
2. Isaiah Berlin, *The Hedgehog and the Fox* (Chicago, IL: Elephant Paperbacks, 1953).
3. Philip Tetlock, *Expert Political Judgment: How Good Is It? How Can We Know?* (Princeton, NJ: Princeton University Press, 2005).
4. Adrian Tschoegl and J. Scott Armstrong, "Review of Tetlock's *Expert Political Judgment,*" *International Journal of Forecasting* (2007), 339–342.
5. Philip Tetlock, *Expert Political Judgment: How Good Is It? How Can We Know?* (Princeton, NJ: Princeton University Press, 2005), 2.
6. Richard Levin, "Top of the Class: The Rise of Asia's Universities," *Foreign Affairs* (May/June 2010).
7. Ibid.

About the Author

Vikram Mansharamani is an experienced global equity investor based in Boston, Massachusetts. He is also a Lecturer at Yale University where he teaches a popular seminar called "Financial Booms and Busts." Dr. Mansharamani has experience in venture capital, investment banking, and management consulting. He has been a board member of numerous for-profit and nonprofit organizations, and currently serves as chairman of Torit Language Center Montessori in Boston. Dr. Mansharamani earned a PhD and MS from the Sloan School of Management at MIT, an MS in Political Science from MIT, and a BA from Yale University. He currently lives in Brookline, Massachusetts.

Index

100 year mortgage, 154, 197, 203

A
adjustment irrelevance, 58–59
Alchian, Armen, 70
Aliber, Robert, 141, 146–148, 152,
    157–158, 161
Allen, Frederick Lewis, 118–121, 125–130,
    133–134, 211
ambiguity, 73
anchoring irrelevance, 58–59
Anderson, Phil, 203
ants, 93–94
Antsey, Michael, 92
Archilochos, 241
Ariely, Dan, 61
Armstrong, J. Scott, 218, 242
art market
    Chinese, 229–230
    Japan, 141–142
The Ascent of Money: A Financial History of the
    World, 173–174
asset prices
    debt deflaiton and, 34–35
    interest rates and, 30
asset-backed securities, 178
Austrian School of Economics, 35–36

B
Bachelier, Louis, 11
Barbara, Robert, 156
Barboza, David, 221, 223–224, 236
base rates, 51–52
Bazerman, Max, 53–54, 56
Beekman, M., 93
Bees, 92–93
Belesky, Gary, 62–63
Benazi, Sepidah, 91
Berlin, Isaiah, 241–242
bias

confirmatory, 65–66
ease-of-recall, 56–57
retrievability-based, 57–58
biology lens, 210
    China, 234–237
    East Asia, 171–172, 211–212
    Great Depression, 133–134, 211
    indicators, 213–215
    Japan, 152–154, 211
    tulipomania, 114–115, 210
    U.S. housing bust, 186–189, 212–213
Black Thursday, 124
Black Tuesday, 124
Bonabeau, Eric, 94
Bookstaber, Richard, 198
boom
    East Asia, 155–158
    mature, 99–100
Booms and Depressions, 34–35
Boudreaux, Donald, 75
Brooke, Chris, 234
bubble economy, Japan, 139–147
bubble indicator
    skyscrapers, 202–203
    Sotheby's stock, 143
bubbles, tulips, 106–109
Budaghyan, Arthur, 224
Buffett, Warren, 45
Buhl, J., 91
business cycle theory, 35–42

C
capital structure, macroeconomics and ,
    37–39
Cave, Andrew, 20
ceilings, prices, 79–80
central banks, 39–42
Central Intelligence Agency. *See* CIA
Chancellor, Edward, 124, 128–130, 132, 134,
    137–138, 141, 144, 153–154, 237